AF255958

EX LIBRIS
THORNCLAW

This Volume is
dedicated to all the strangely beautiful
families like my own.

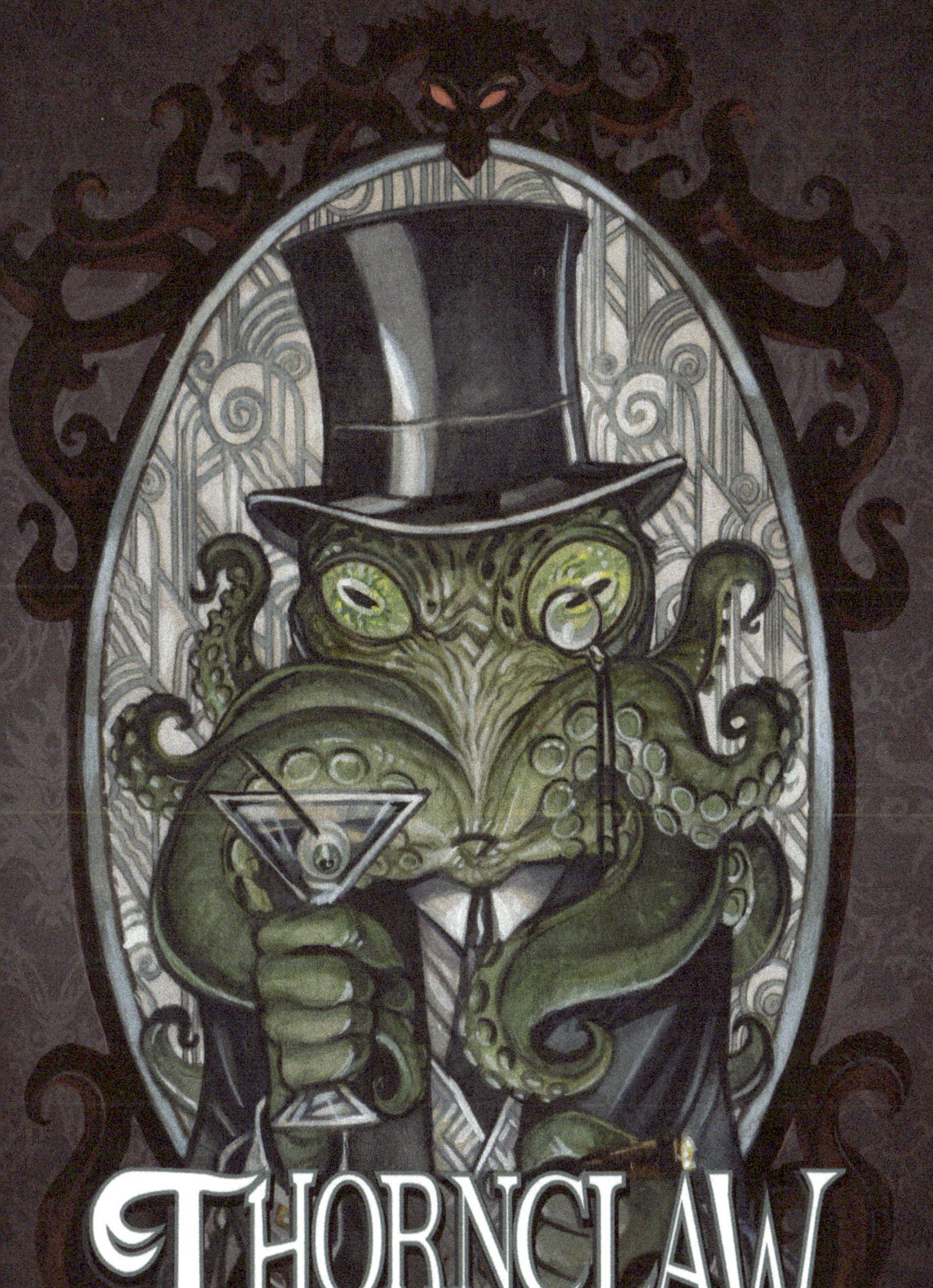
THORNCLAW
MANOR

Welcome to Thornclaw Manor

This ancient labyrinthine house on the divide between dream and reality is the nexus point of the universe, the crossroads between our world and the worlds of myth and legend. Inside the old mansion live the Thornclaw Family, a very old and venerable extended family of Fairies, Demons, Lovecraftian horrors, Cryptids, and things from beyond.

They find our world and our modern trappings intriguing, compelling them to cross over and check us out, often with eerie effect. They leave no sane witnesses, only legends, stories, strange dreams, and myths.

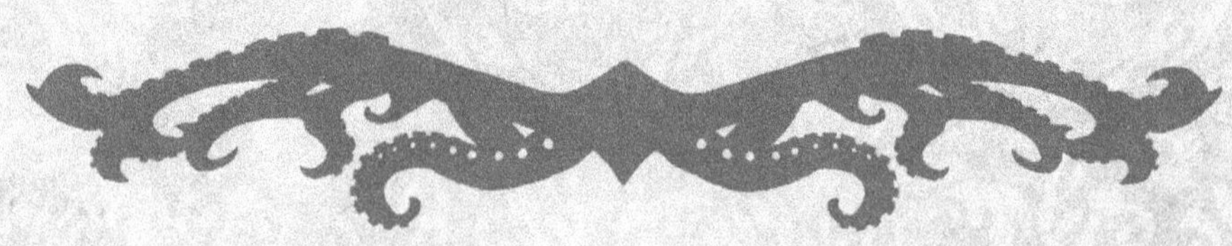

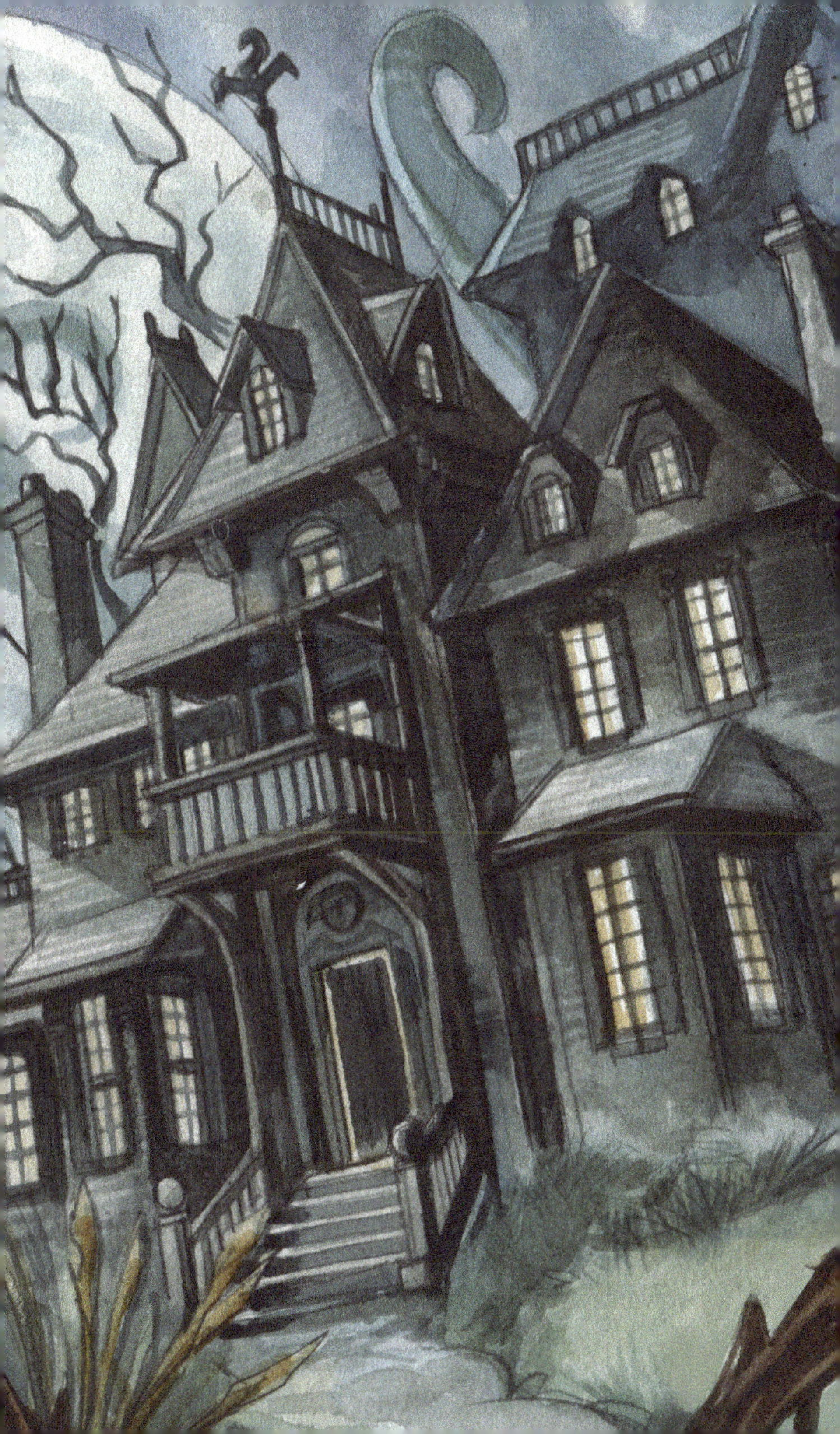

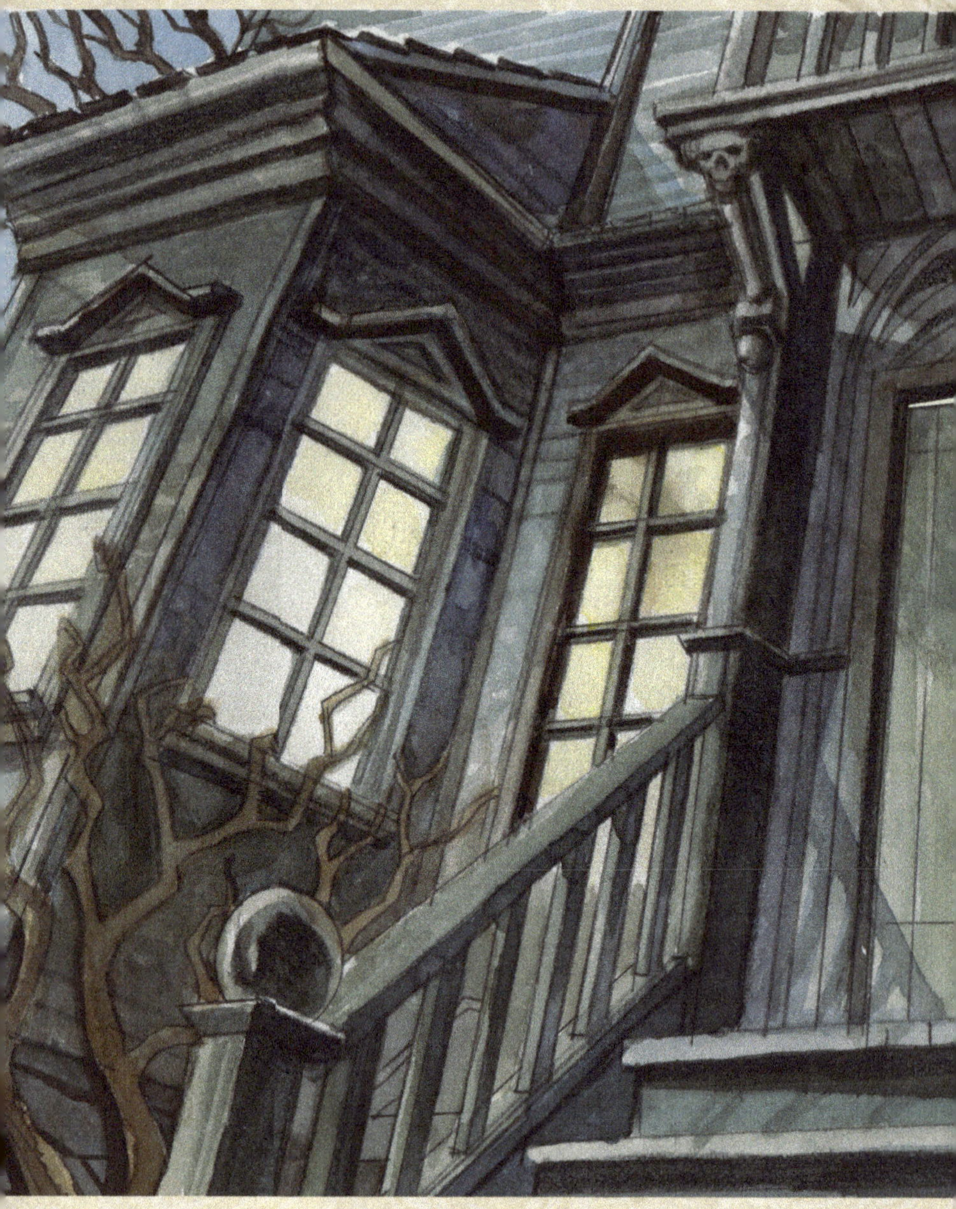

I was asked by the Dowager, the matriarch of the clan who holds the purse strings, to create portraits of the family and to record the strange and disturbing creatures that live just outside our human reality. By sharing their pictures and writing down their stories, she wishes to create an understanding between our world and theirs. She claims they mean no harm, truly, but I suspect there is something deeper to her request.

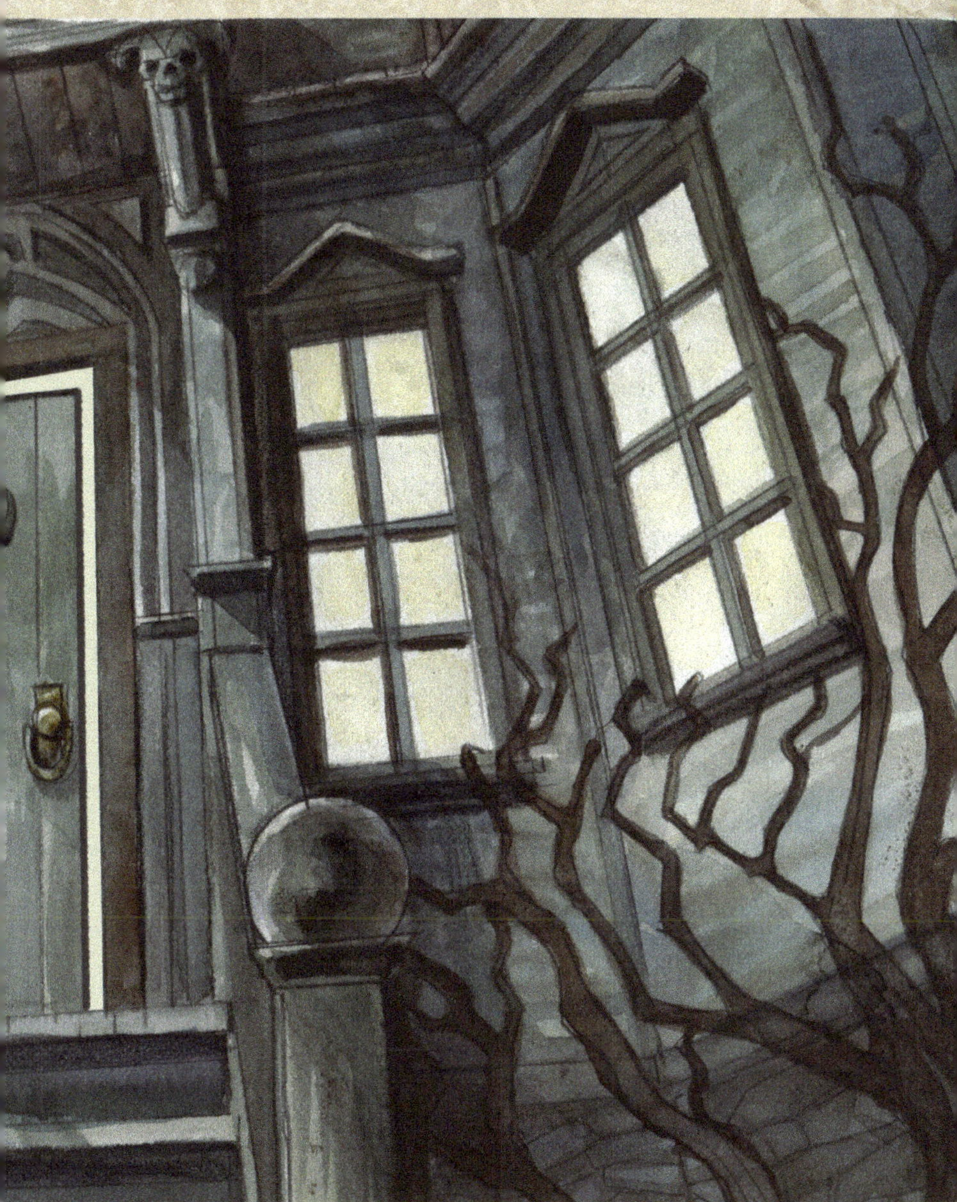

Within this tome is a collection of biographies and portraits of the Family that has been revealed to me so far. The more I get to know them the more I recognize there are bizarre and frightening things beyond what is in this book. Perhaps I will be able to bring reveal more to our world if I survive.

One final word, Be warned, inside this book you may find disturbing answers to your questions about the true nature of the universe, or worse yet, you may find more questions.

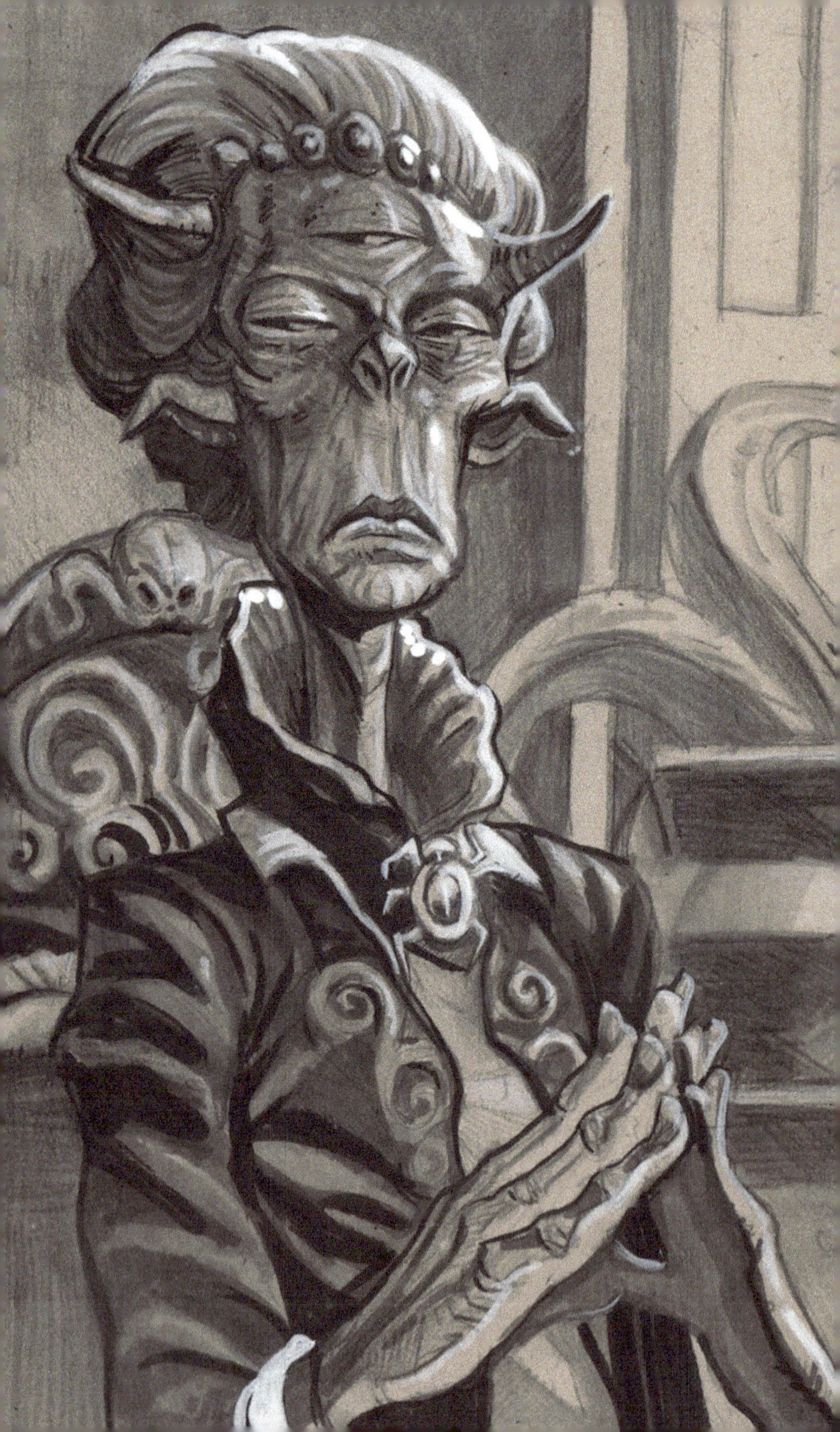

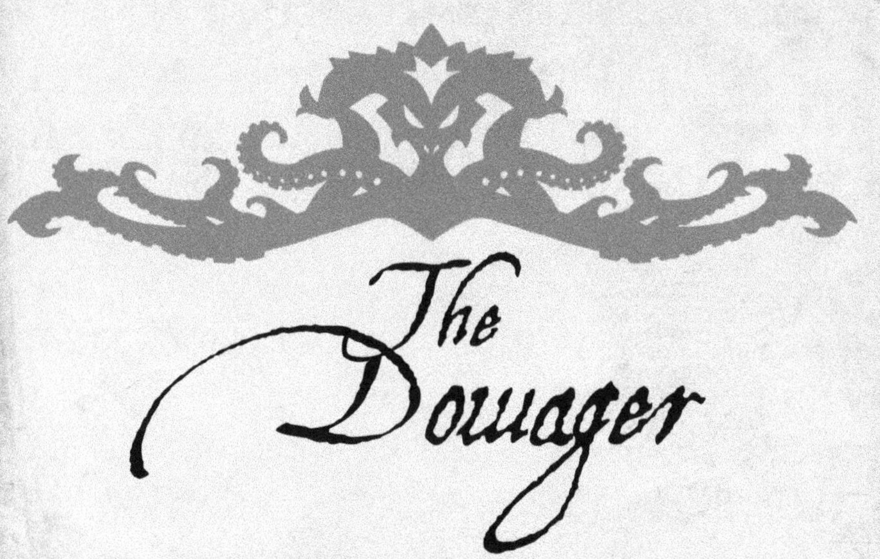

The Dowager

The matriarch of the Thornclaw Family, she has been alive for millennia. She is shrewd and sometimes cruel and she always has a plan. She sits at the center of the Thornclaw family controlling the dynasty of otherworldly beings from the high-backed chair in her chamber. She is watched over by her doctor and the Apothecary who work to ensure that she will live for another millennium, but the three-eyed elder being can see that her end is in sight. She sees herself as the bulwark against chaos and through her order, she has allowed the humans of our world to survive and prosper. Her control of the Manor allows her to maintain control of the realities of the universe, but she believes the stars are aligning against her and that a new age must come to replace the old. She has searched among her brood for her successor, but she continues to find them wanting. As the forces of chaos scratch at her front door, she fears there will be no one to protect the universe she has worked so hard to maintain.

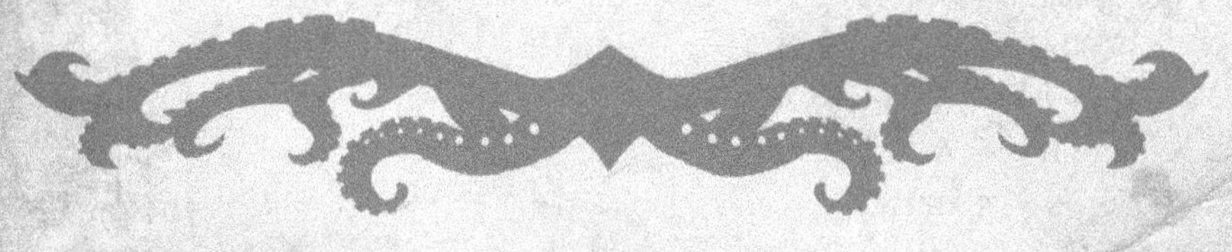

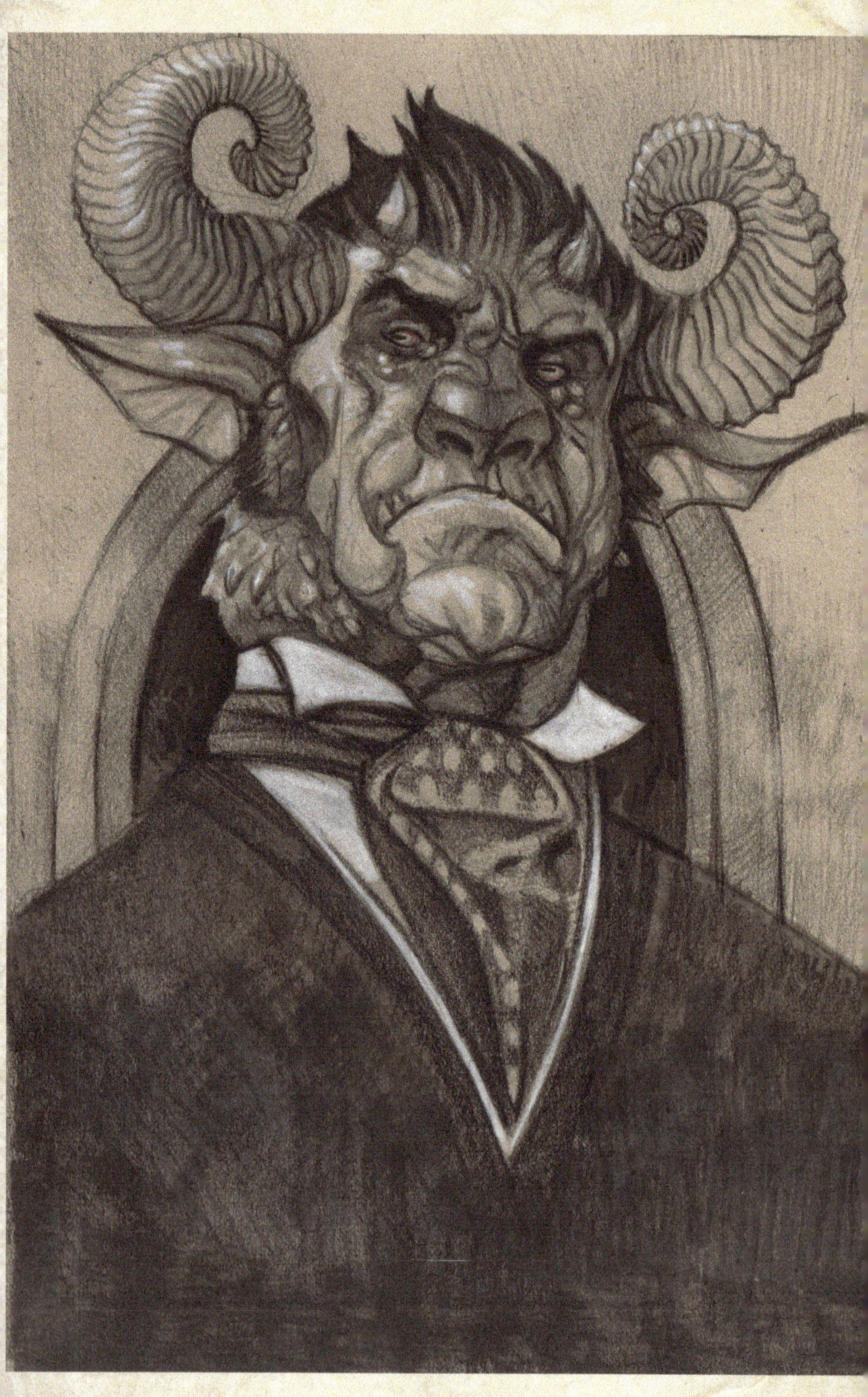

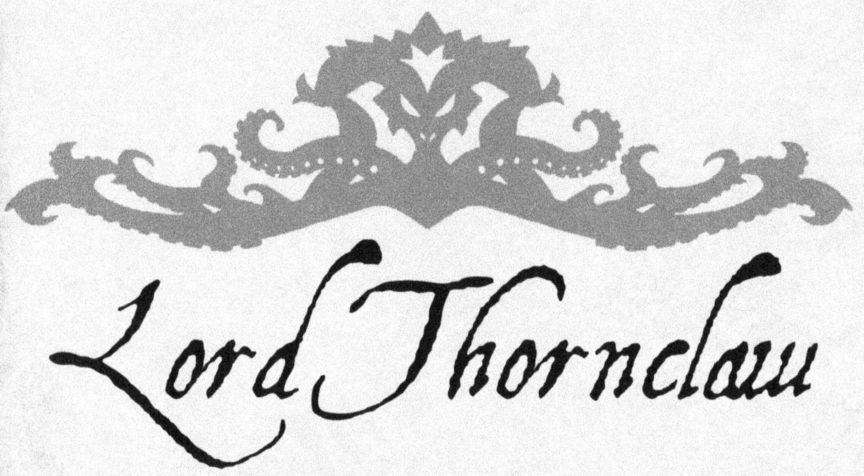

Lord Thornclaw

His giant size and brusque manner only hide the simple sweetness of the Lord Thornclaw. Highly emotional he is easily sent into blind rages and fits of sadness, his heart worn boldly on his sleeve no matter how hard he tries to maintain a powerful, reserved presence. His love for his Manor is exceeded only by his love and loyalty to his family. The Dowager believes him to be far too weak- hearted to become the leader of the Thornclaw clan at her passing and while he stays by her side through the ages, his loyalty will most likely never be returned.

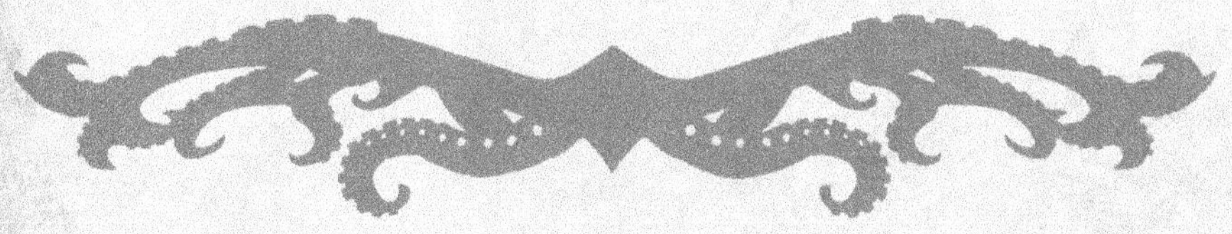

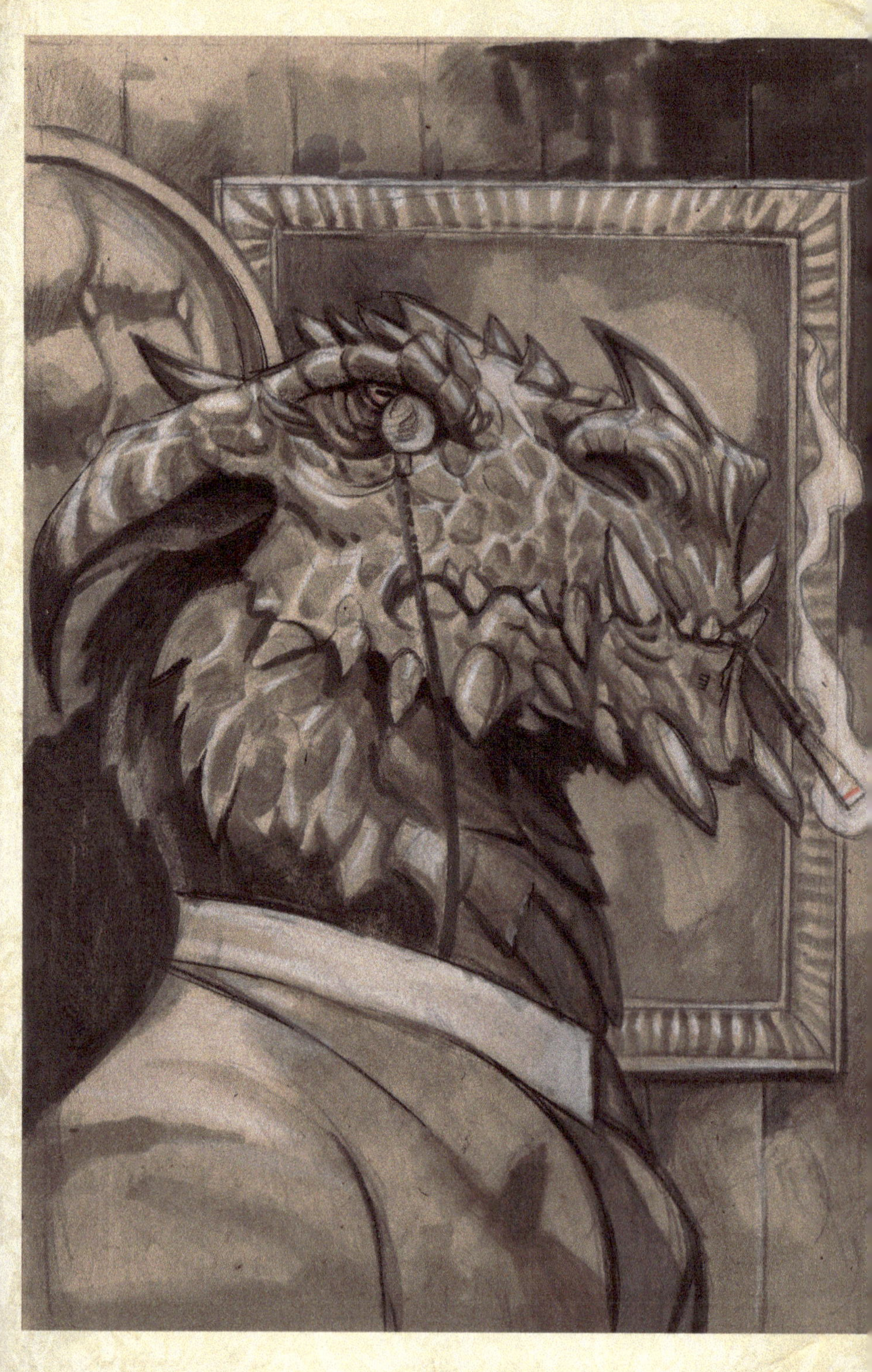

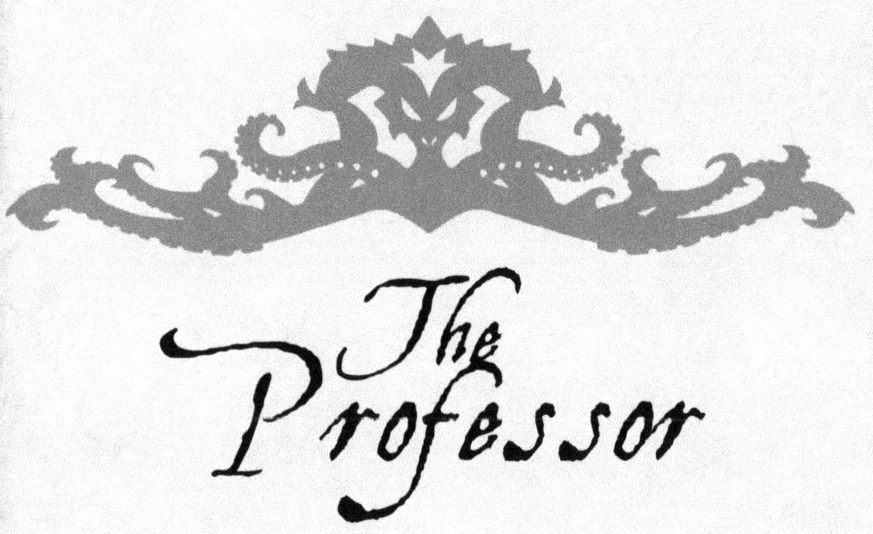

The Professor

A second-generation Thornclaw, the Professor has made a living out of his habit of reading into others' motivations. As a psychoanalyst for the Thornclaw Clan, he probes into the subterranean depths of the monstrous psyche. Watch what you say, he is listening.

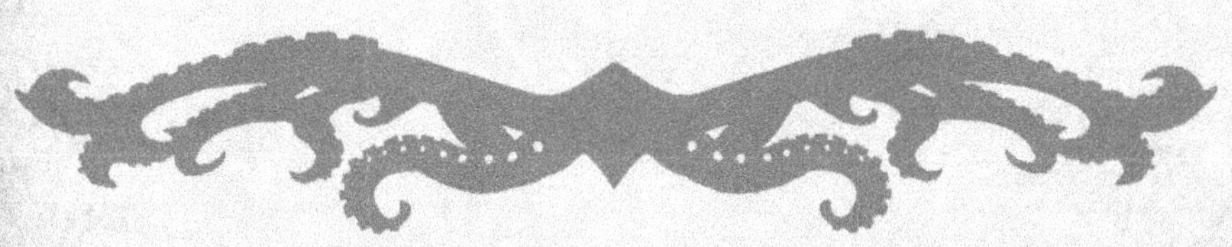

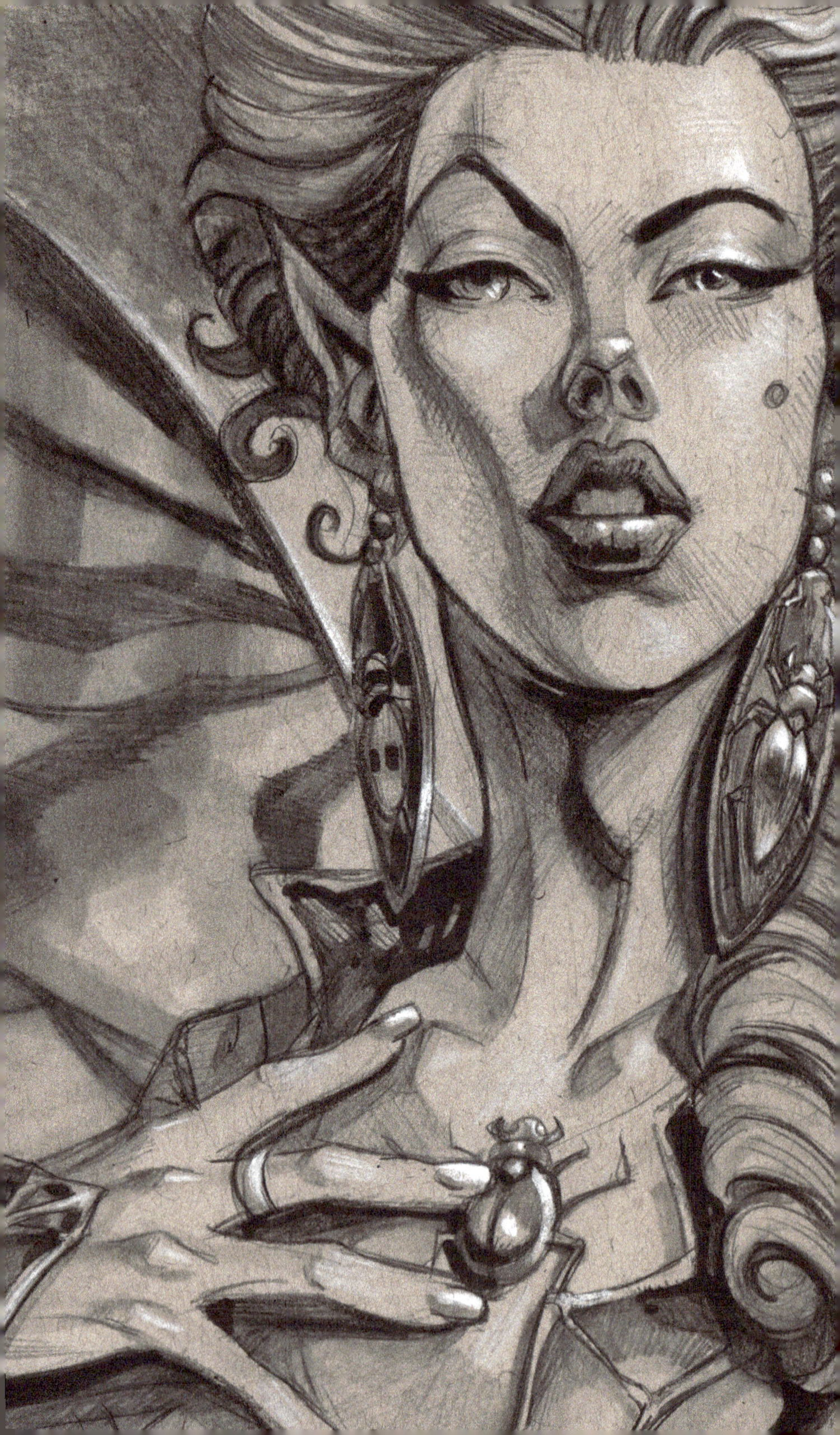

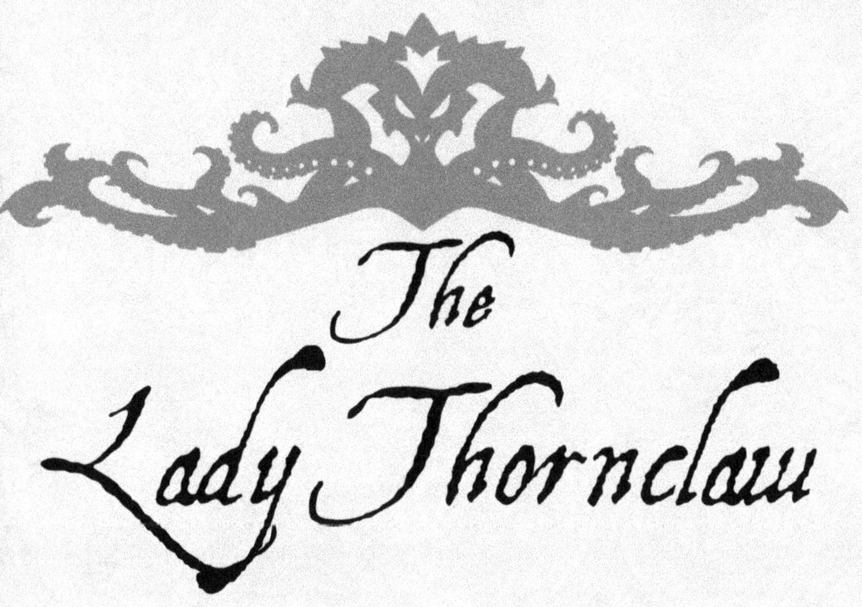

The Lady Thornclaw

Wife of the Lord and daughter of the Fae, she exalts in the luxury and glamour of the life of The Lady. While she plays the part of the dizzy wife who is dazzled by the sparkle and shine of wealth and jewelry, she plots to put her husband into positions of power where she can manipulate him. Maneuvering on the sidelines she plots to get her hands on the power and wealth of Thornclaw Manor.

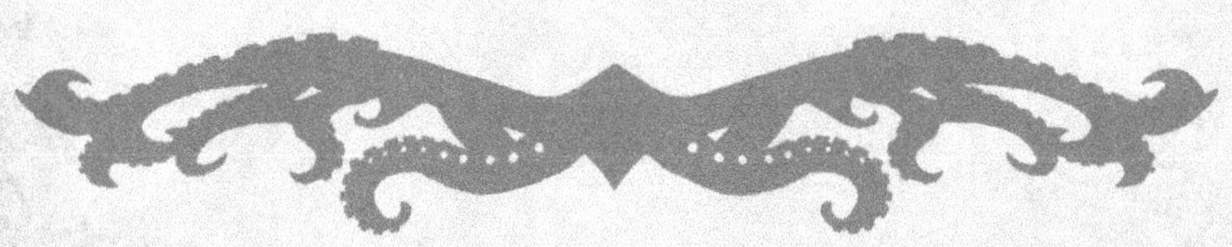

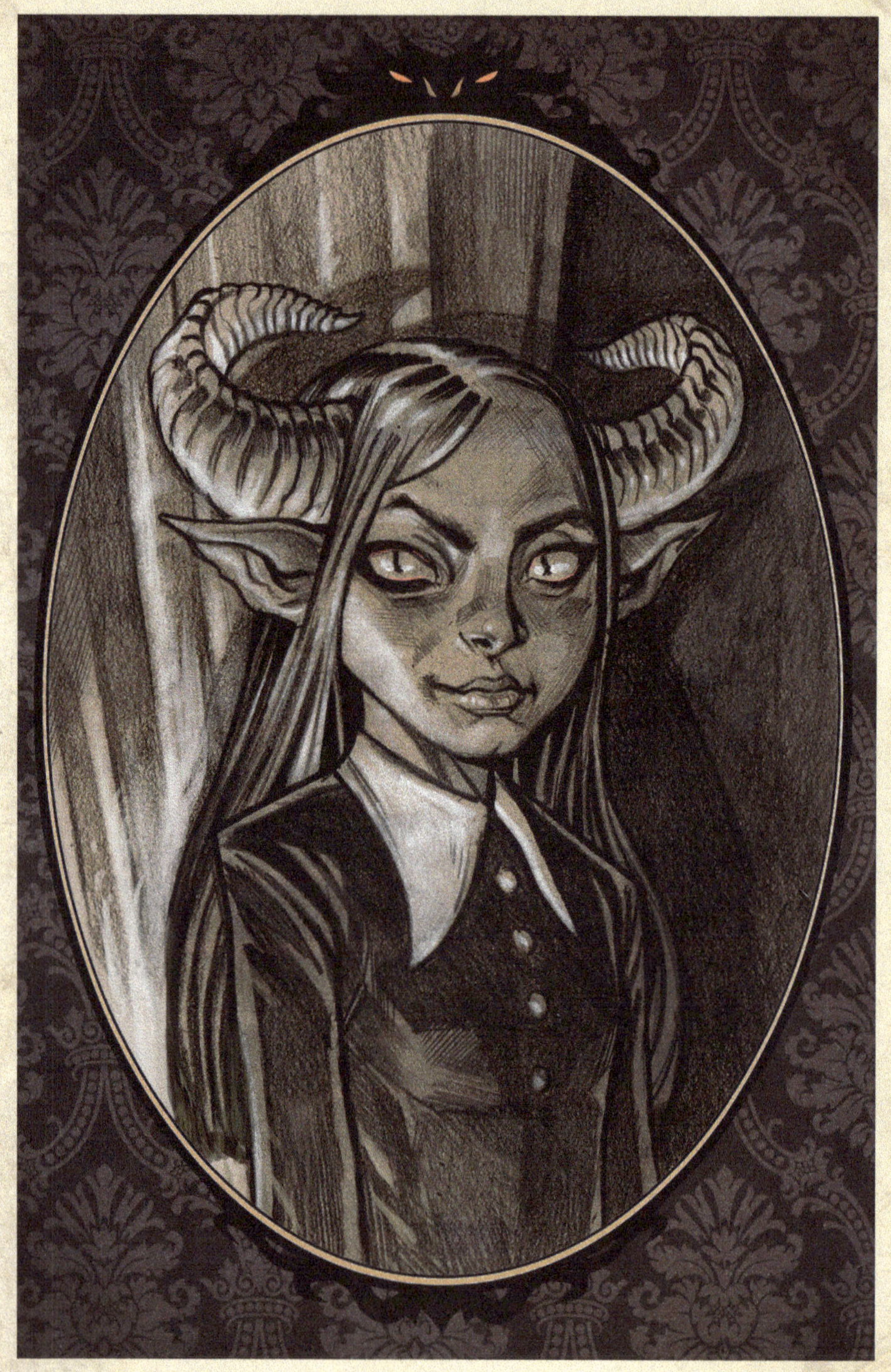

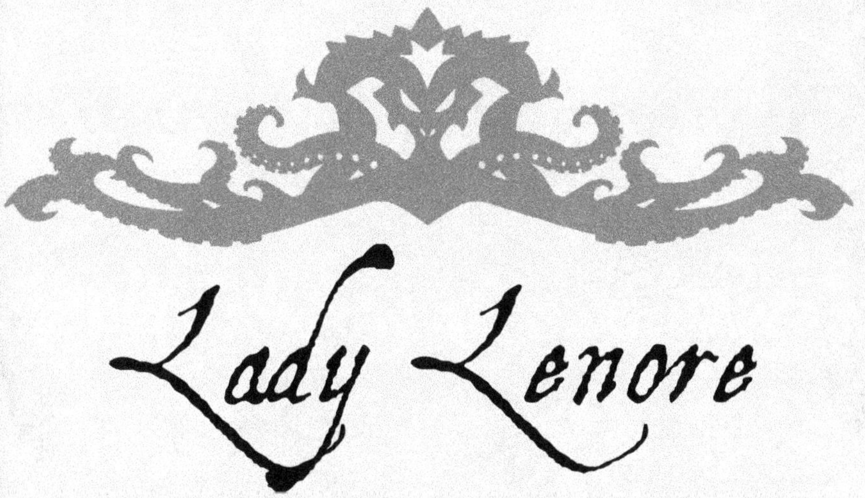

Lady Lenore

She's the youngest daughter of the Lord and Lady Thornclaw.
She's made of sugar and spice and everything devilish. She
seems sweet and playful at first, but watch out, her "games"
and "pranks" often are deadly serious. She often sits at the side
of the Dowager, listening to her tales of the old days. Beware to
anyone who tries to get between them.

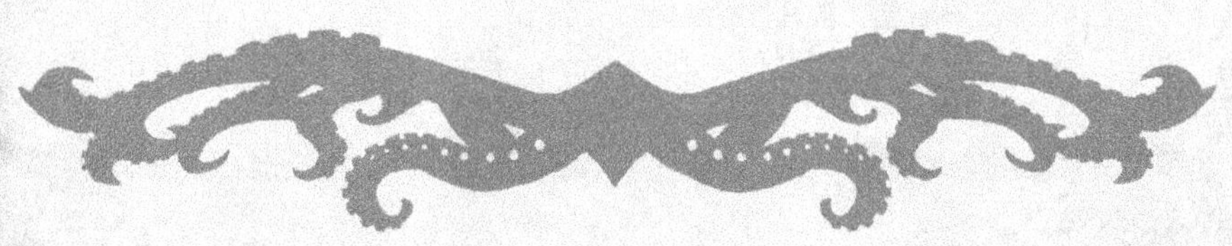

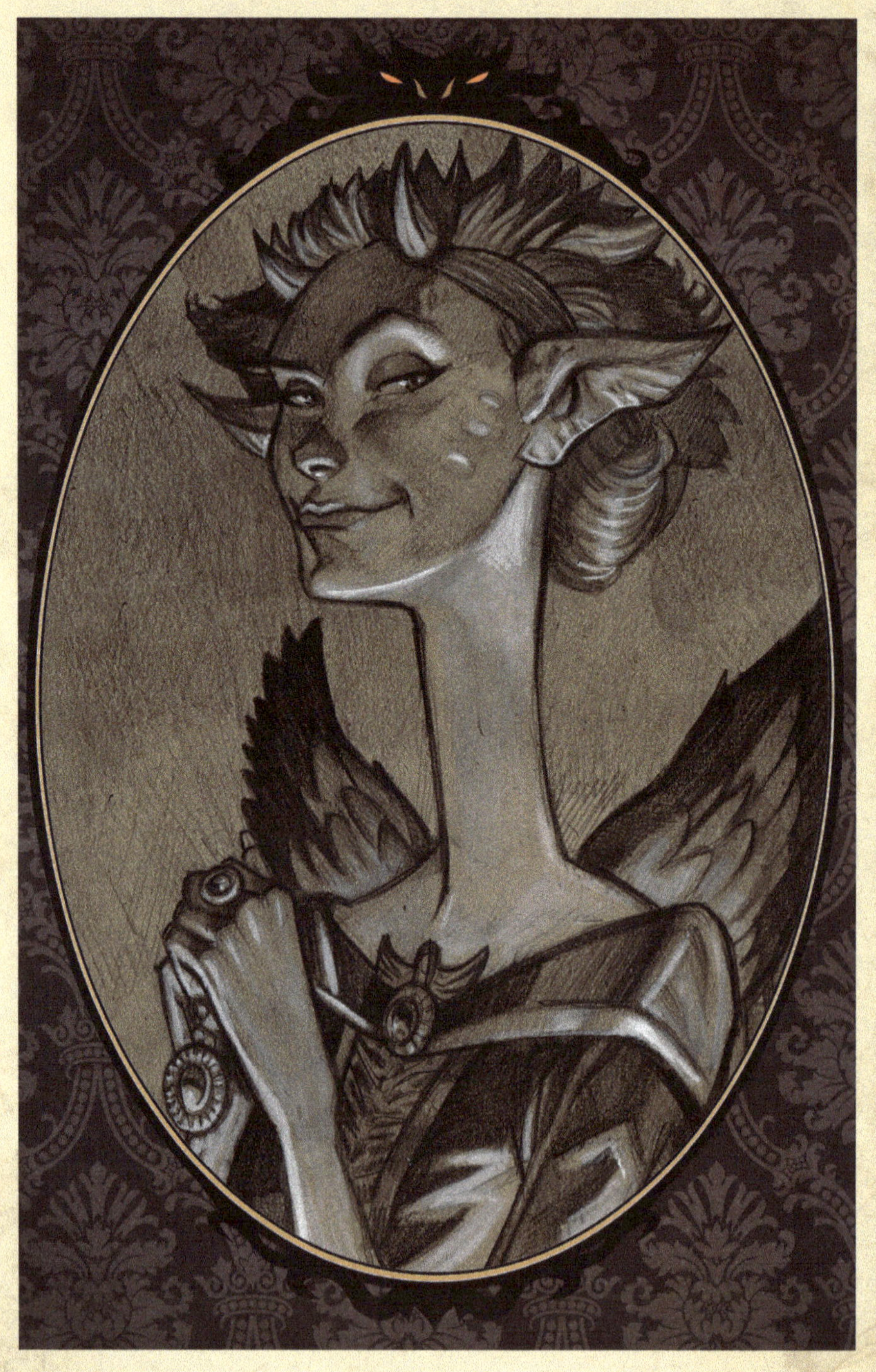

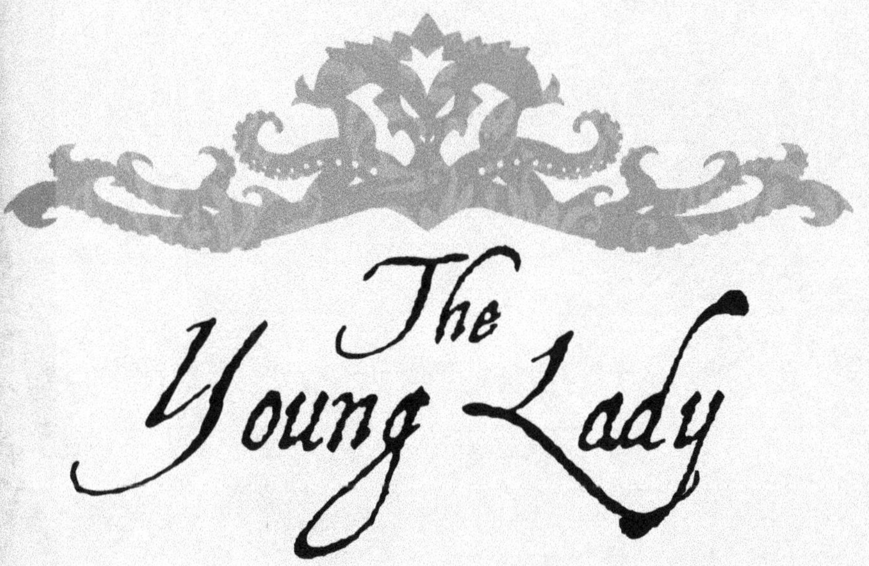

The Young Lady

The eldest daughter of Lord Thornclaw, she is sweet and kind and happy to give a kind word to everyone she meets. But, in the competition for her grandmother's affections, and maybe her fortune, she is fierce. Don't take her sweet smile for granted.

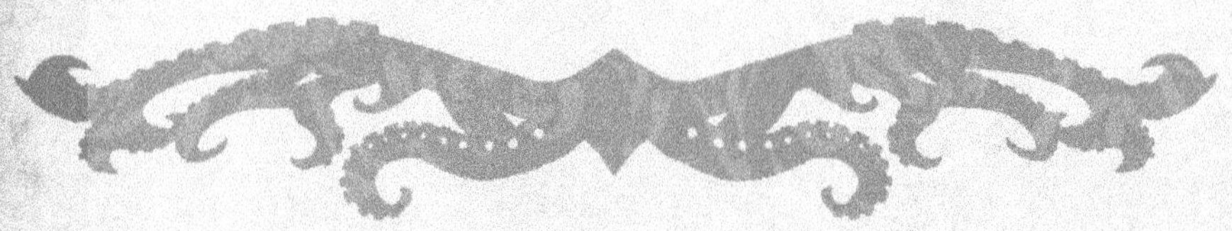

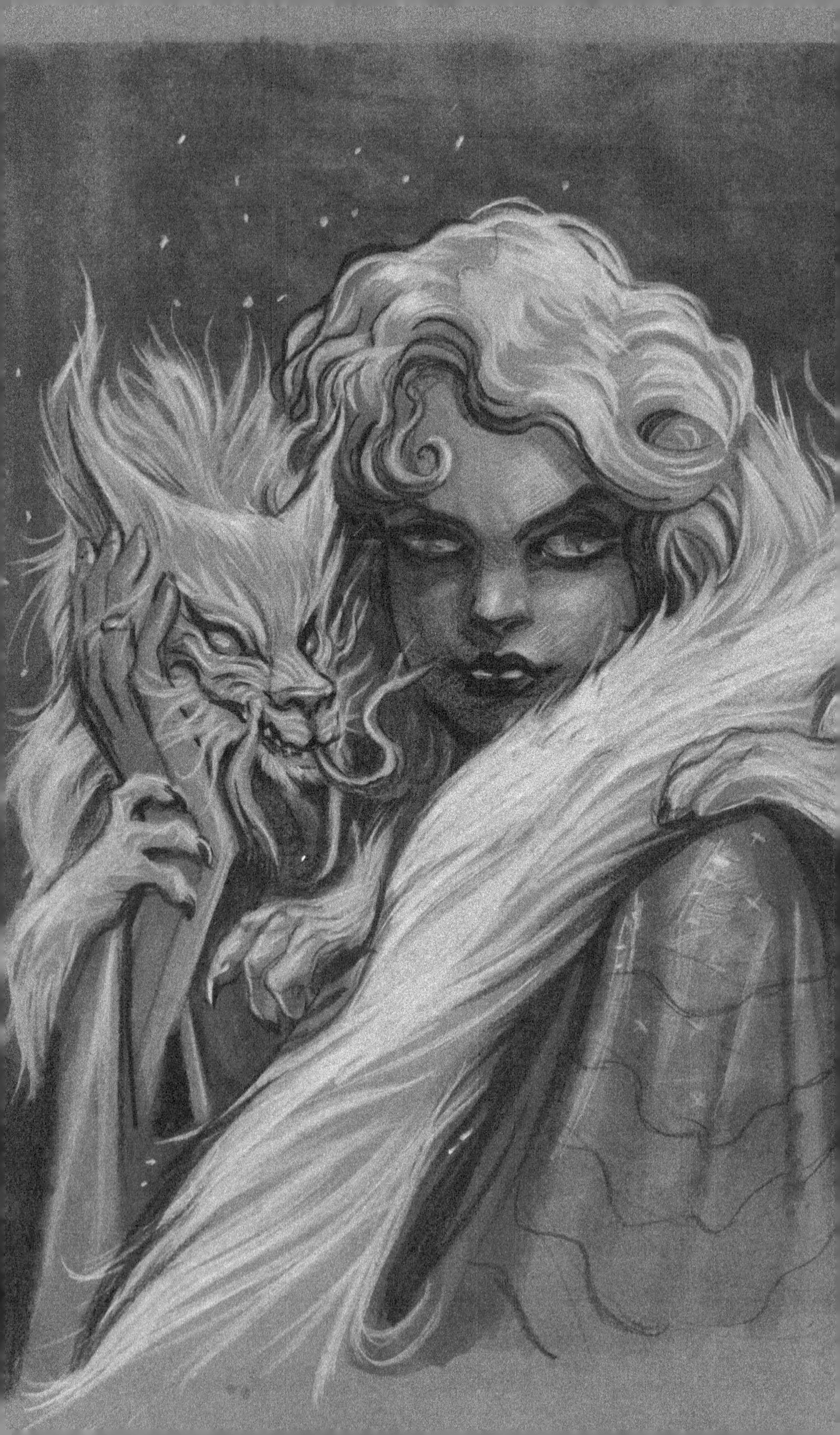

Whisperer

The Whisperer charms his prey with promises of wealth and power. His prey never quite see themselves as victims since after listening to his charming advice they are always invited to the loveliest of parties in the halls of power. As the Victim enjoys herself, The Whisperer, wrapped about her neck, listens plots and manipulates.

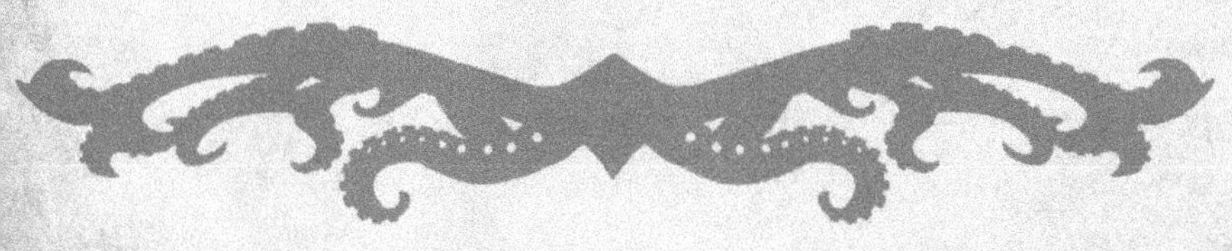

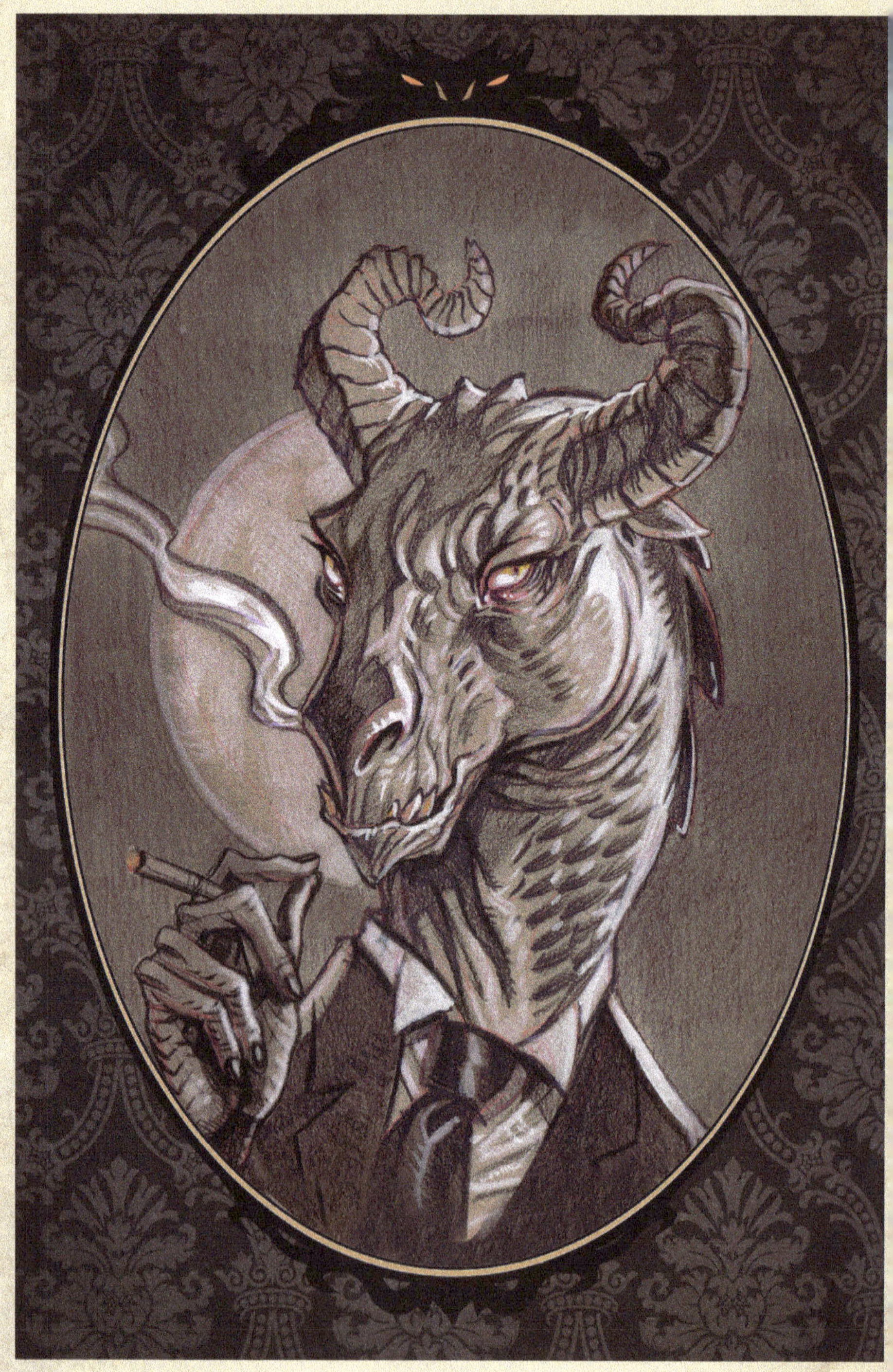

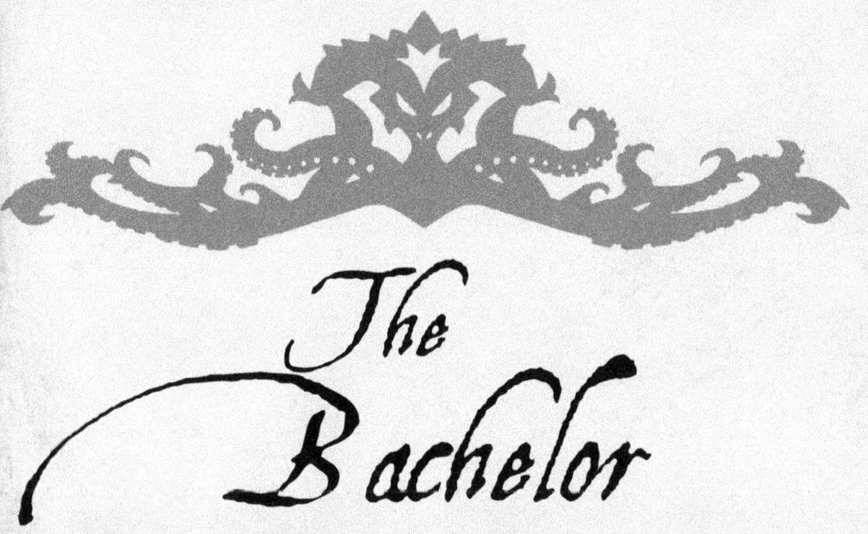

The Bachelor

Sly and smooth, the charming Bachelor is the eldest grandson of the Dowager Thornclaw. His exquisitely-tailored suits and sharp look is a way of hiding his con man career. His slick words work wonders with his Marks, as well as the ladies . . . and the men . . . and whomever catchies his fancy, but the Dowager can always see right through him. He'll need all of his wits to get his claws on the family fortune.

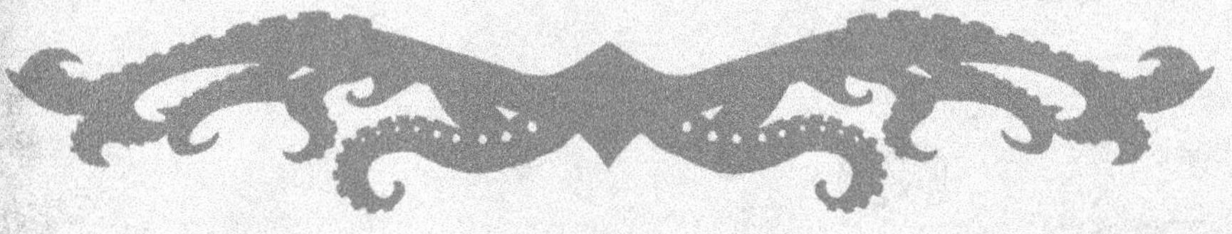

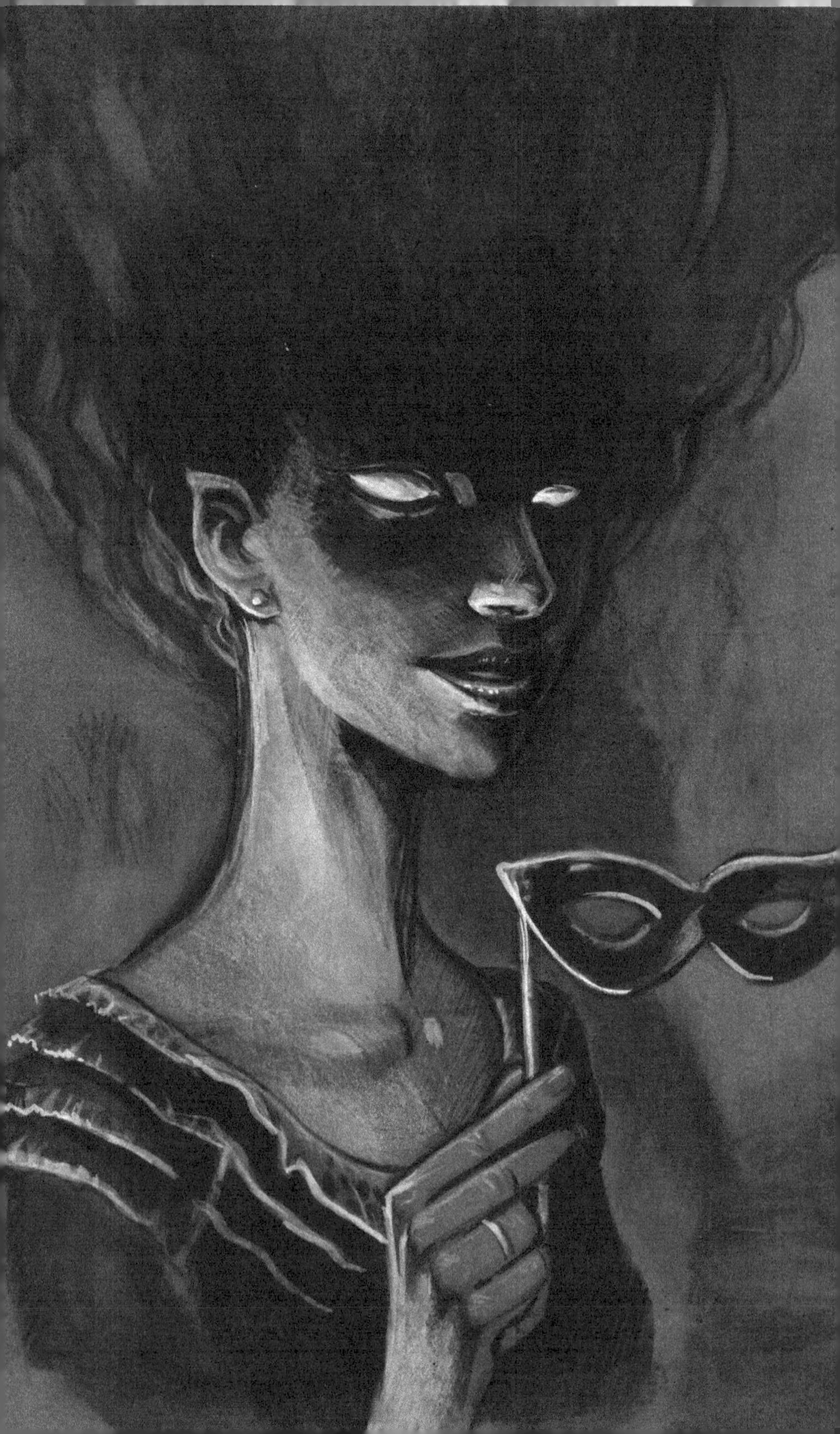

Countess Fogworthy

Since the mysterious and untimely death of her husband, a nephew of the Dowager, The Countess has had a second life living in a haze of parties and masquerade balls on the arm of many a powerful entity. Her "devil may care" attitude may mask a shrewd manipulator looking to climb socially through the Thornclaw Clan, some believe, upon the bodies of its members.

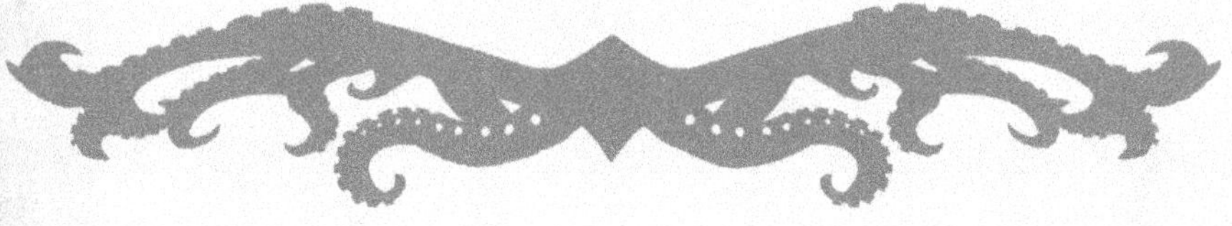

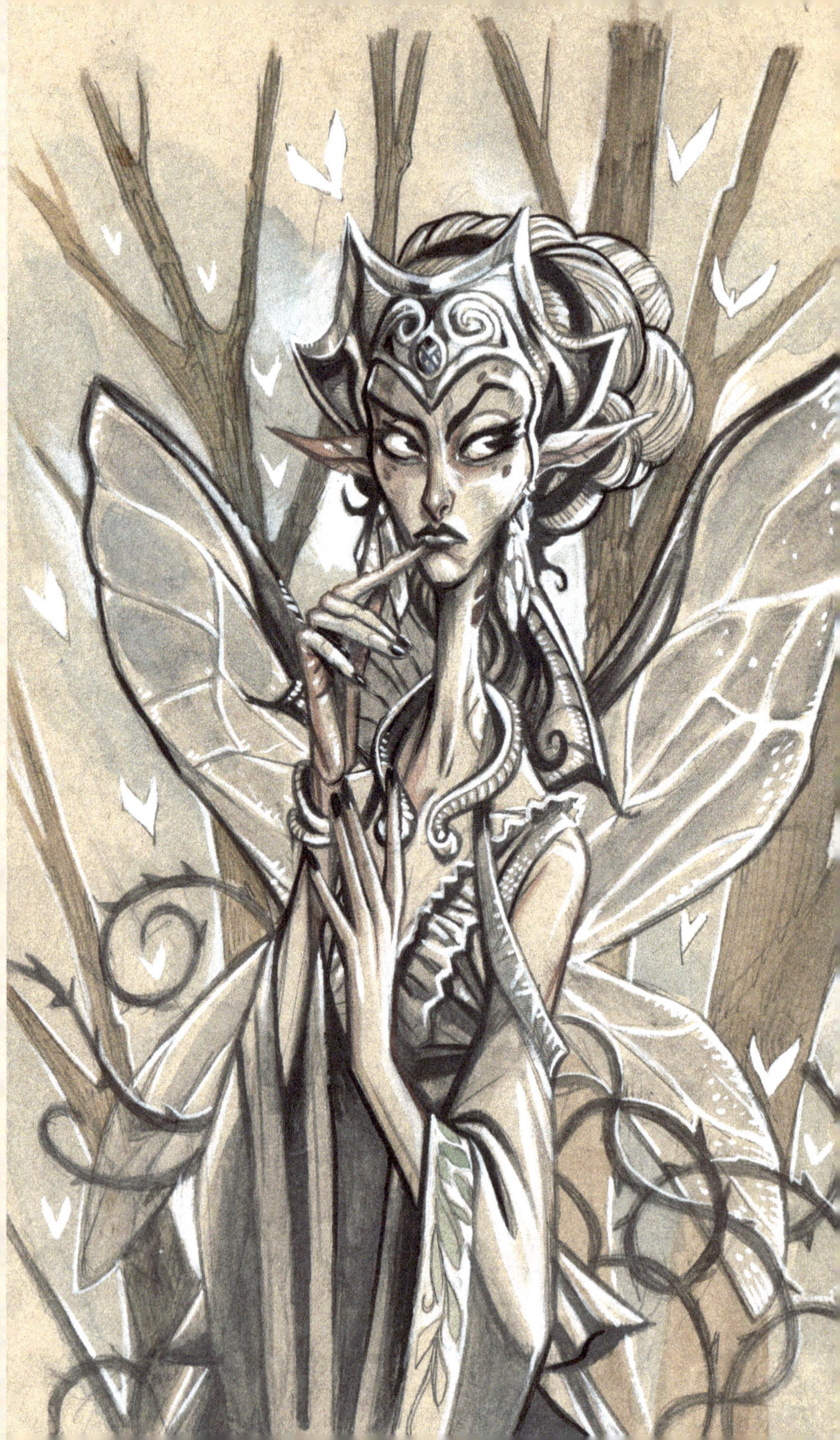

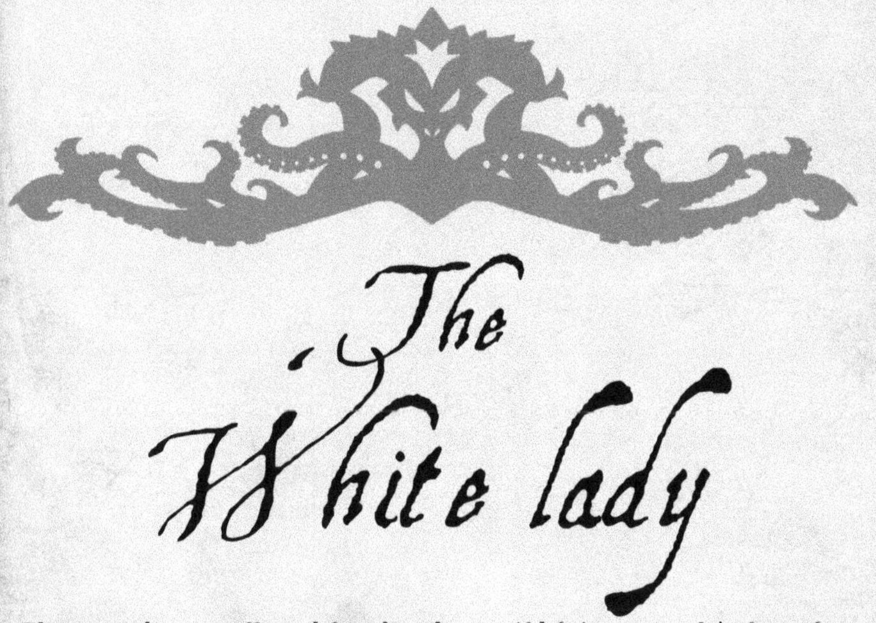

The White Lady

She may be small and fae, but her wild fairy people's love for her is large and strong. She is a sister to the Woodwitch and the ThornedWitch and Thornford, but their family connection doesn't imply a deep love for each other. Her diminutive people who live in the Near Forest are on constant alert to encroachments of the Unseelie Fae, and their fierce loyalty means they will protect their lady with all of their magicks. Her domain is near the gates of Thornclaw manor and she enjoys a comfortable Laissez-faire relationship with the Dowager, although the Dowager's influence can sometimes grate upon the ego of this erstwhile queen.

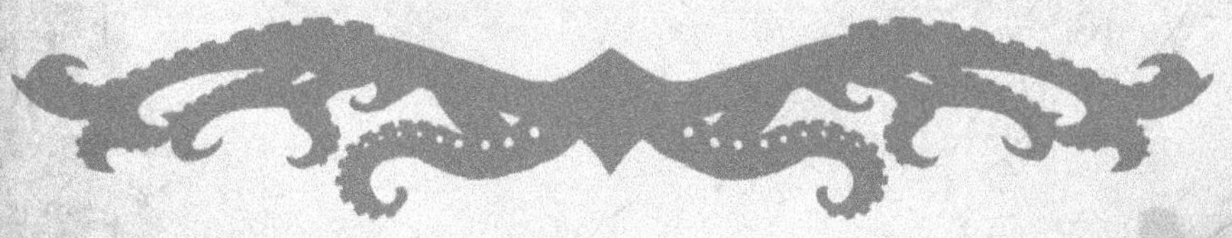

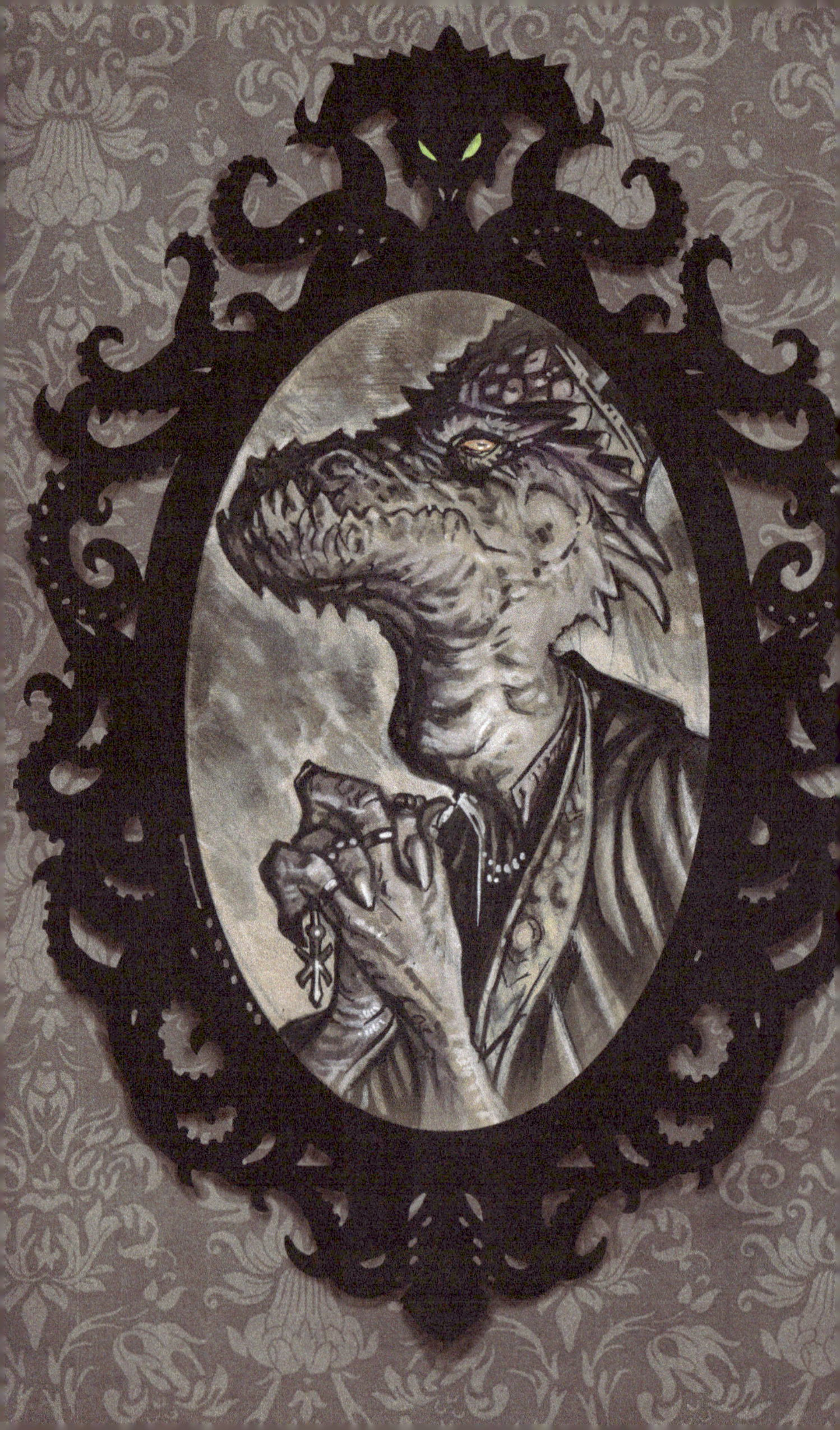

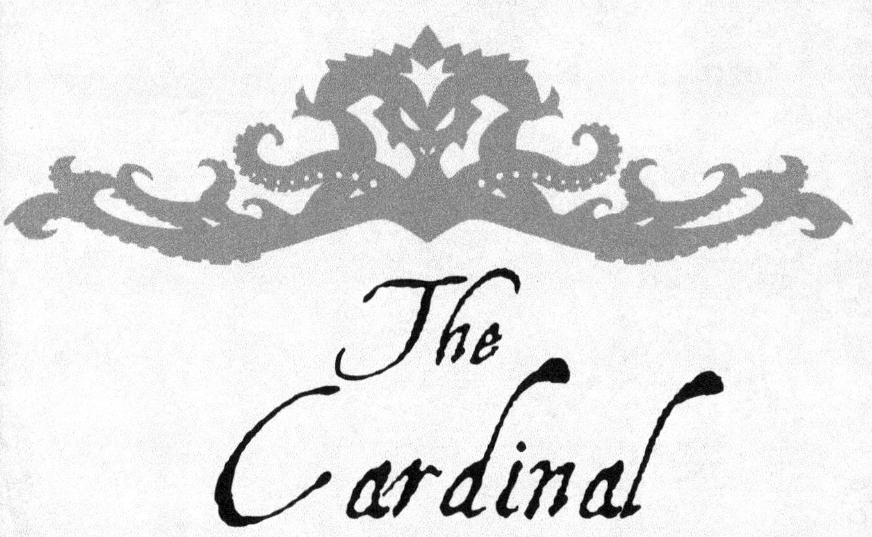

The Cardinal

As the second in command to the Dowager's sister, the High Priestess, the Cardinal acts to further the goals of the cause of Chaos. Unbeknownst to Her Highness, the Cardinal walks a thin line as the Dowager's eyes and ears in the Church. Both powerful beings believe they can trust him, but can either of them be certain of his loyalties? One thing is certain, he enforces the will of the Church with an iron fist as its Grand Inquisitor.

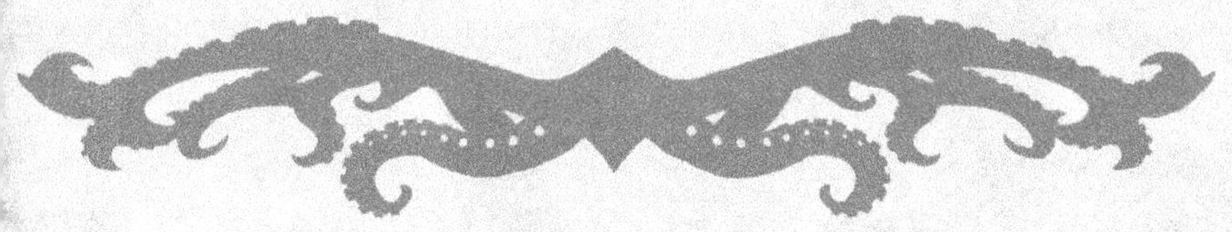

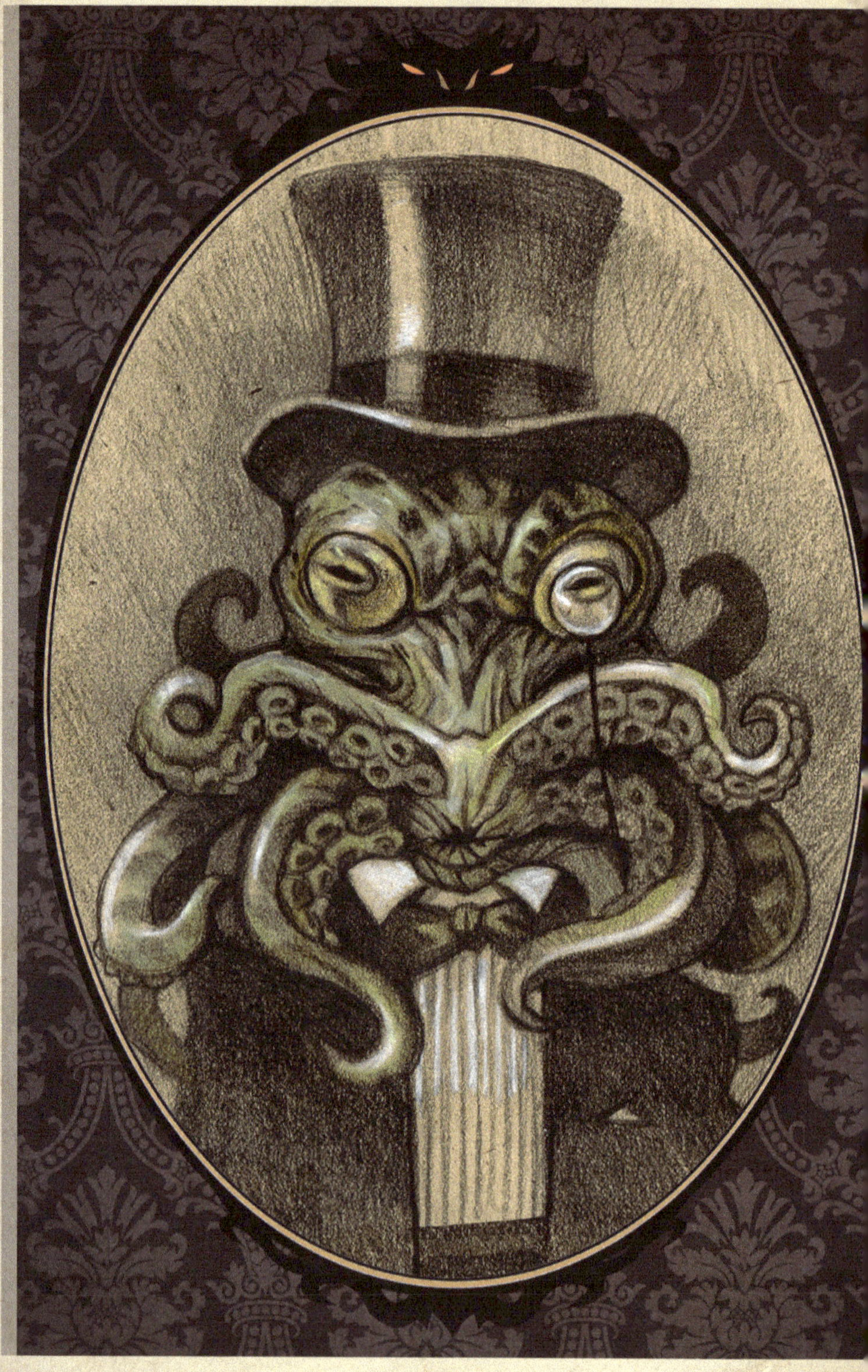

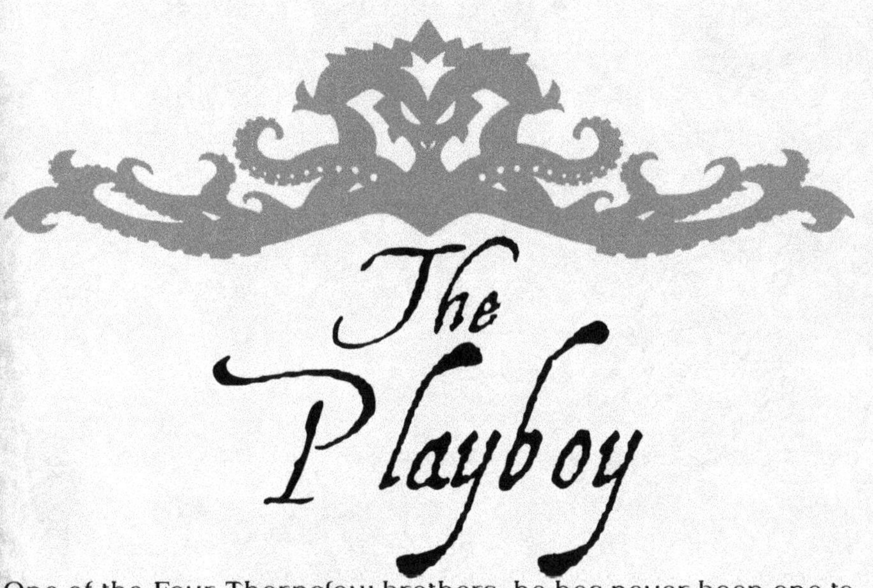

The Playboy

One of the Four Thornclaw brothers, he has never been one to take responsibility too seriously, but now that His mother (The Dowager) is aging, the matter of the inheritance has made him much more family-minded. His mysterious and transgressive club, The Antediluvian, plays home to the universes creative underground and sometimes the dark menace of the Underworld. He can often be found sitting at his table in the back of the club holding court with his hangers-on, drinking, playing cards, and making deals.

His Motto:

"I may sleep for a thousand years, but when I rise, it's time to party!"

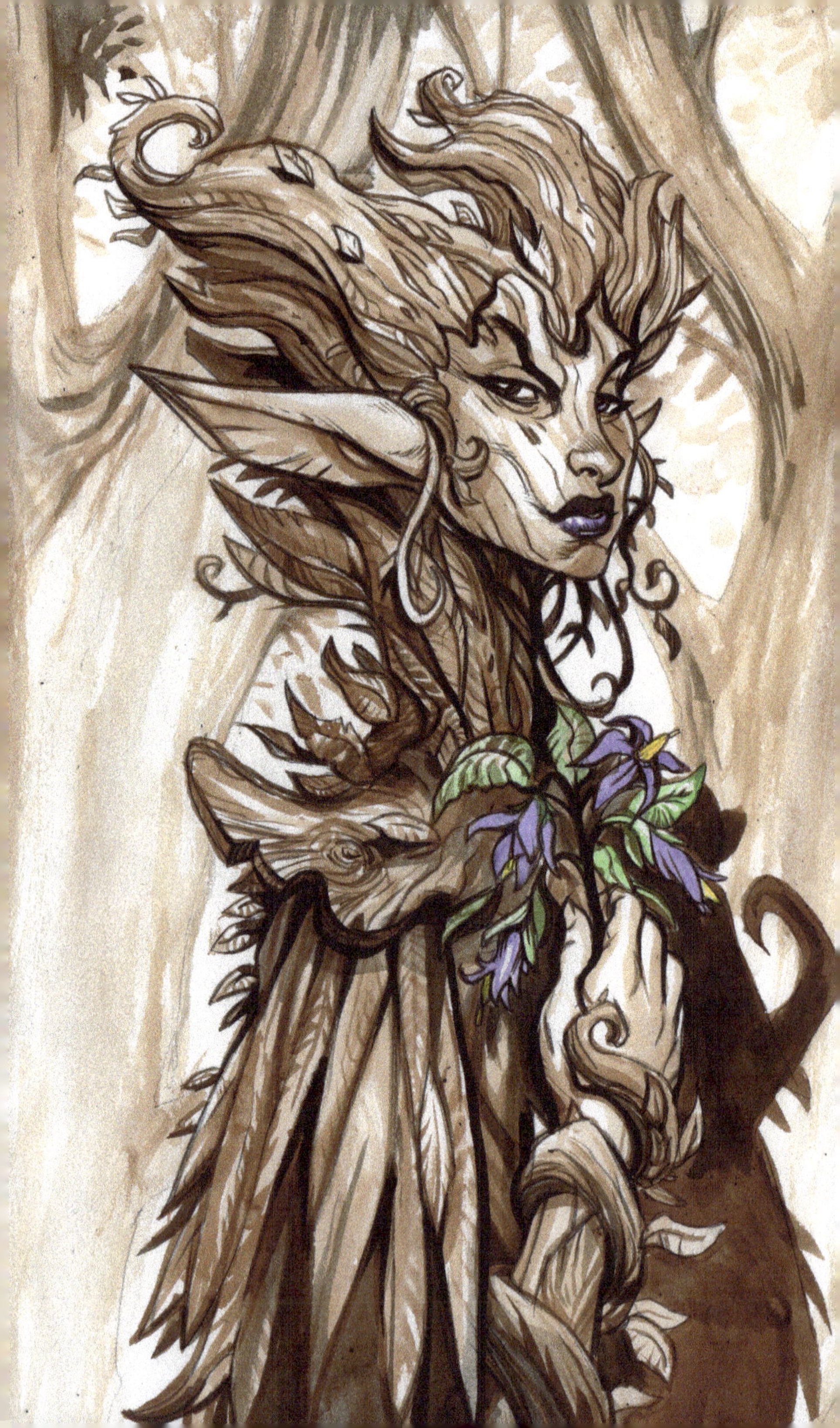

The Wood Witch

A cousin of the dowager, NightShade the Witch Queen lives in the Dark forests around Thornclaw Manor. Never feeling comfortable with a more civilized life, she lives among the wild fae near the creatures and plants she uses in her potions. She and the Dowager have never seen eye to eye, but a piece of the fortune would buy lots of "eye of newt."

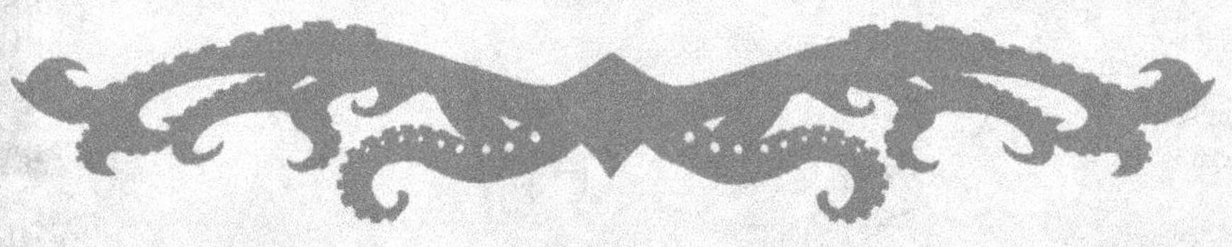

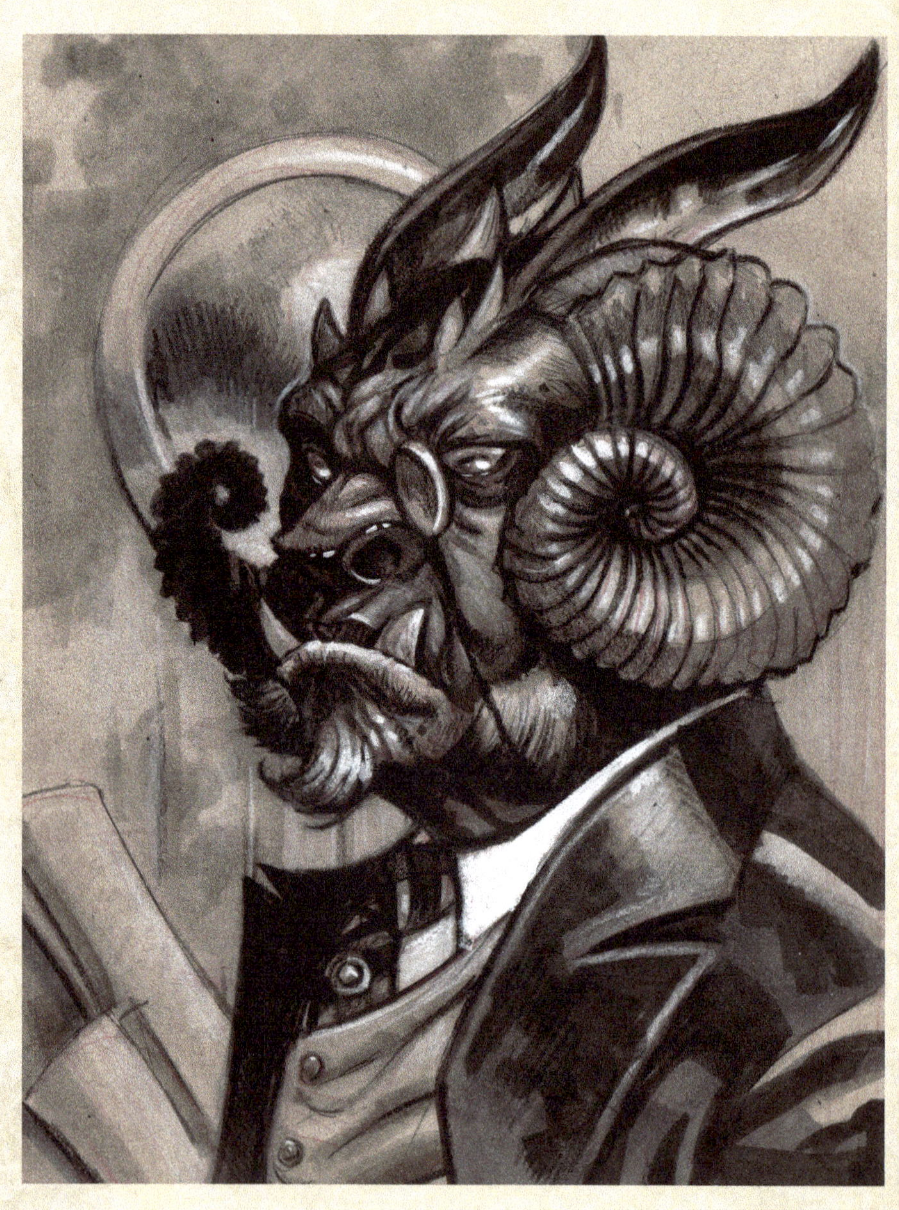

The Architect

The Architect, at the Dowager's request, is constantly building additions onto the manor and is seemingly never done. Anyone trying to figure out his maze-like plans are apt to go insane from his use of non-euclidean geometry to design the labyrinthine and maddeningly confusing layout of the monstrous abode. It is said that visitors should beware of wandering the house alone, they may never find their way out. Some say you can hear the calls of lost beings echoing through the night as they seek an exit from the ancient home.

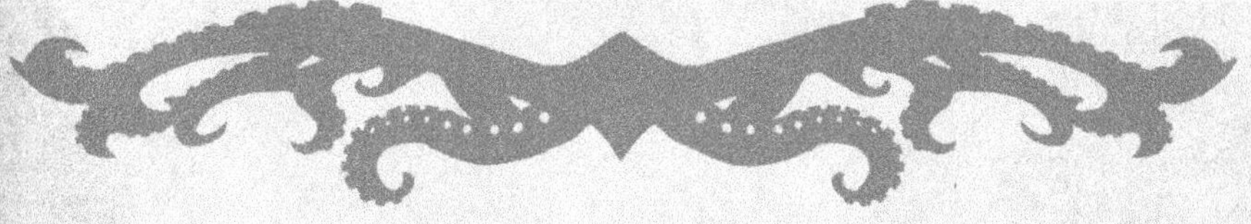

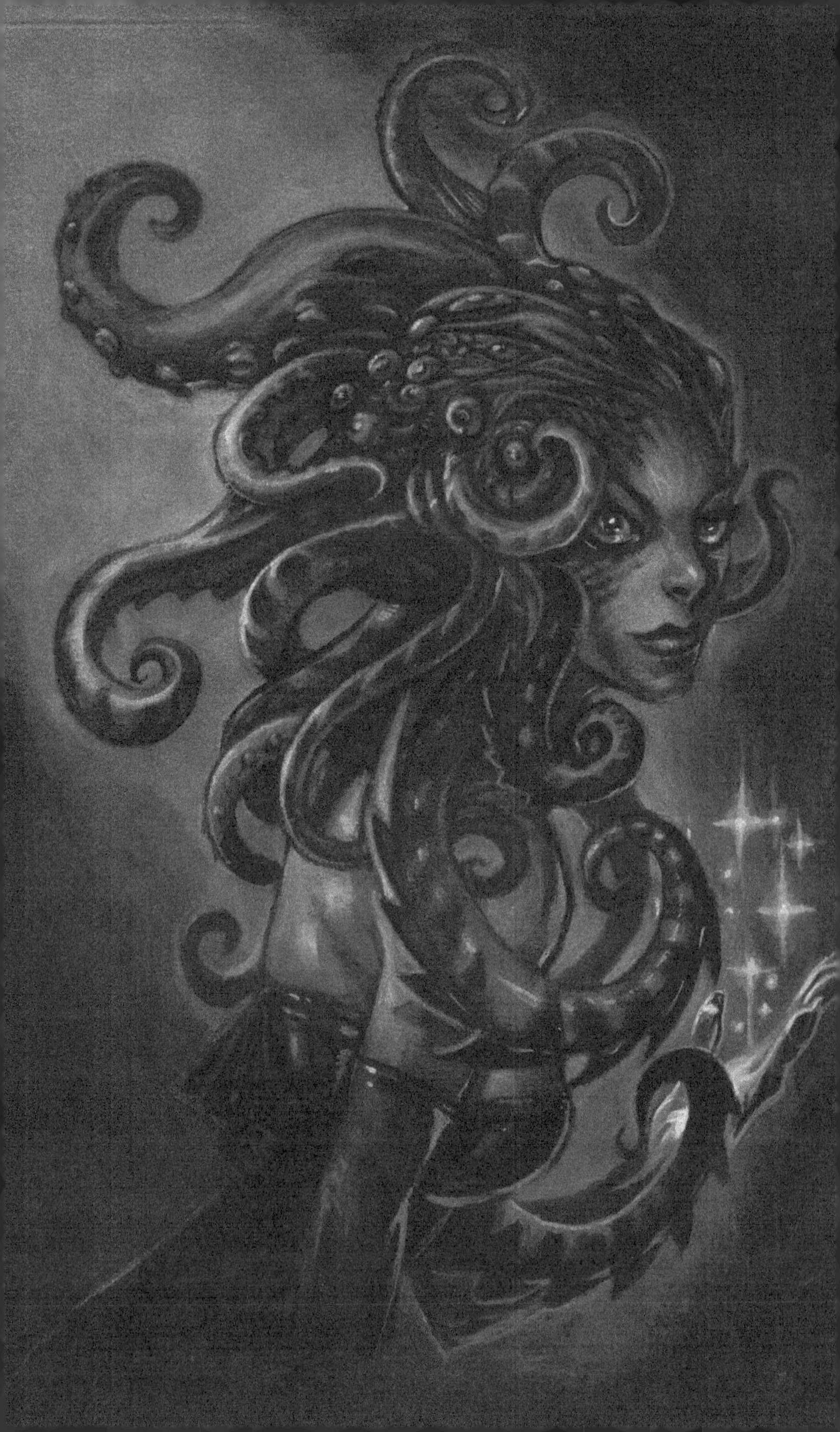

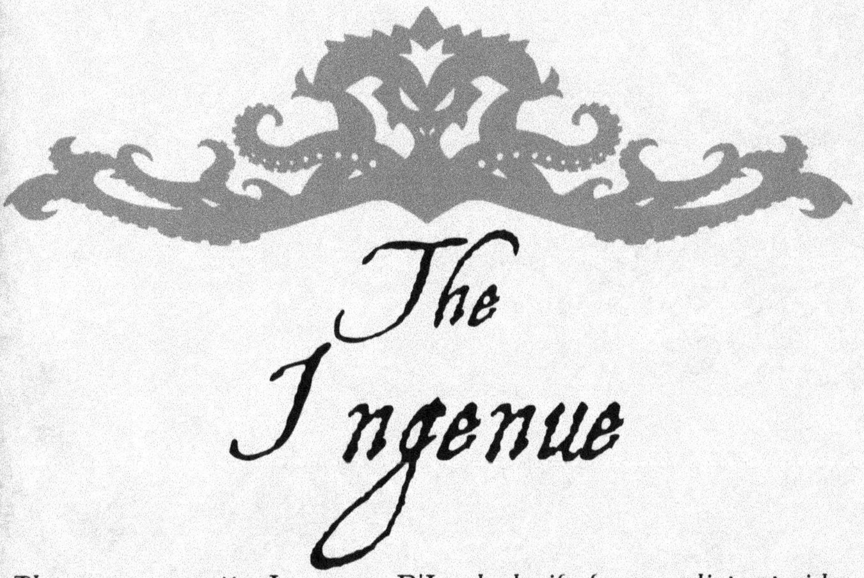

The *Ingenue*

The young, pretty Ingenue, R'Lyeh, hails from a distant side of the Thornclaw lineage. Only having recently arrived at Thornclaw Manor, there is much about her that is shrouded in obscurity. Her mystical connection to the stars and her arrival so close to the Dowager's end make it hard for her to fit in with the already suspicious Thornclaw clan.

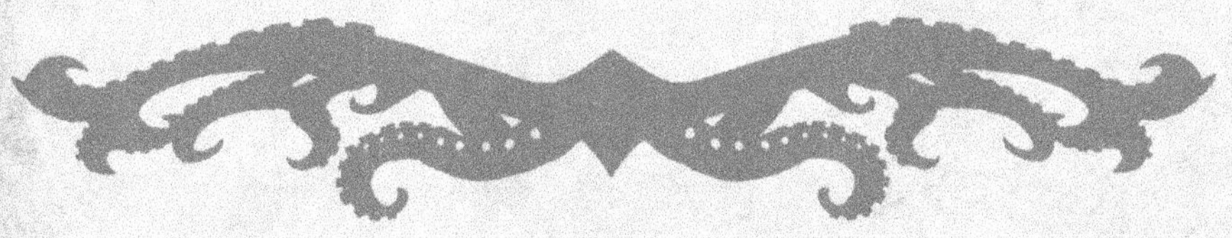

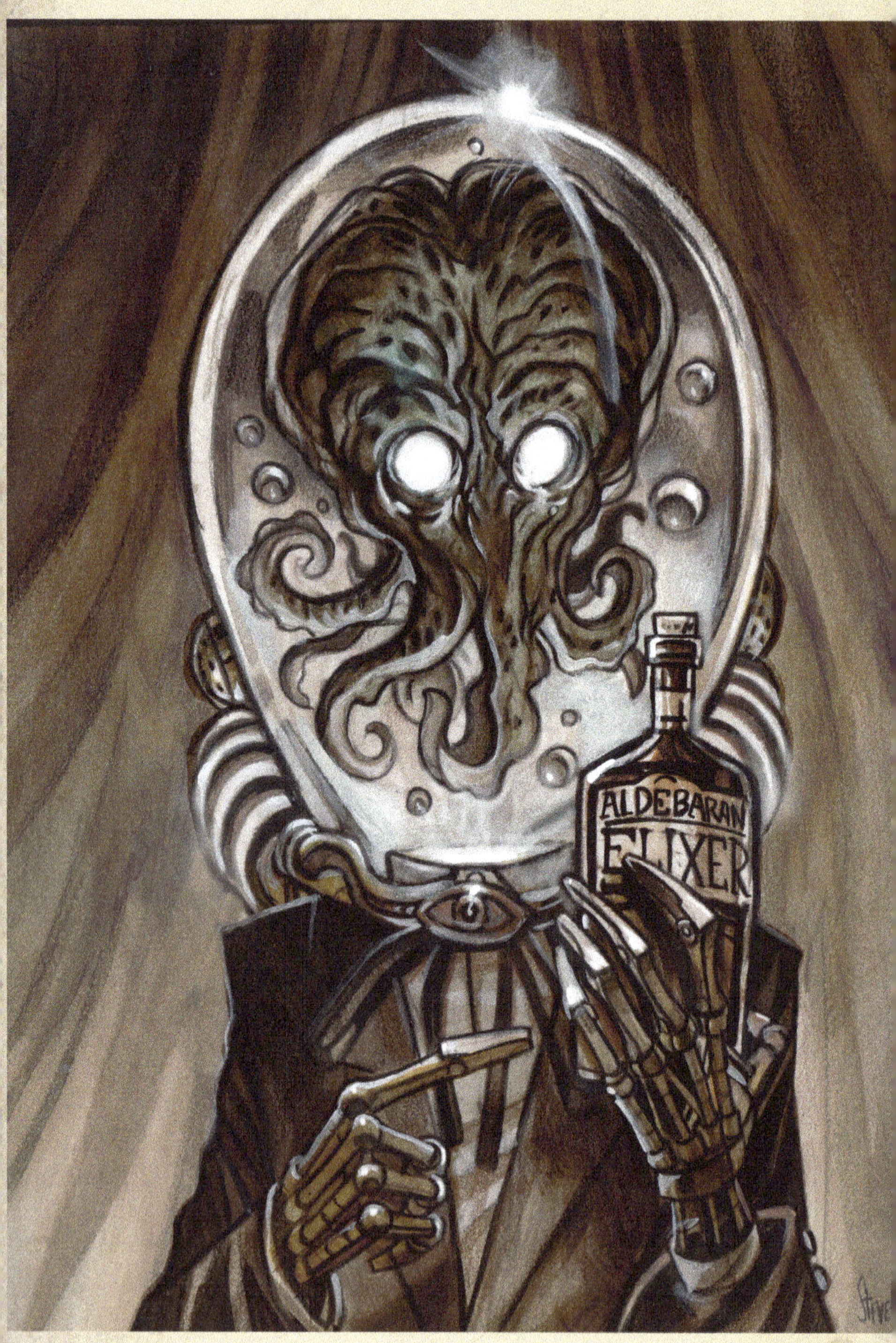

ALDEBARAN
ELIXER

The Magician

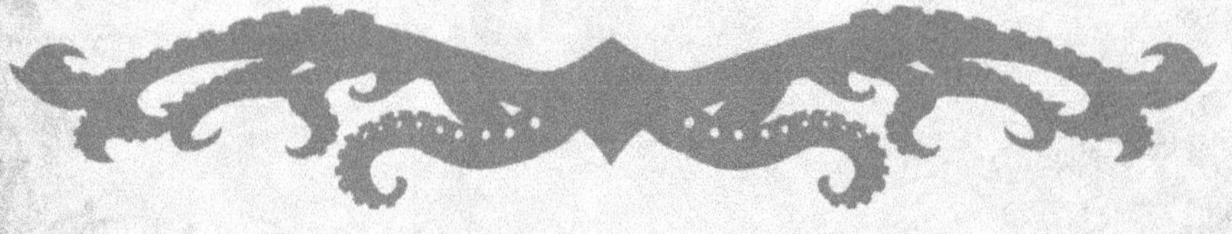

This braincased "dimensional traveler" searches the multiverses for elixirs and potions to uplift the weary and heal the sick...for a price. He takes good care of the Dowager, who keeps him in his extravagant lifestyle. Just make sure he doesn't try to sell you his Aldebaran snake oil.

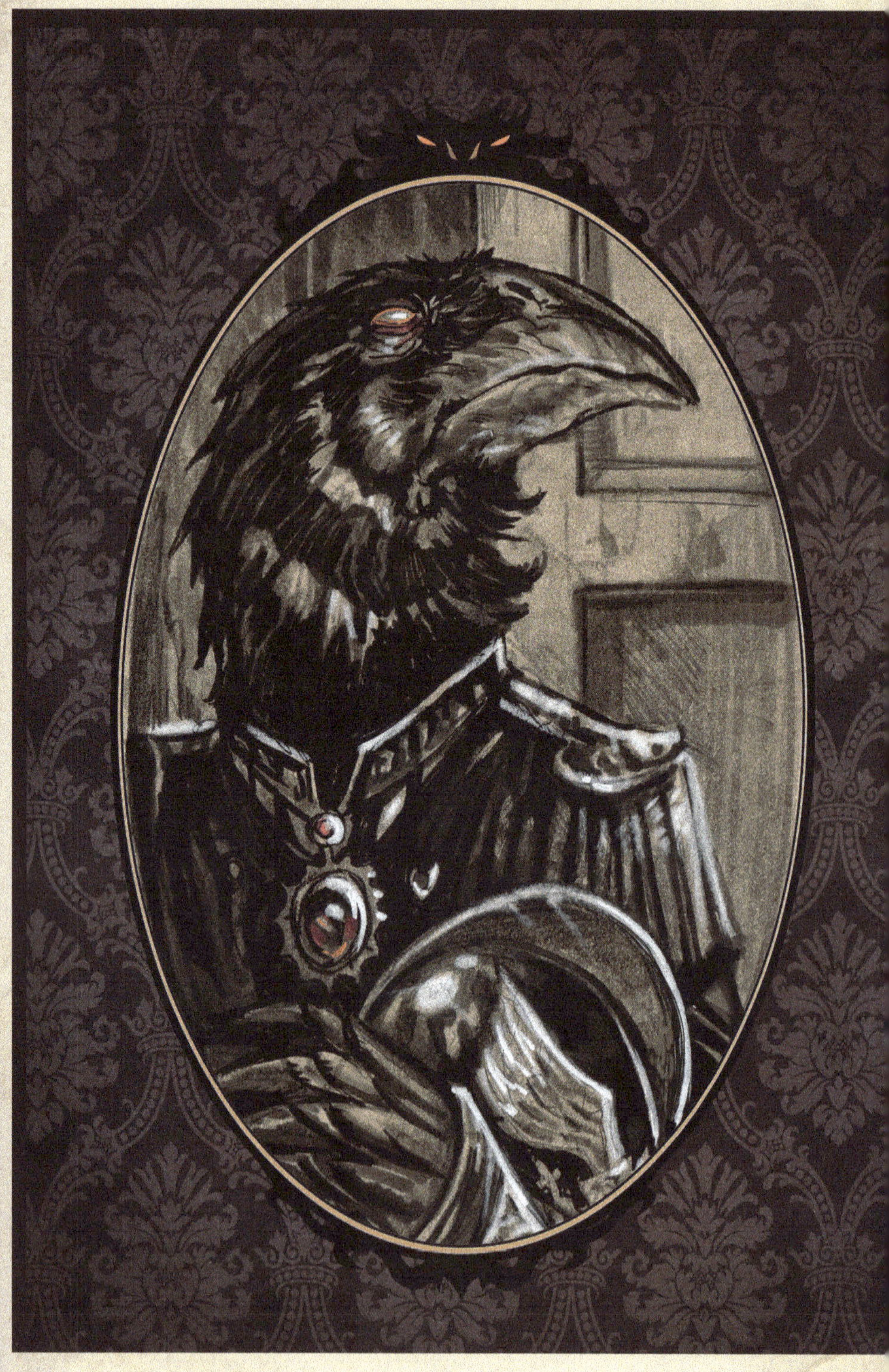

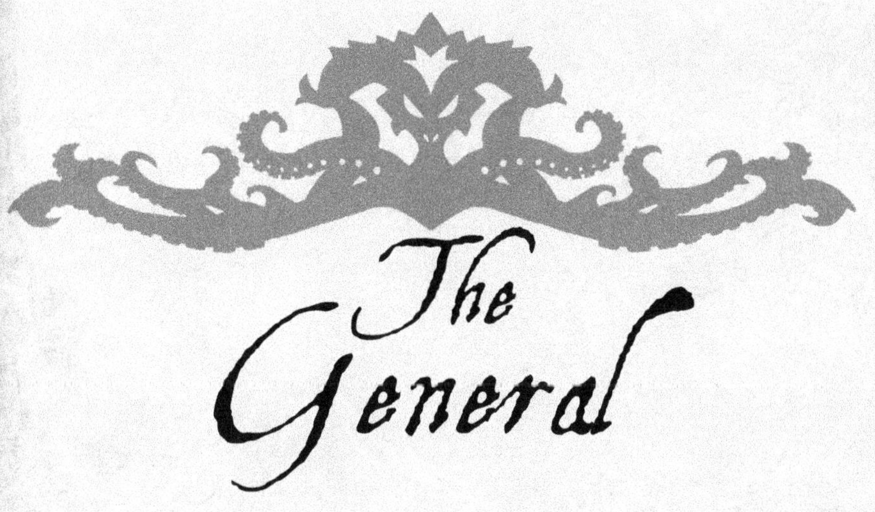

The General

This proud old warbird has many stories of valorous battle and he will regale you with them all night, sometimes twice, provided you keep him plied with a good scotch. He is tough and serious, just do not take his forgetfulness for weakness, he is every bit as sharp as his beak.

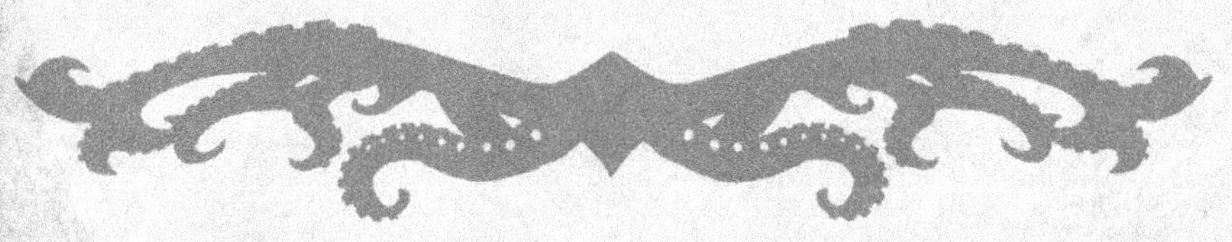

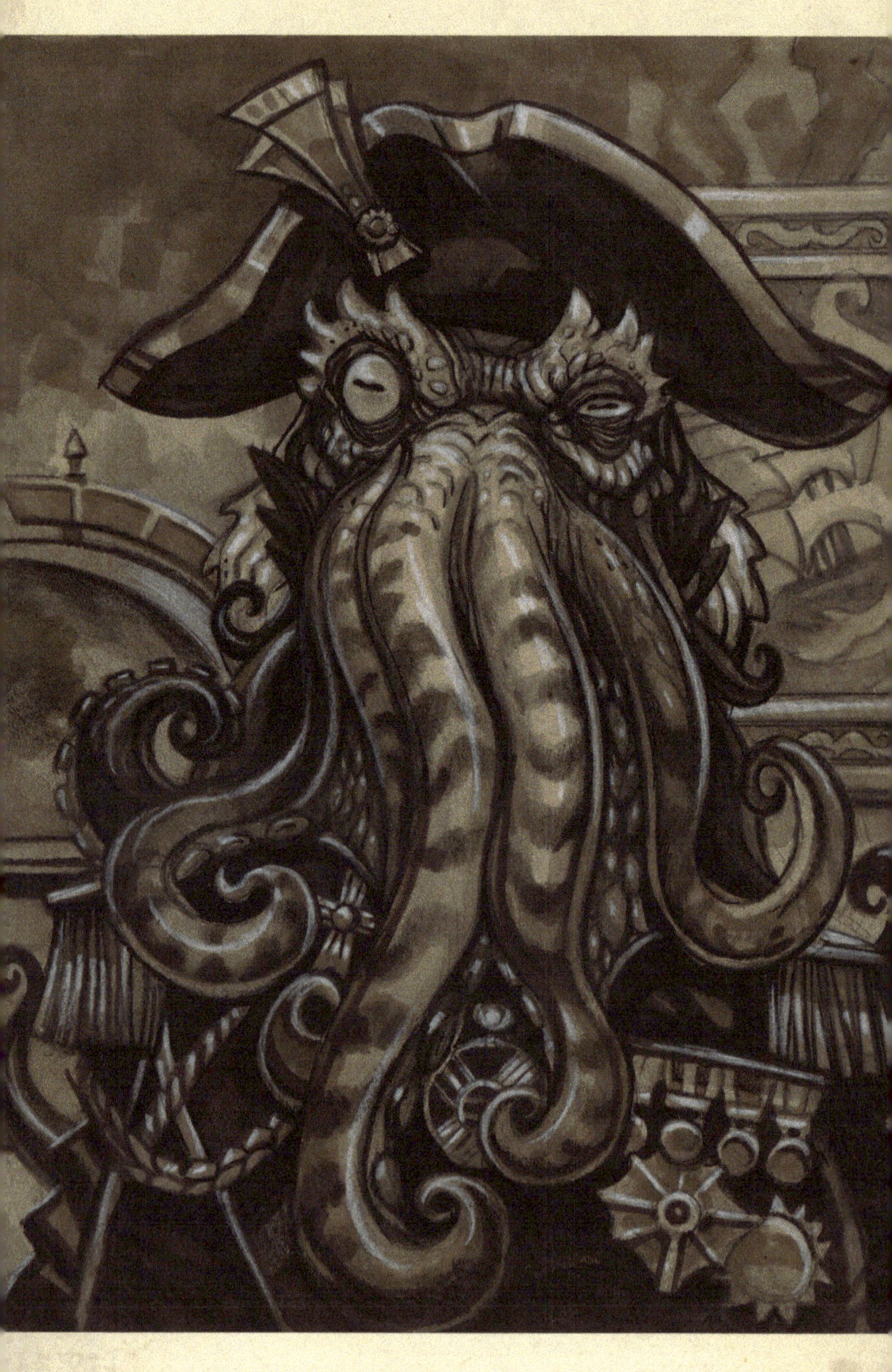

The Admiral

The Admiral has been the scourge of the high seas for countless millennia. His military reputation is only outmatched by his reputation as a blowhard. When he deigns to rise out of his underwater city to attend a feast, be warned: if he begins telling stories of the good old *ancient* days, run for the sake of your sanity.

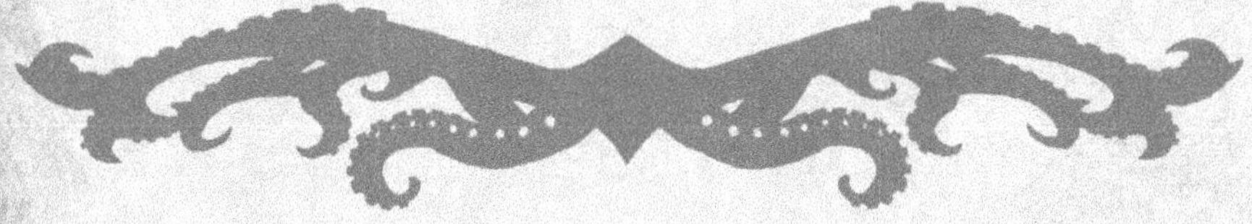

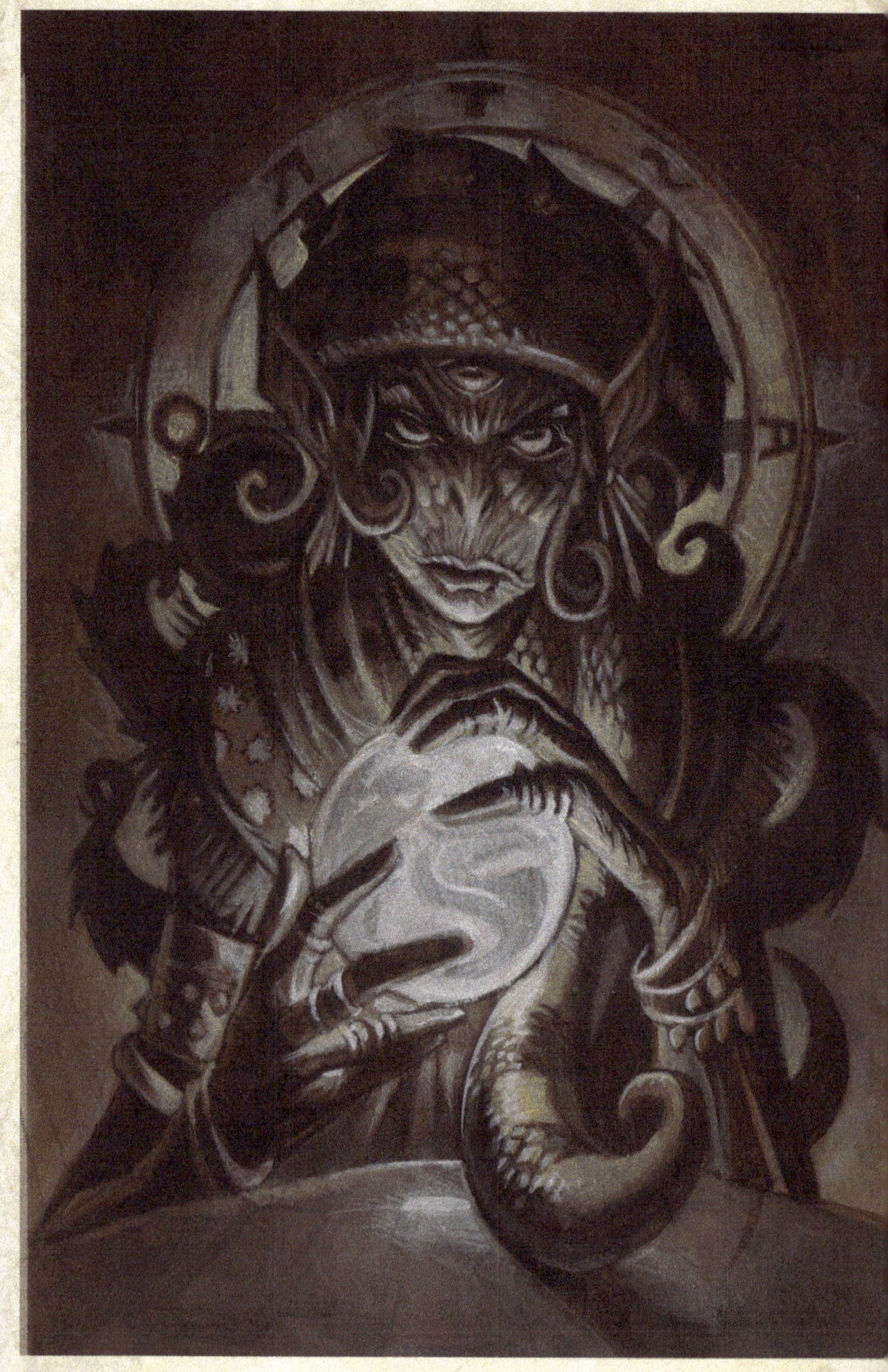

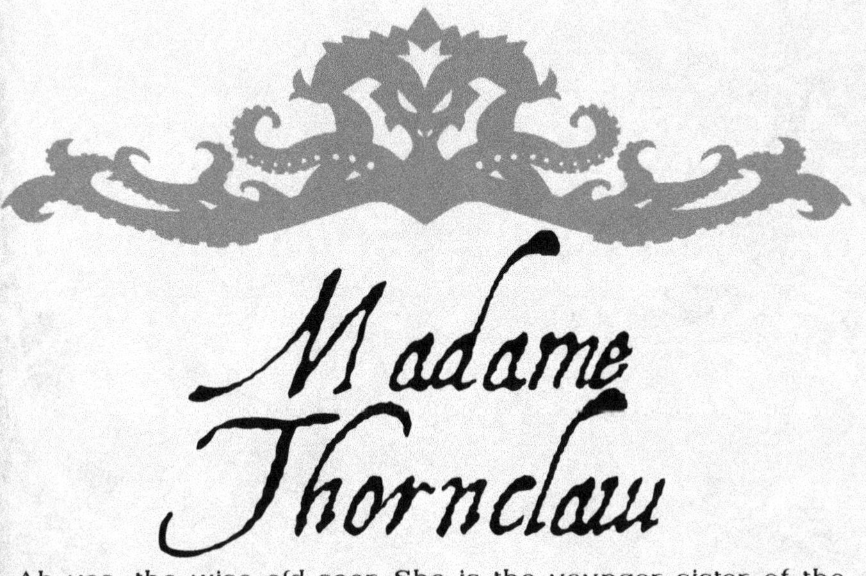

Madame Thornclaw

Ah yes, the wise old seer. She is the younger sister of the Dowager Thornclaw and sees all. The only thing that seems beyond her ability to predict is how she can get her hands on the family fortune after her sister passes. Beware, those who get their fortunes told often end up . . . unfortunate.

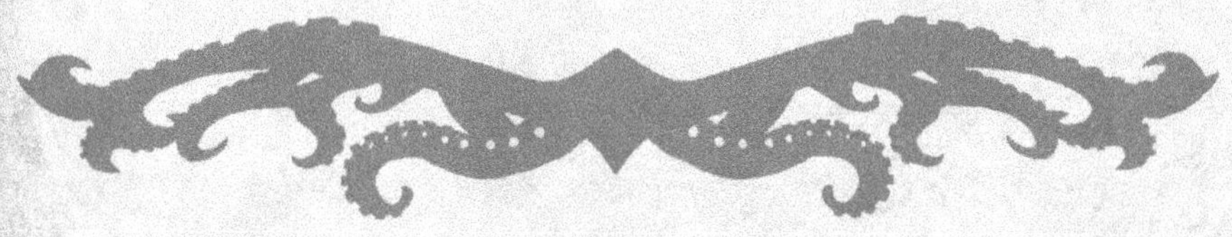

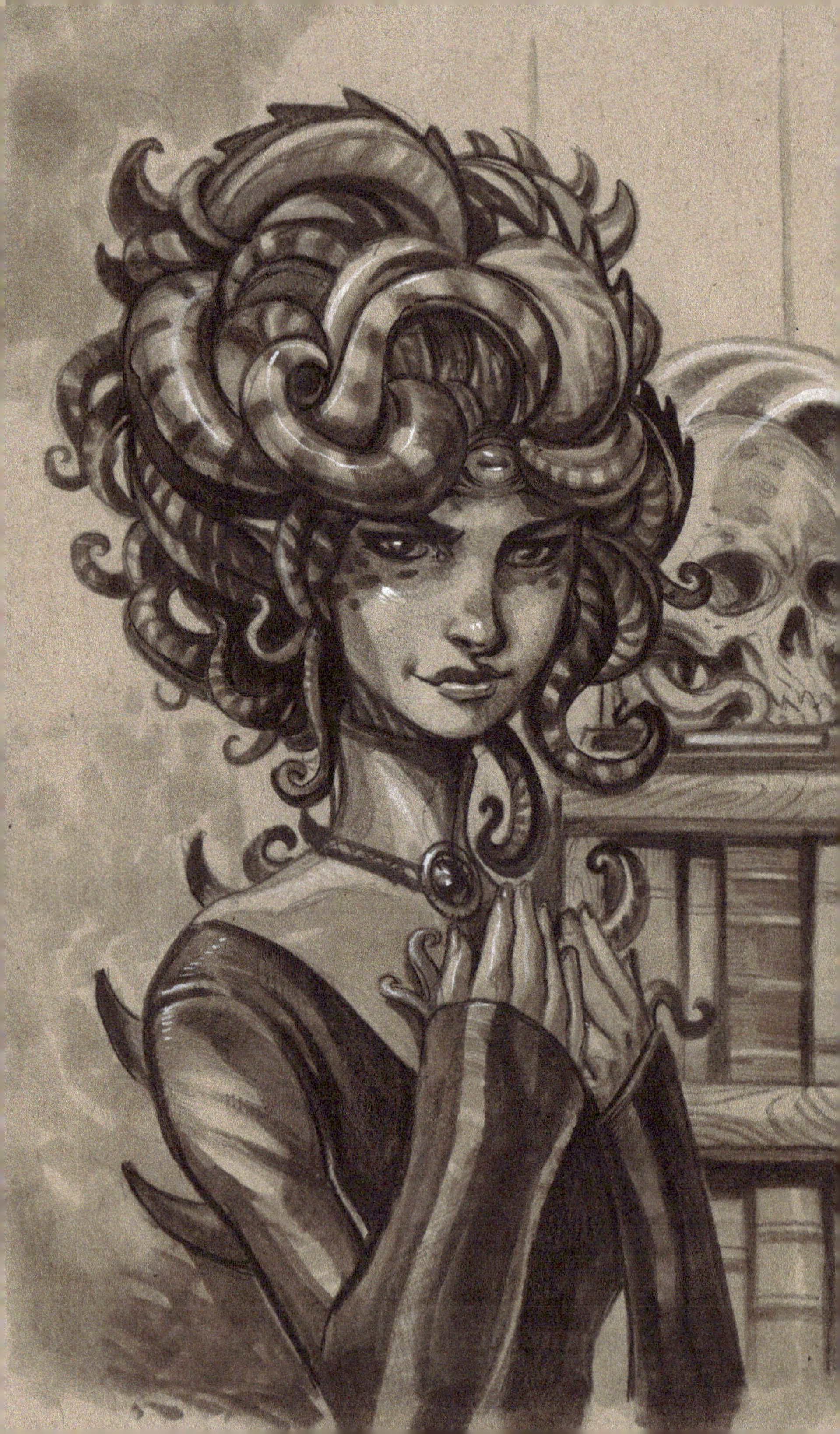

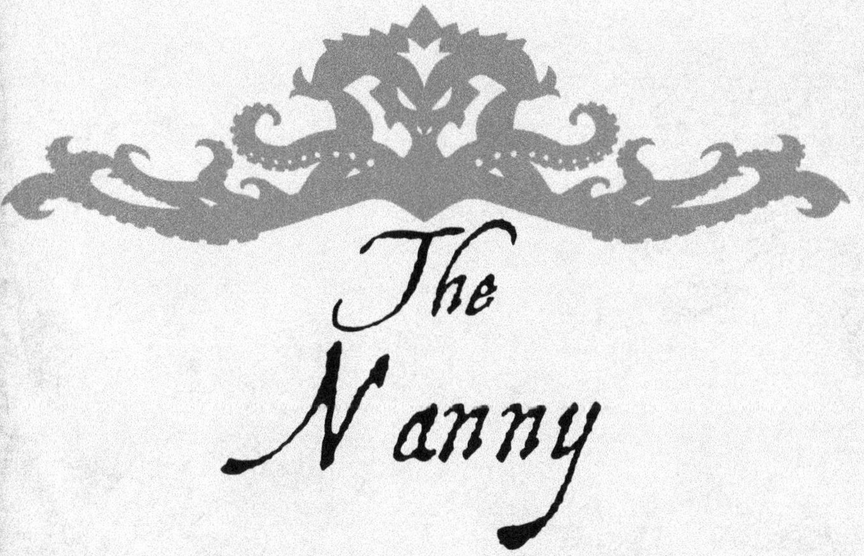

The Nanny

The beautiful Nanny has been with the family for as long as they remember. With Lenore getting older, she finds herself less needed, forgotten even. Not to be left out of the intrigue, the lovely Nanny has often been seen spending time with Lord Thornclaw, much to the Lady's chagrin. It is said the lure of money and power has often corrupted the young, but what if the corrupted is the hand that rocks the cradle?

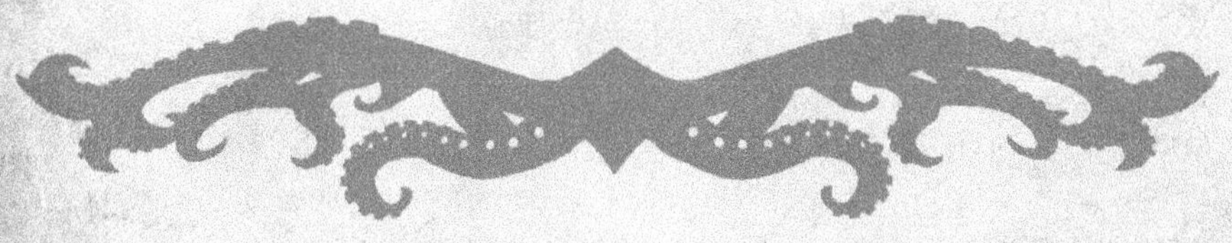

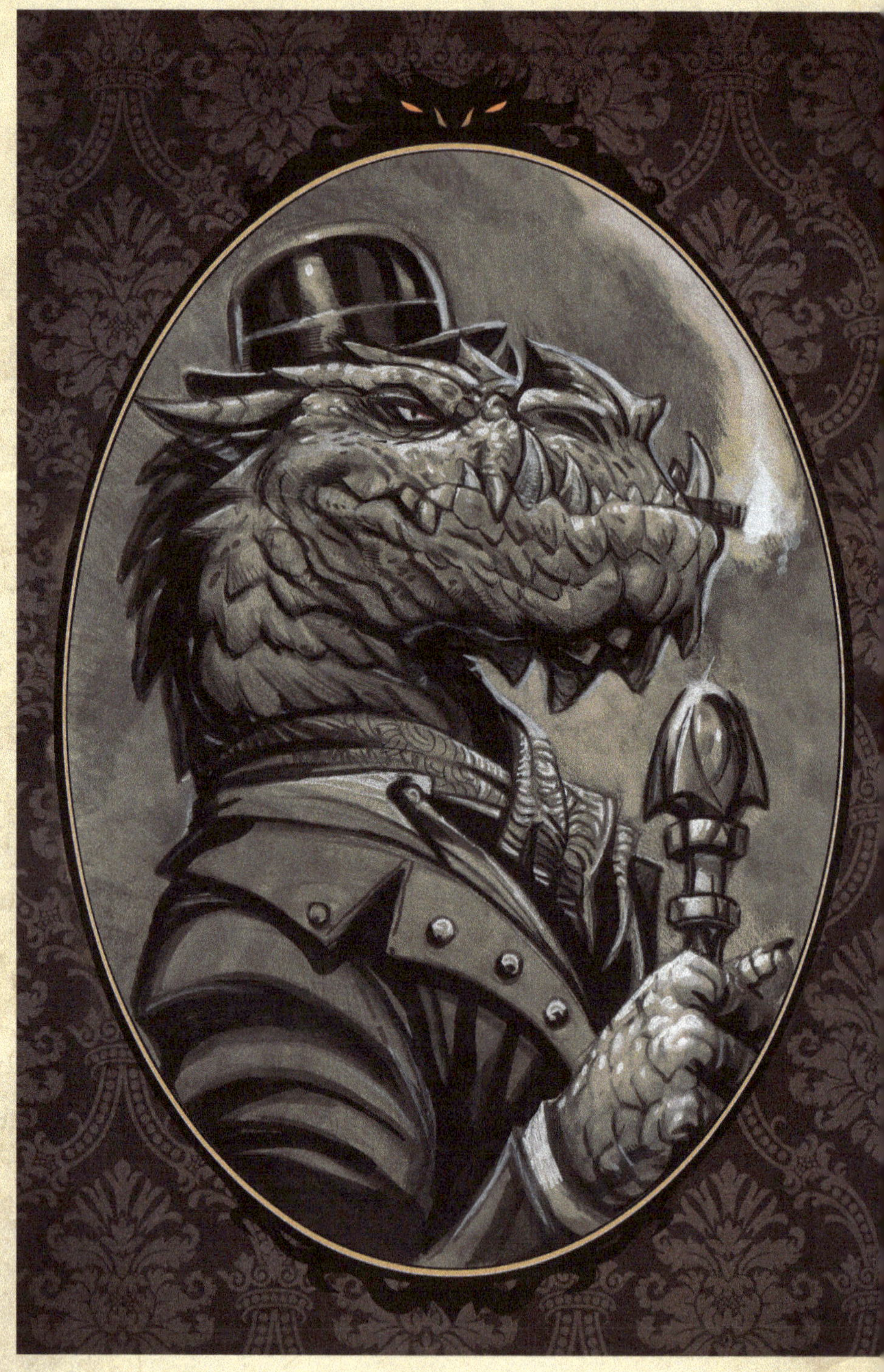

The Boss

A member of a long lost line of the Thornclaw Clan, the not-so-gentle gentleman known as The Boss has only recently come back into the family fold . . . and into the family money. His rough manners and street lingo make it hard for him to be accepted in polite company. His life up to now is unknown, but rumor has it he walks on the darker side of the law. Best not get on his bad side.

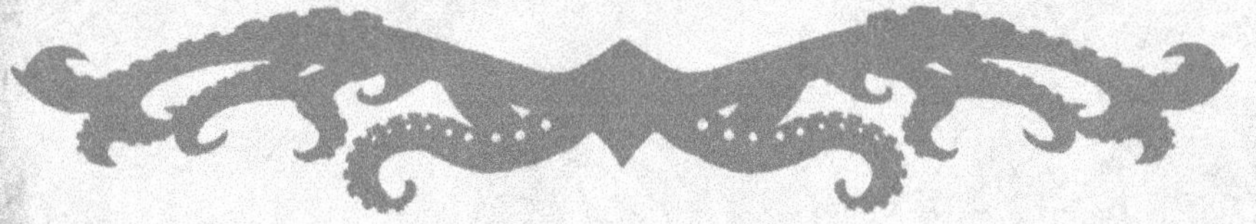

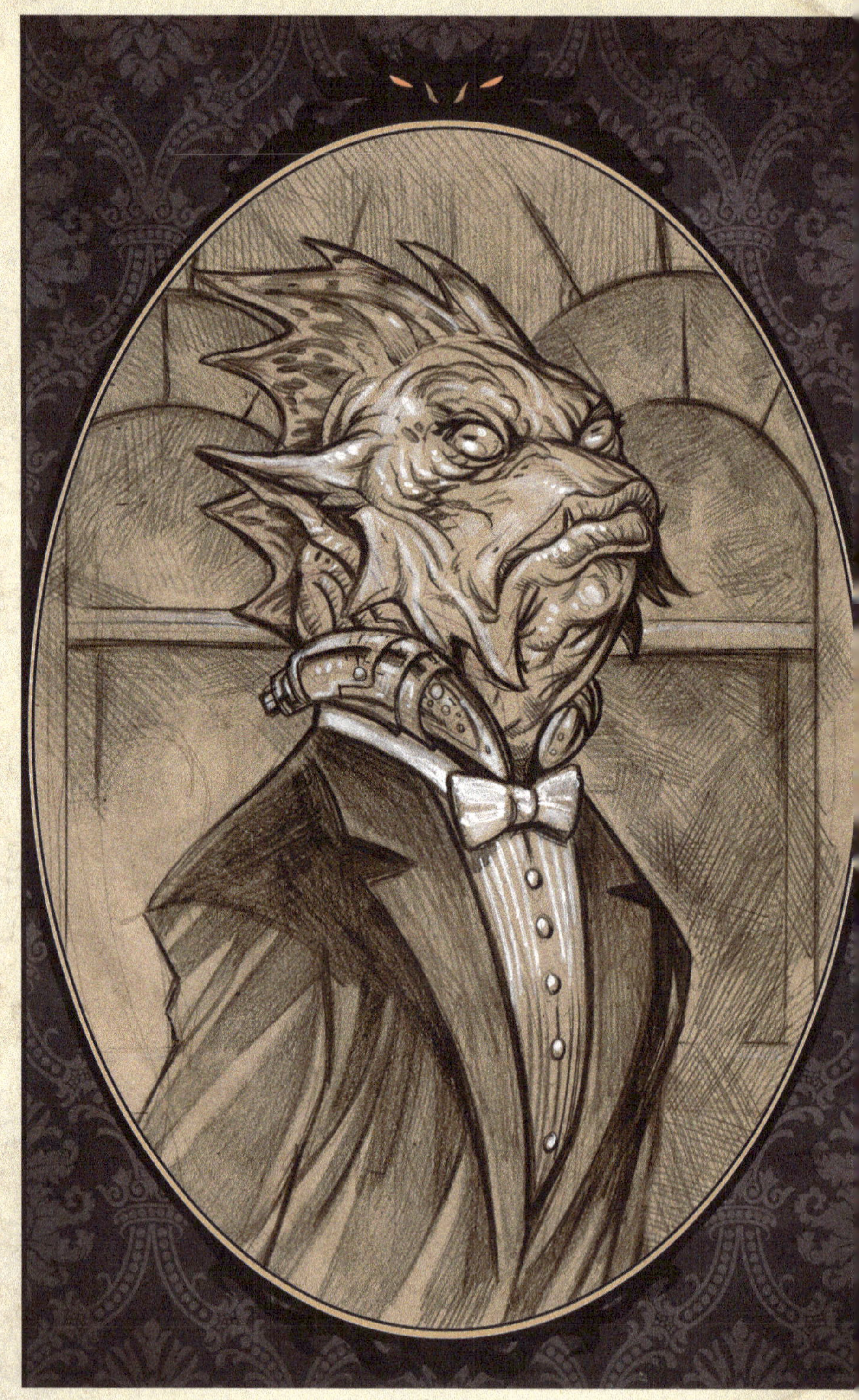

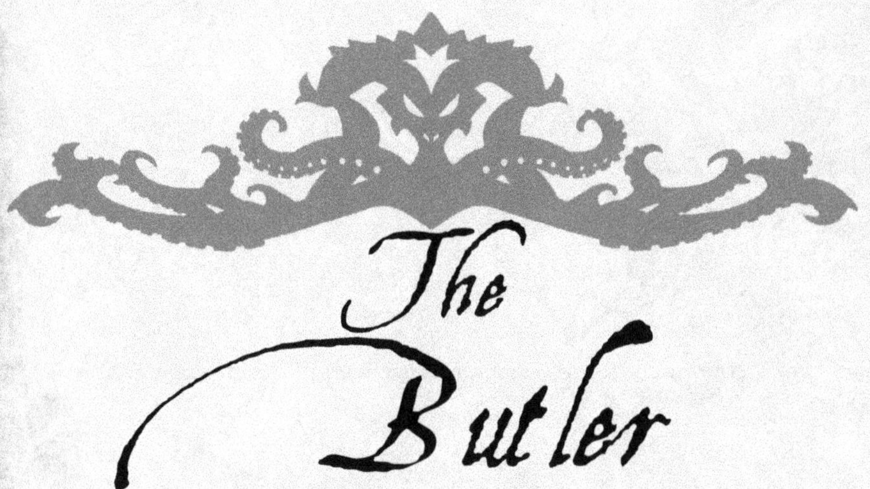

The Butler

He has served the Dowager's family for countless ages and has become the Dowager's secondhand man and confidant. Anyone who enters the house is immediately aware of his watchful eye and ability to predict a guests wishes and fulfill them before being asked. Being "the help" he is overlooked by much of the family and guests and is often privy to their plots and private conversations. He silently collects information and knows everything that goes on inside the walls of Thornclaw Manor. His professional and austere manner often leave guests wtih the impression that he is a "cold fish." Don't ever dismiss the old adage, "the Butler did it," because he probably did.

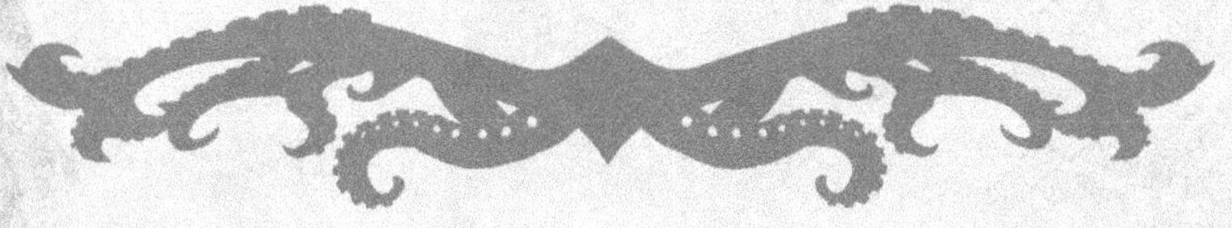

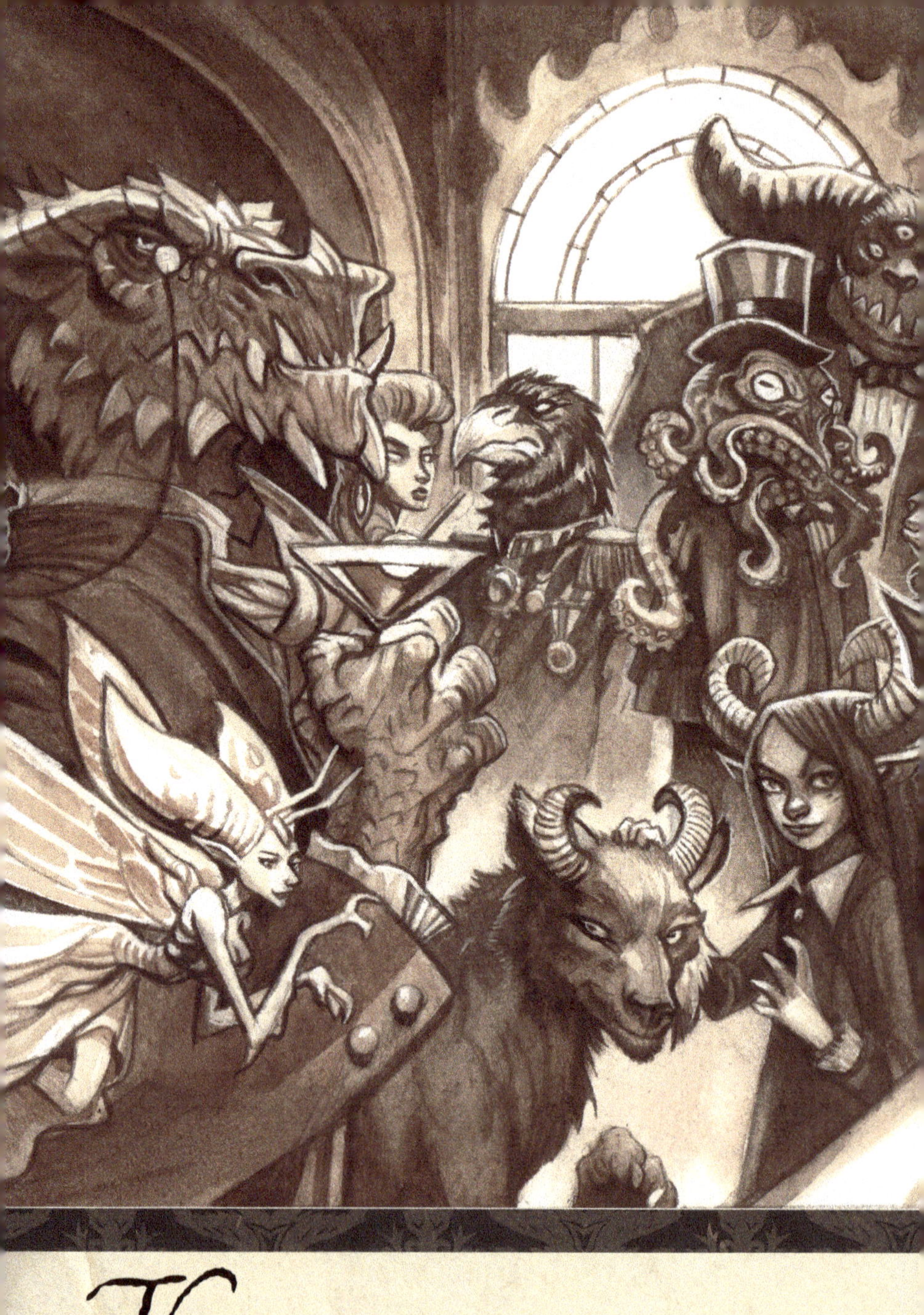

The Solstice Ball

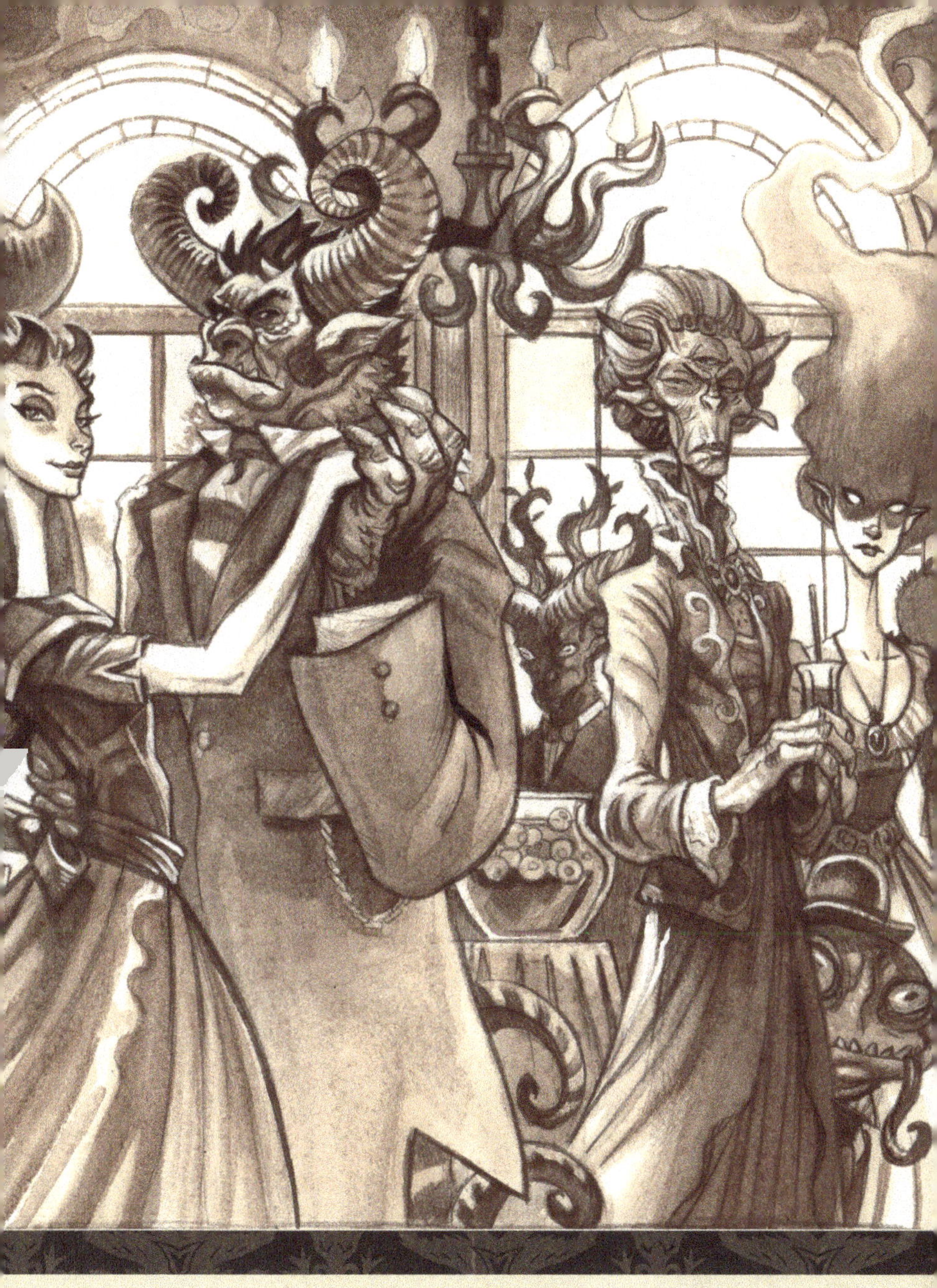

Every year the family gathers from around the universe to celebrate the Solstice. Petty squabbles and bitter rivalries are put away for the event and through often gritted teeth the family holds the Grand Ball. While exquisitely bizarre hor' douvres and drink is passed around, the band, led by Unlce Dagon plays its shrill morbid tunes. Austere smiles and sideways glances hide scheming minds as they dance and frolic through the night..

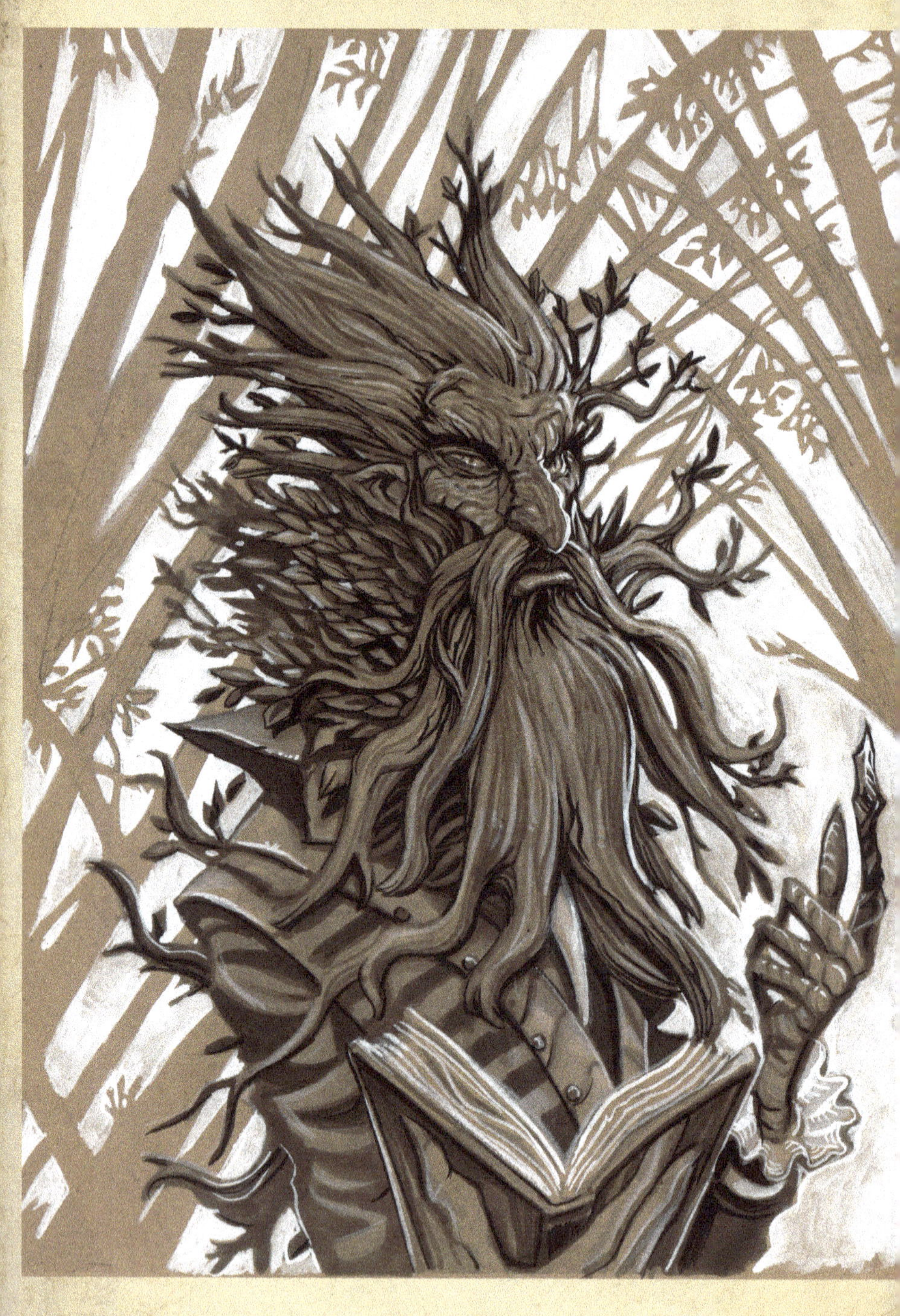

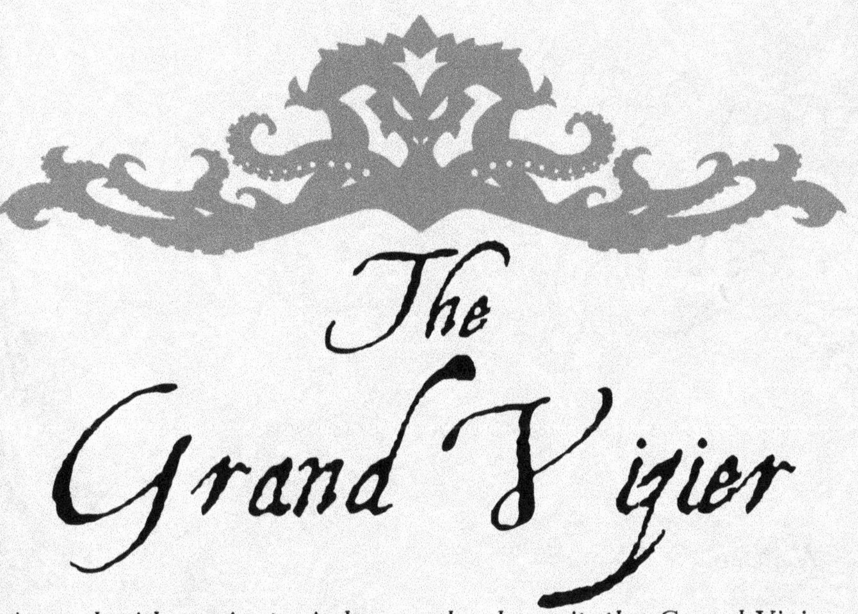

The Grand Vizier

Armed with ancient wisdom and a dry wit, the Grand Vizier doles out his advice to Kings, Queens, and anyone who will listen. He lives in the near forest surrounded by his library santuary. His walls of books protect him from the intrigues of the Manor. This Brother of the Dowager has seen hundreds of generations pass and is always confused and confusticated by how little the "saplings" seem to heed his sage words. History is riddled with the failures of those who didn't listen.

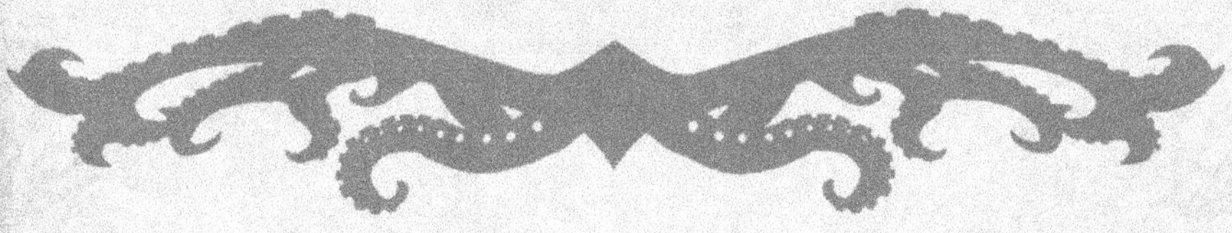

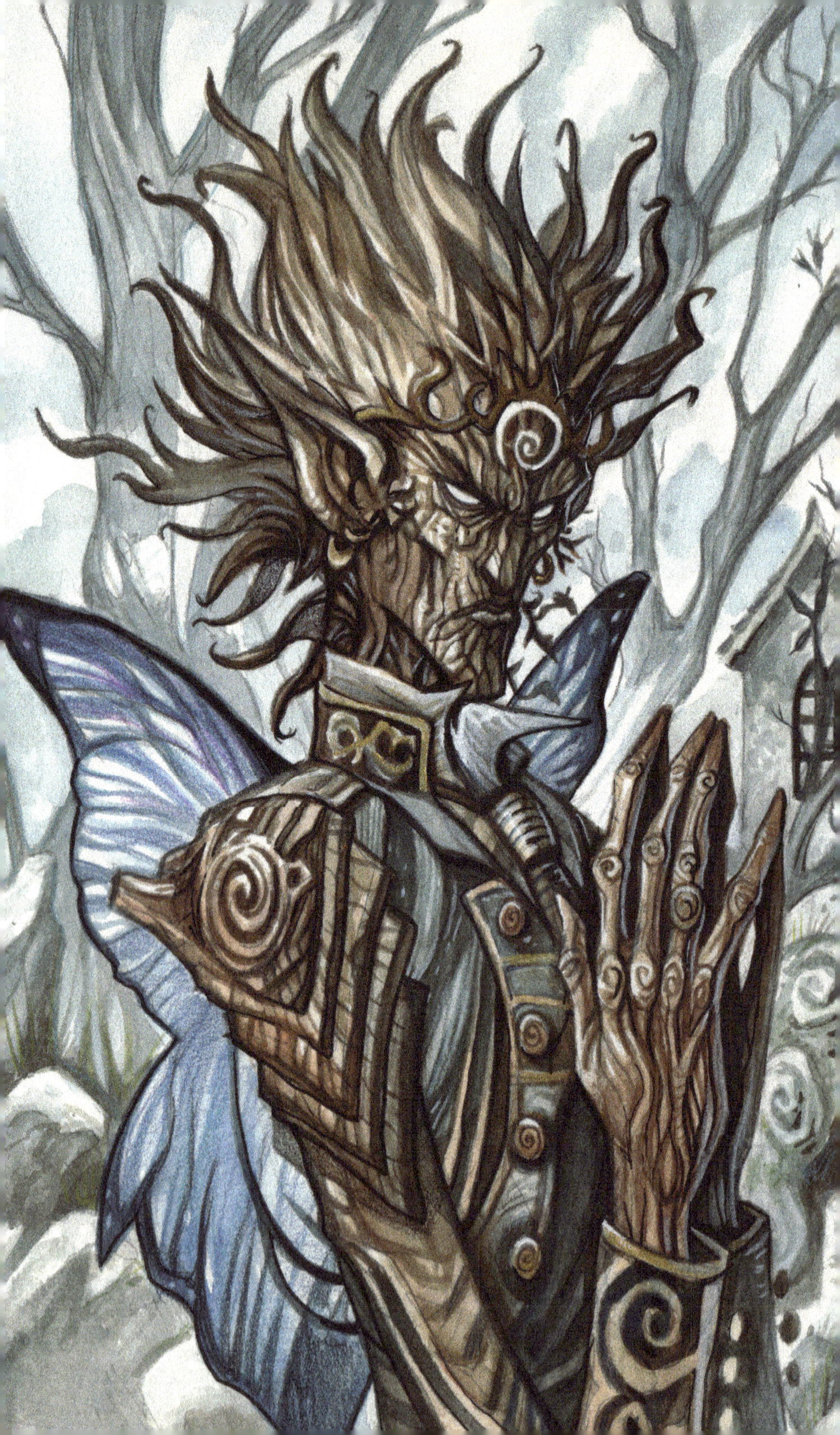

The Thorn Lord

Proud and noble, Luthan The Thornford, brother of the Hexen and Nightshade rules the Unseelie from the Dark forest with a grim and serious manner. HIs warlike manner has caused trouble between the Unseelie and the other Fae, and though his realm is protected from much of it's influence he covets the power the old Dowager projects from the gates of Thornclaw Manor. He would be much happier if he were to sit in the Dowagers High-Backed Chair.

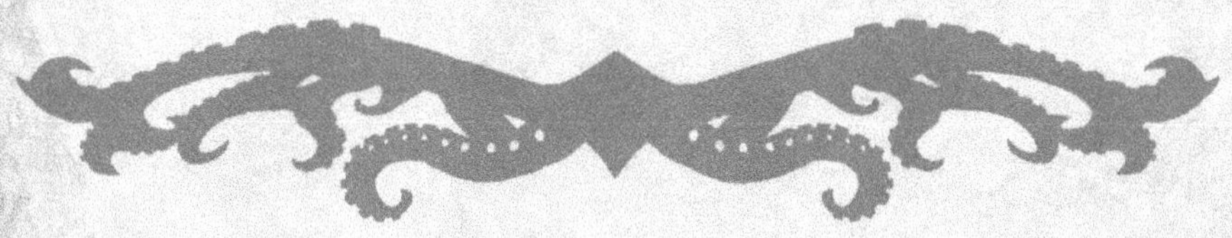

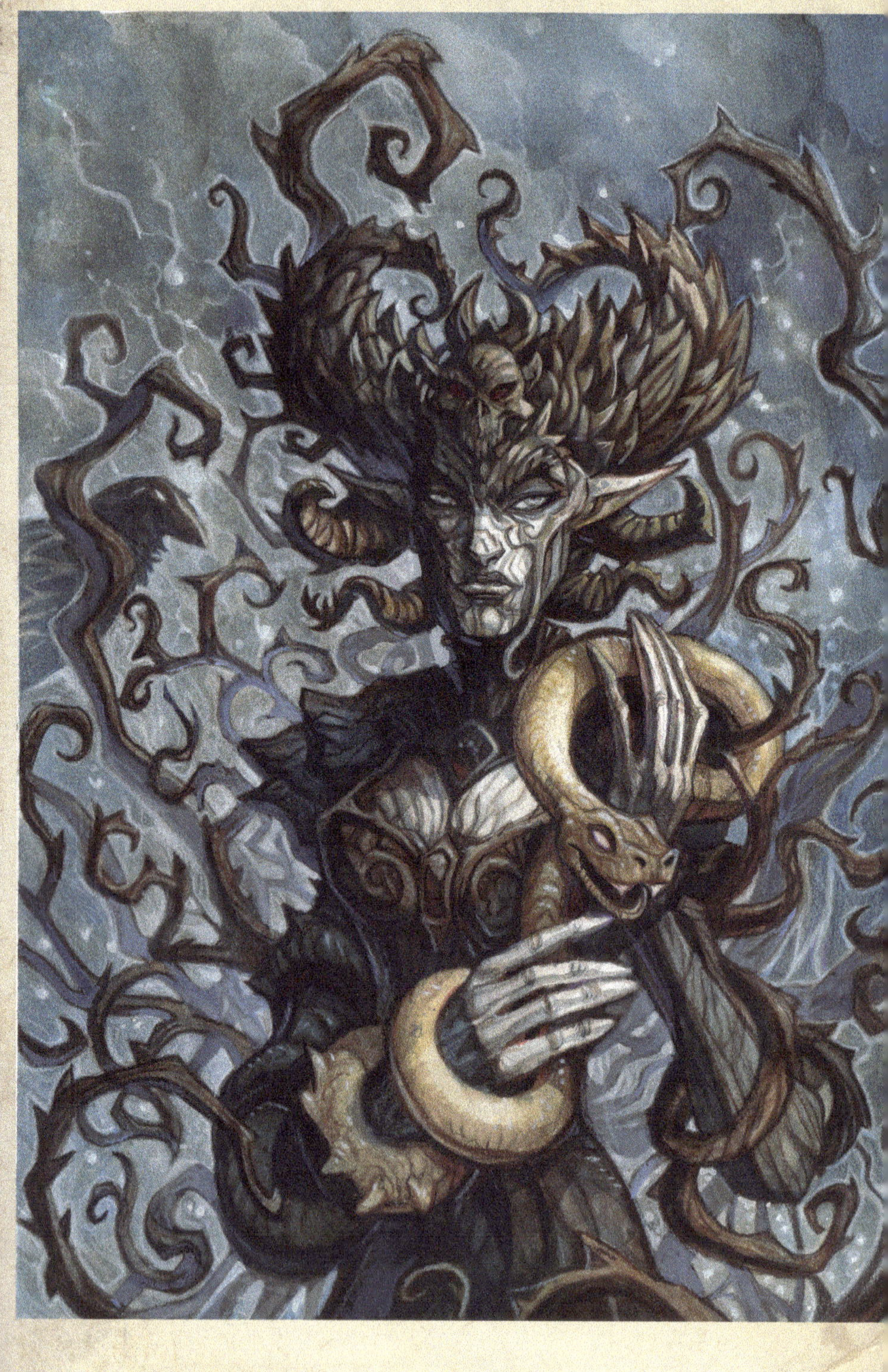

The Thornwitch

Sister of Nightshade the WoodWitch, Hexen is darker and more prone to foul moods and dangerous intent. She commands the Unseelie fae and the beasts of the Dark Forest to do her bidding. On first meeting she will seem kind almost sickly sweet and generously bestows gifts upon those who visit her woody realm. But like the apple from Snow White , her gifts always come with a price. Beware her serpent companion Signa, she slips her way around the universe collecting wisdom and
stories to tell her mistress.

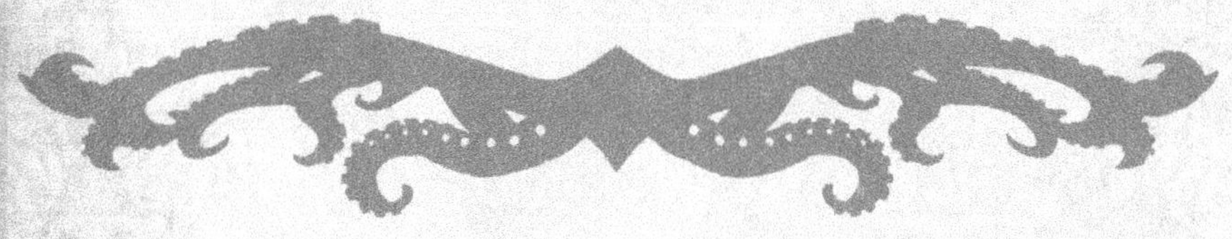

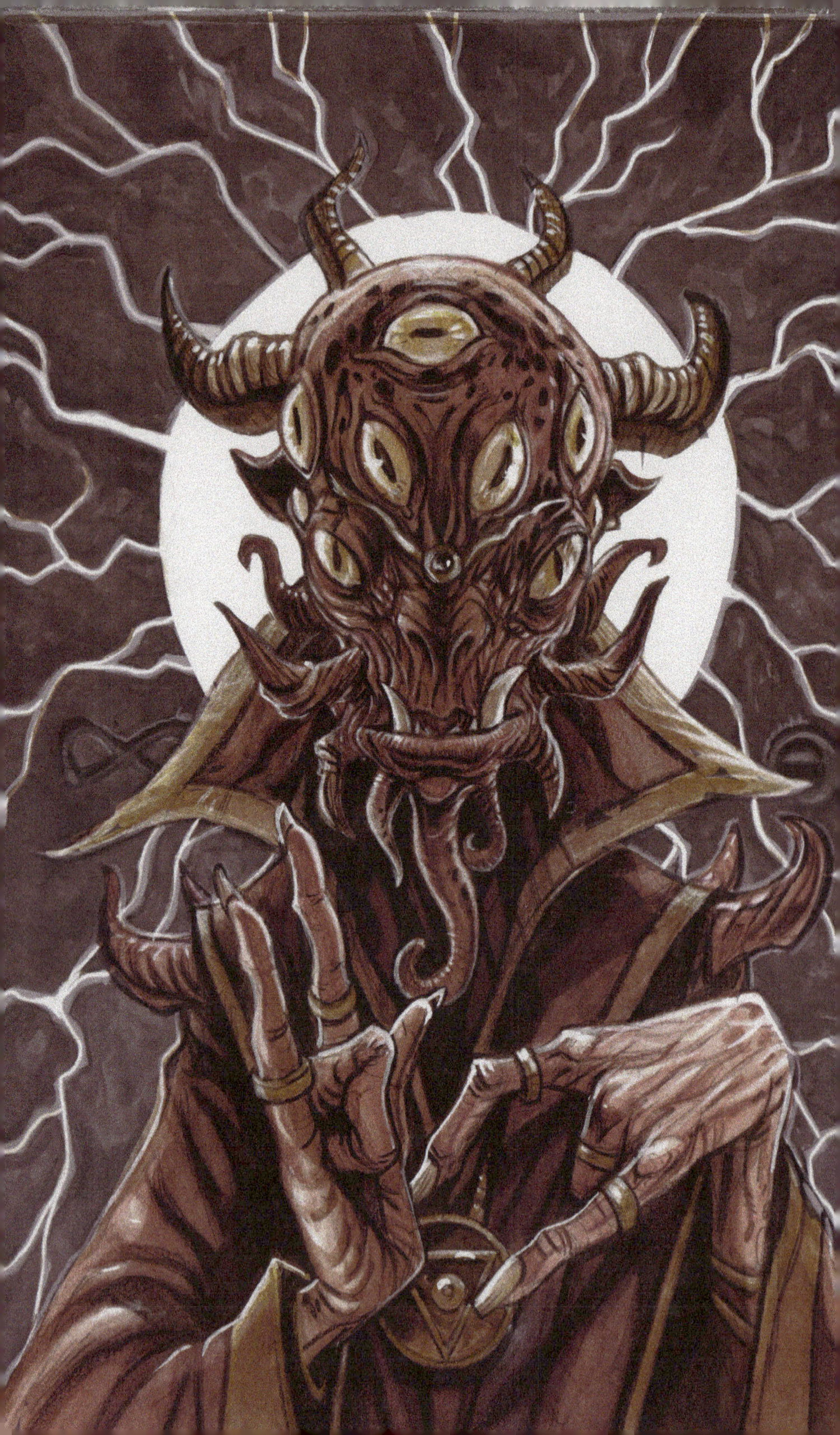

The Sorceror

This master of arcane secrets uses his many eyes to see into other realities, pasts, and futures. Many come to this keeper of secrets to learn the doings of their friends and enemies from afar, and to request aid in altering their fortunes. But be warned though this most solicitous of mystical benefactors will aid most anyone who requests his help, all of his seemingly selfless actions imply a web- like tapestry of manipulation hidden from even the most scrutinizing eye. Put simply, there is nothing you can keep hidden from his piercing gaze and his help will certainly be woven into his indiscernible plans.

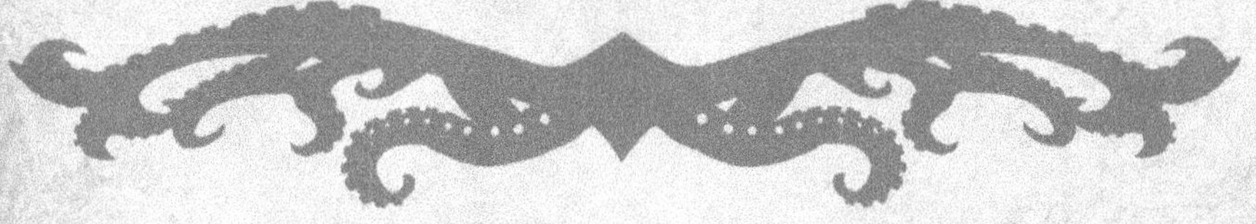

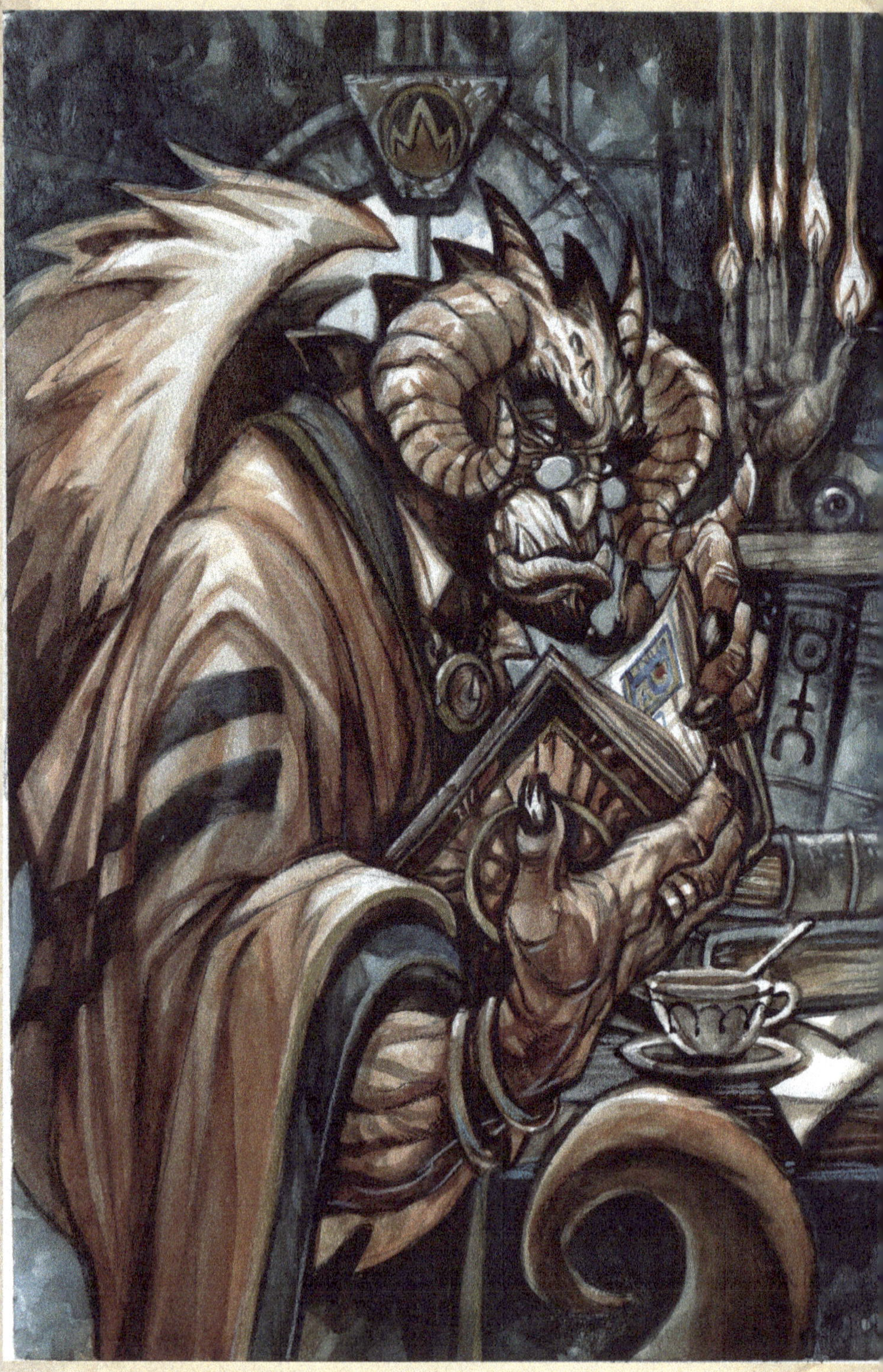

The Scholar

This kindly gentleman is willing to share the obscure knowledge he has been searching for. He hides his obsessive need for information and the dangerous practices he must enact to find his intellectual prizes in his dank and monstrous chamber in the Manor's tower.

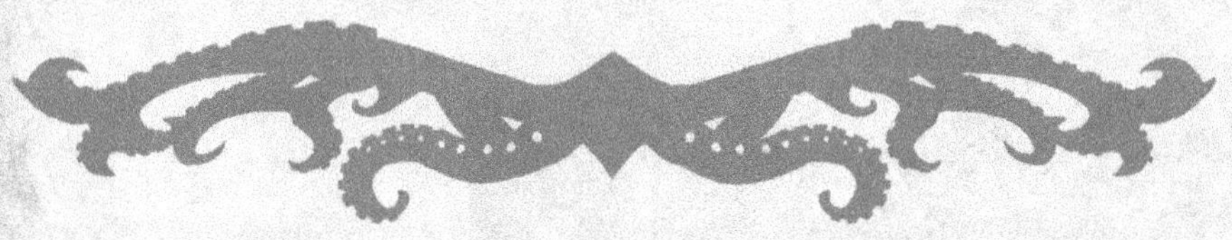

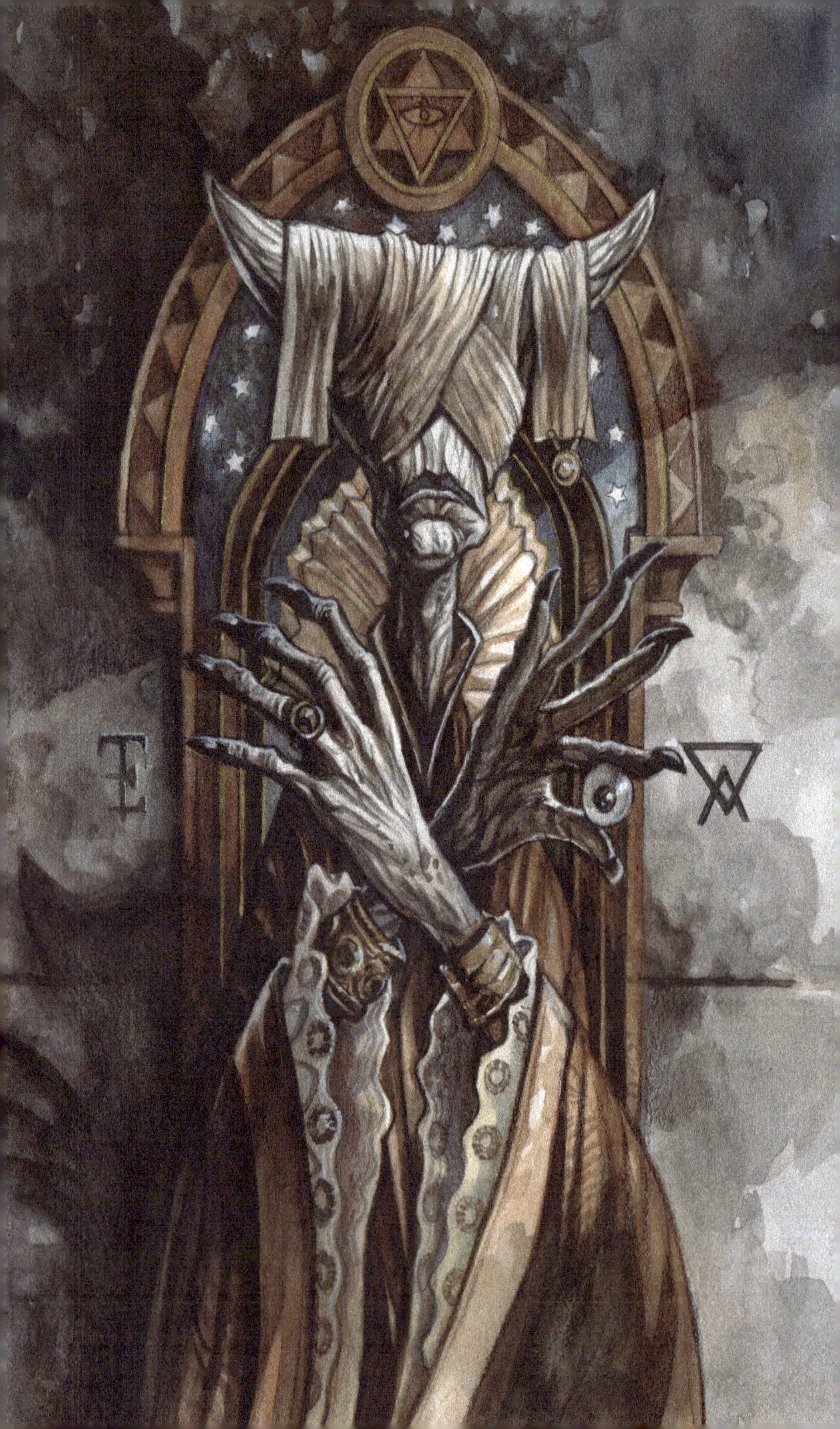

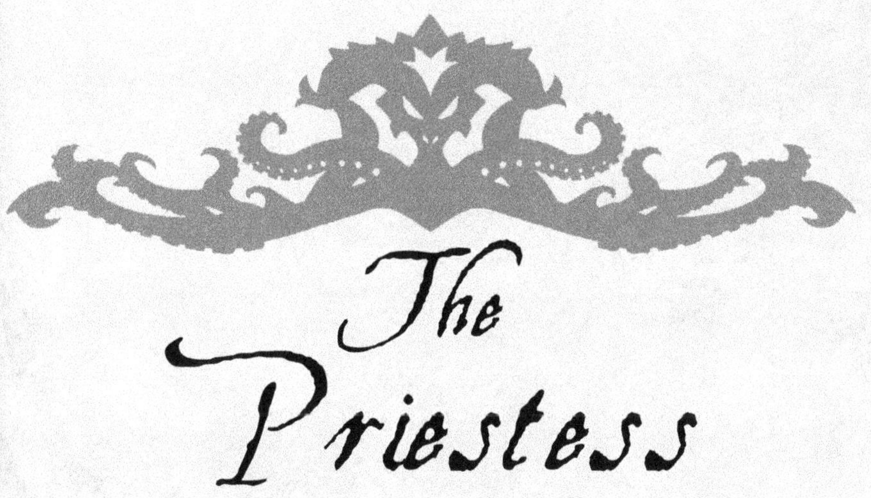

The Priestess

She was sent away to the Black Monastery at the far side of the dark wood as a child by the command of their parents to the delight of her older sister, the future Dowager. Over the centuries since her banishment, she has ascended to the highest levels of the Church, as an inquisitor and now the high priestess. The Priestess believes that too much leeway has been granted to the weak and puny humans over the years and that the order that the Dowager has placed to keep reality secure is ultimately killing the universe. As long as she lives, she will covet the power and fortune of the Thornclaw dynasty and will stop at nothing to overturn the current reality.

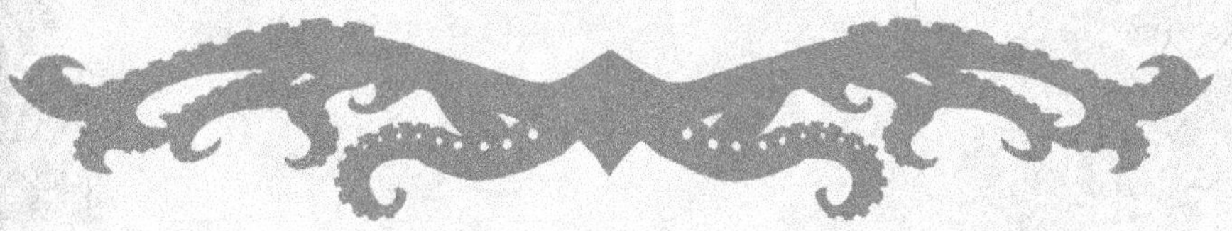

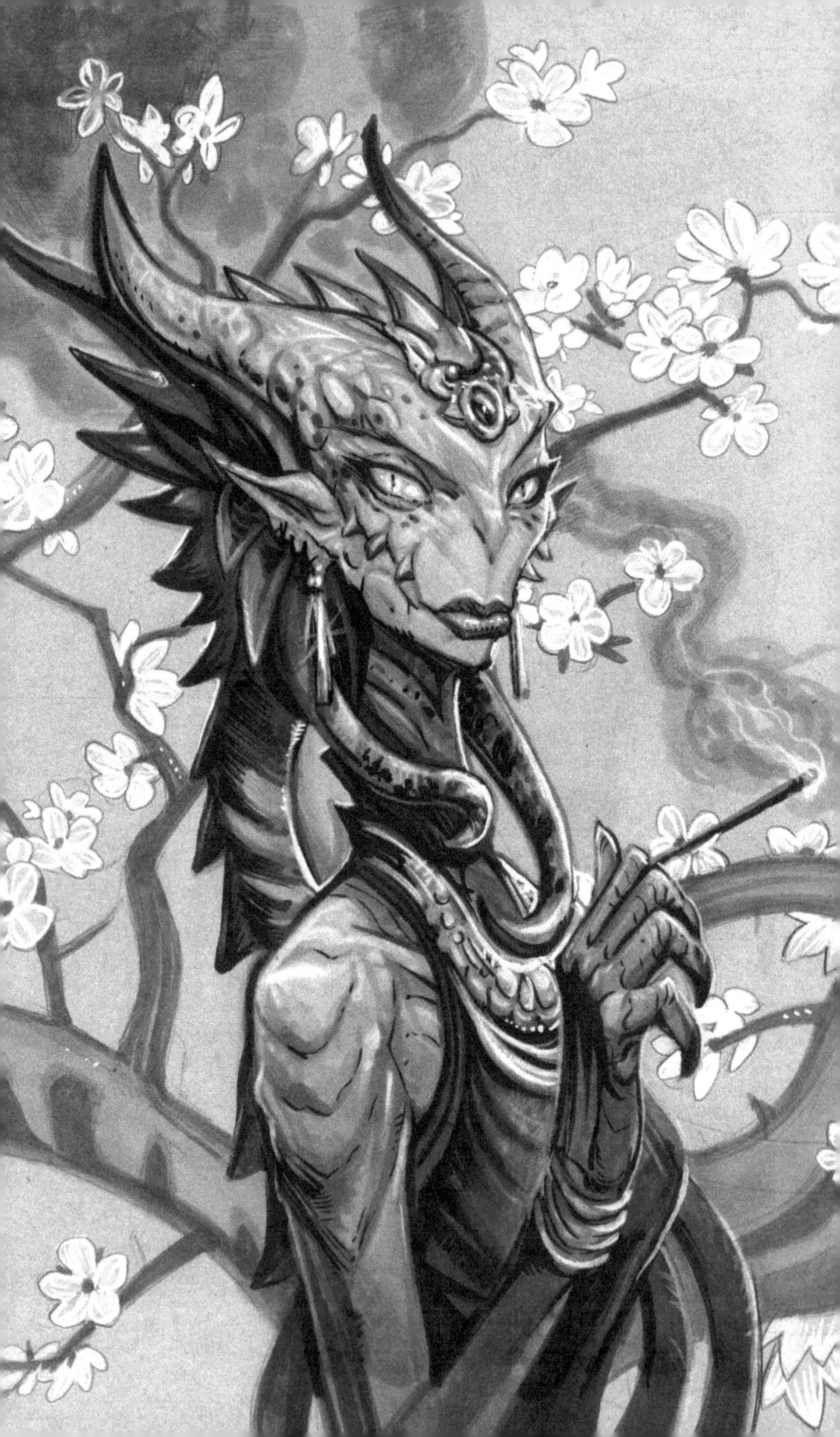

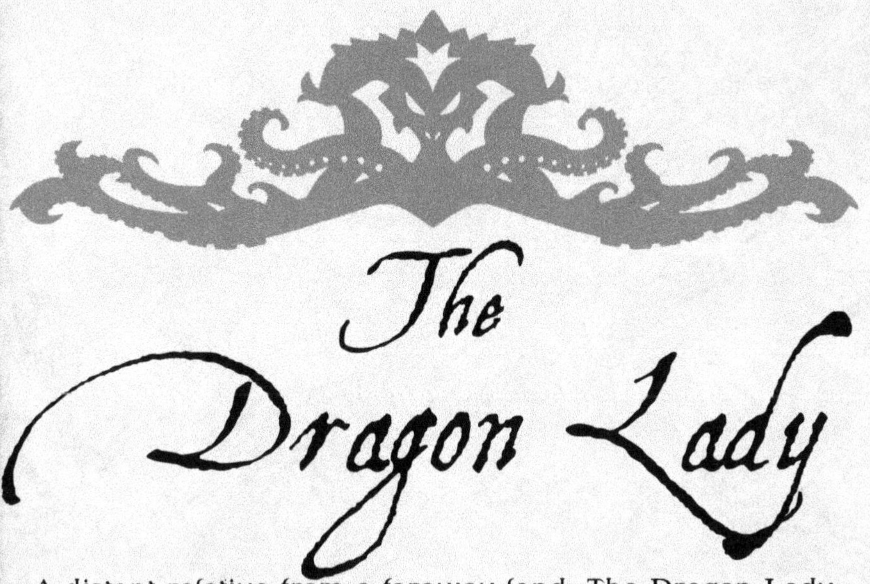

The Dragon Lady

A distant relative from a faraway land, The Dragon Lady slithers into Thornclaw Manor with an air of mystery. Her sensuous ways and her vicious wit make her a formidable conversationalist, as well as a danger to anyone she sets her eye upon.

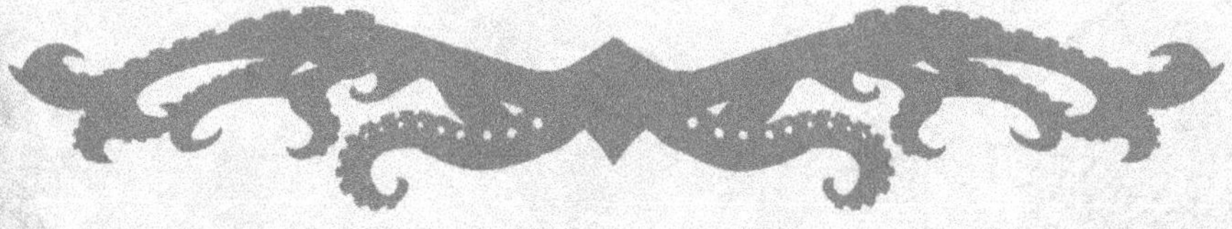

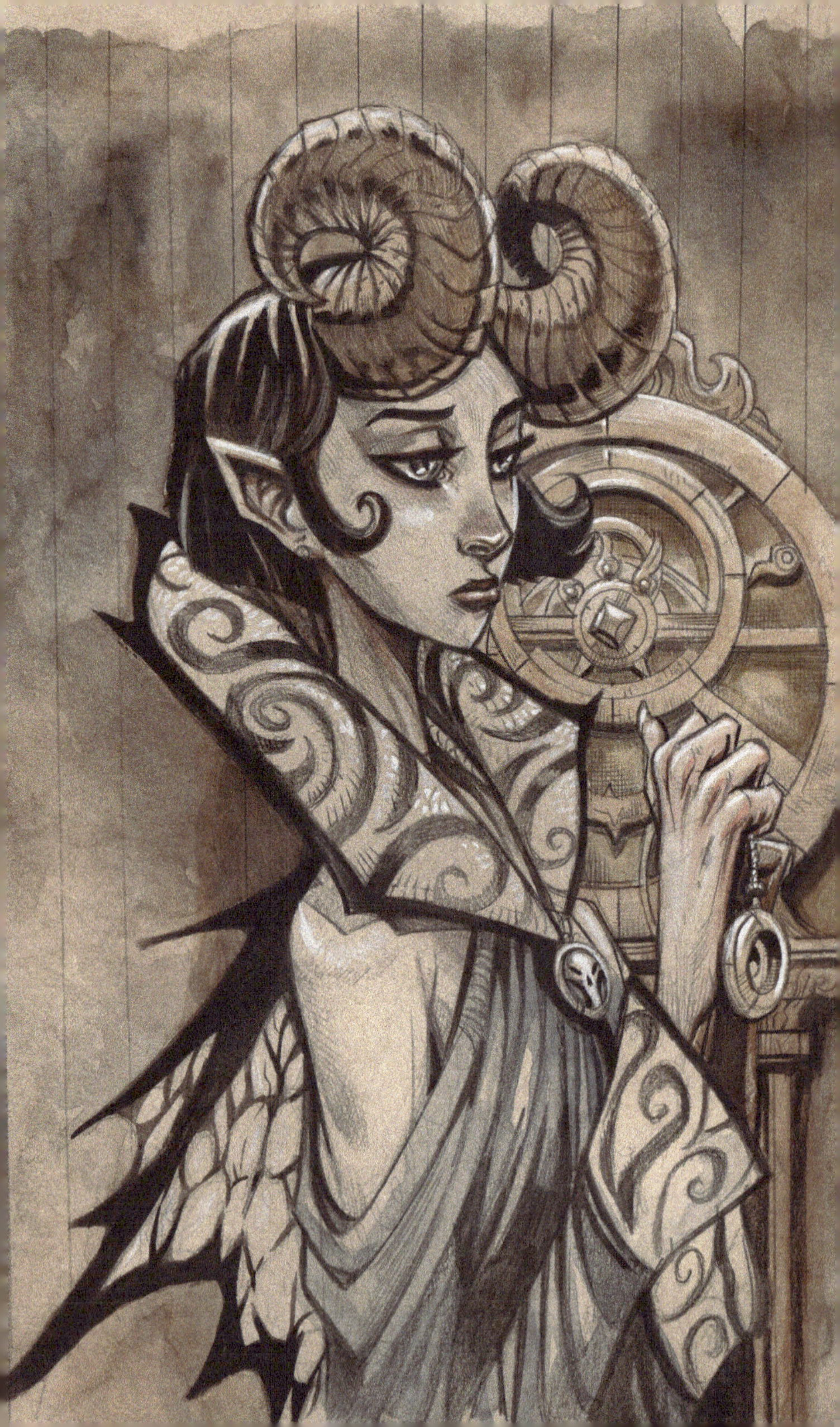

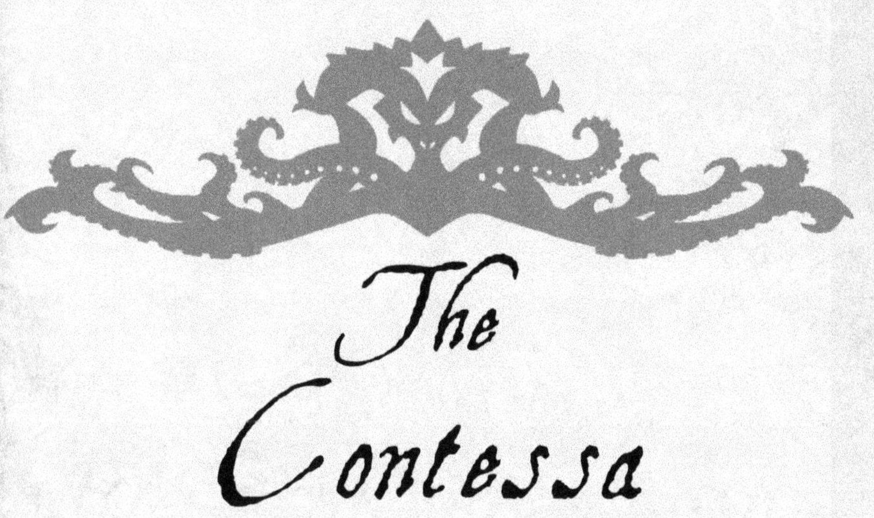

The Contessa

A distant cousin who visits the Manor for months at a time. There is an air of wild sadness in her eyes as she lurks around the halls of the great manor in search of some mysterious treasure and muttering quietly under her breath about unknown cities and and long disappeared beings only heard of in ancient tales whispered by the dead.

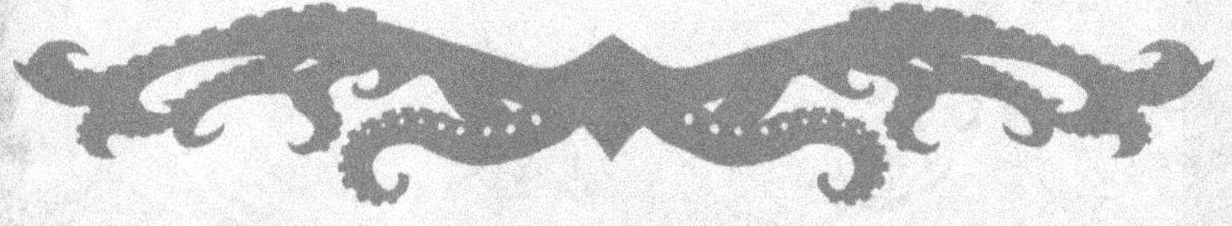

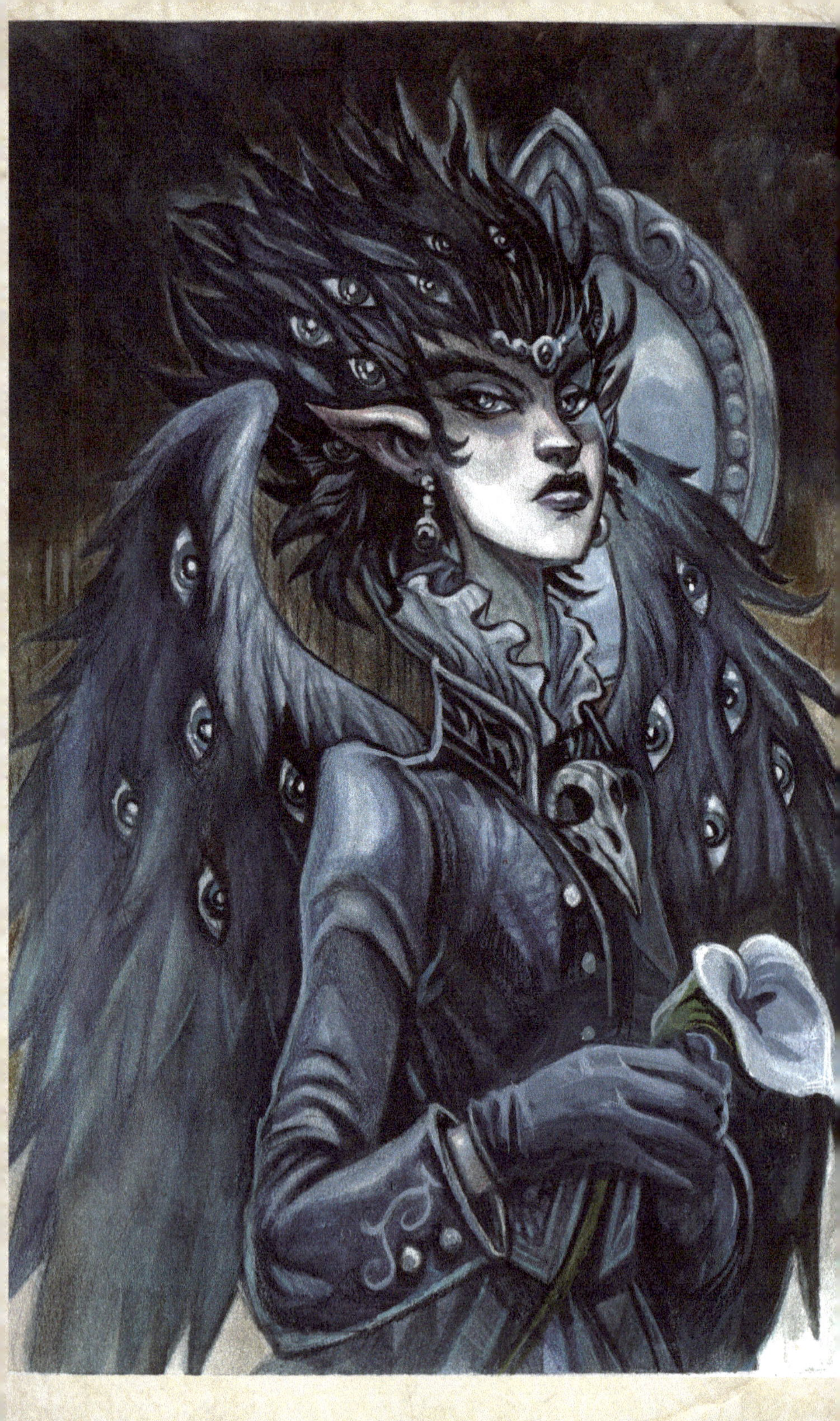

Ligiea
Lady Darque

Sweet, kind, and a beautiful conversationalist, this lady will make you feel seen. Her lovely wings flutter gently in the breeze as the thousands of eyes dappled throughout her feathers follow your every move. Her affection for beautiful souls makes her a wonderful companion, but if you love your life you'd better hope you don't meet her for a very long time.

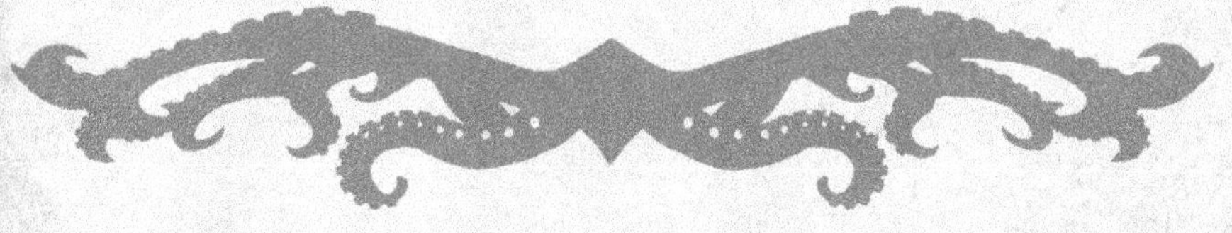

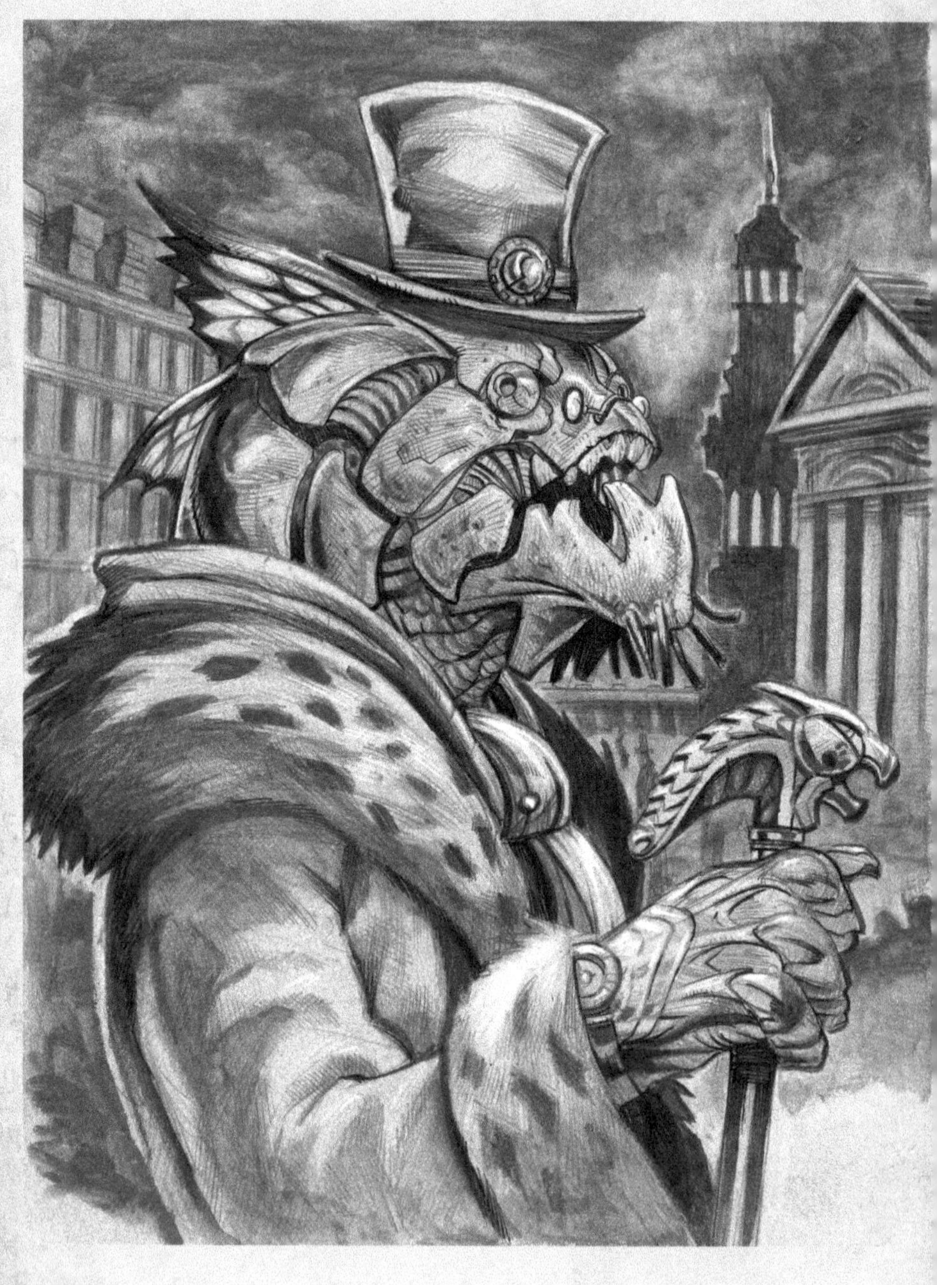

The Gentleman

A haughty old financier of strange and sometimes terrible ventures. This ruthless capitalist controls the fate of nations and peoples throughout the Universe from behind his desk, or while he dines at his personal table at the famed Demonicos Steakhouse.. His bank is thought to have propped up despots and underwritten revolutions. Those that he invests in must beware that his money always comes with unusual yet firmly binding strings attached.

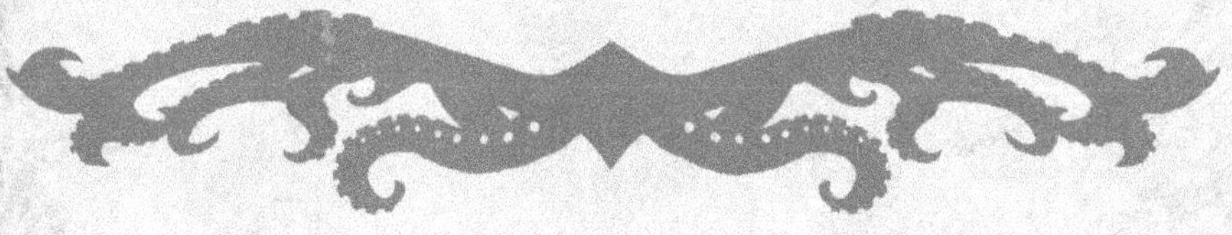

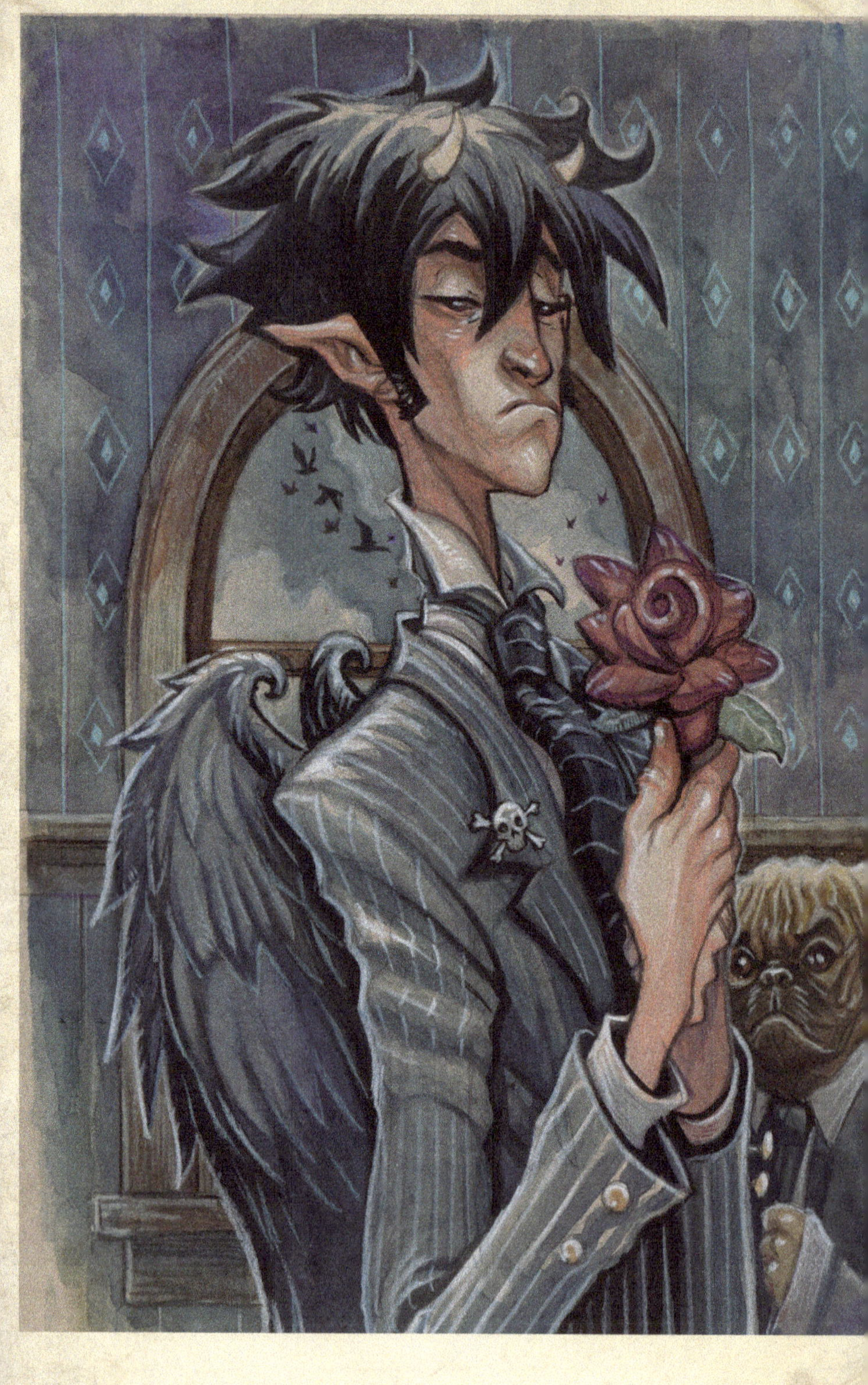

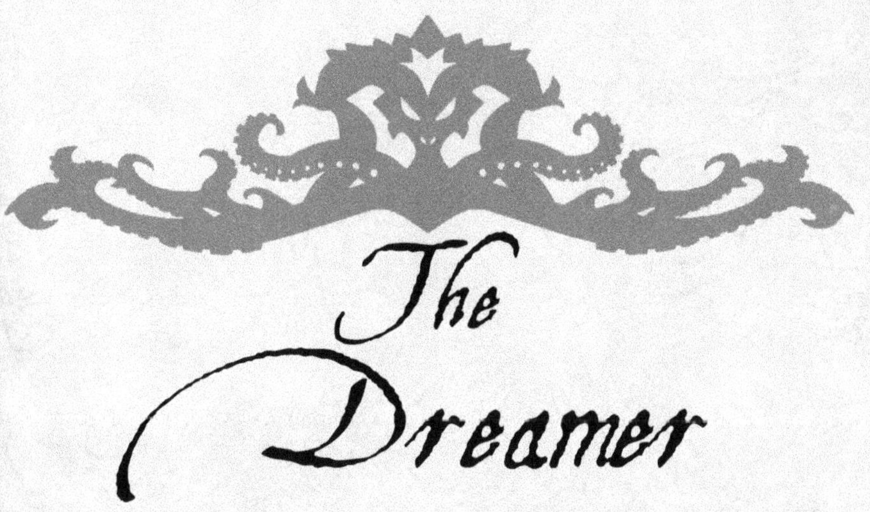

The Dreamer

The eldest child of Lord and Lady Thornclaw, he has been known to fall deeply and tragically in love with a person or an idea at the drop of a hat. His emotions run hot and cold as he flits from one idea, person, or belief system to the next. His fleeting desires burn brightly like wildfire. He can be your greatest ally one minute while he is in love with your spirit and your greatest detractor once you fall from grace in his eyes. Rejecting his love is almost as dangerous as accepting it.

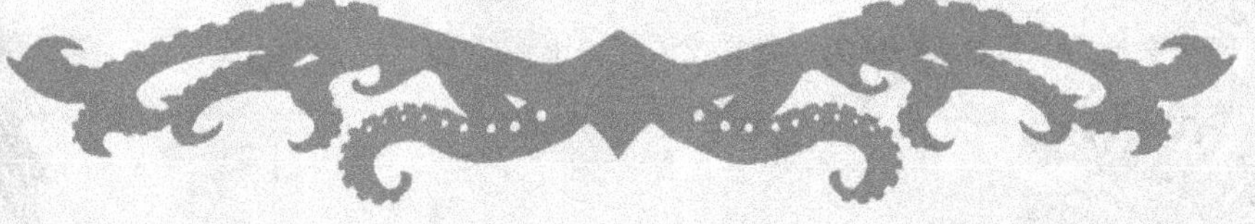

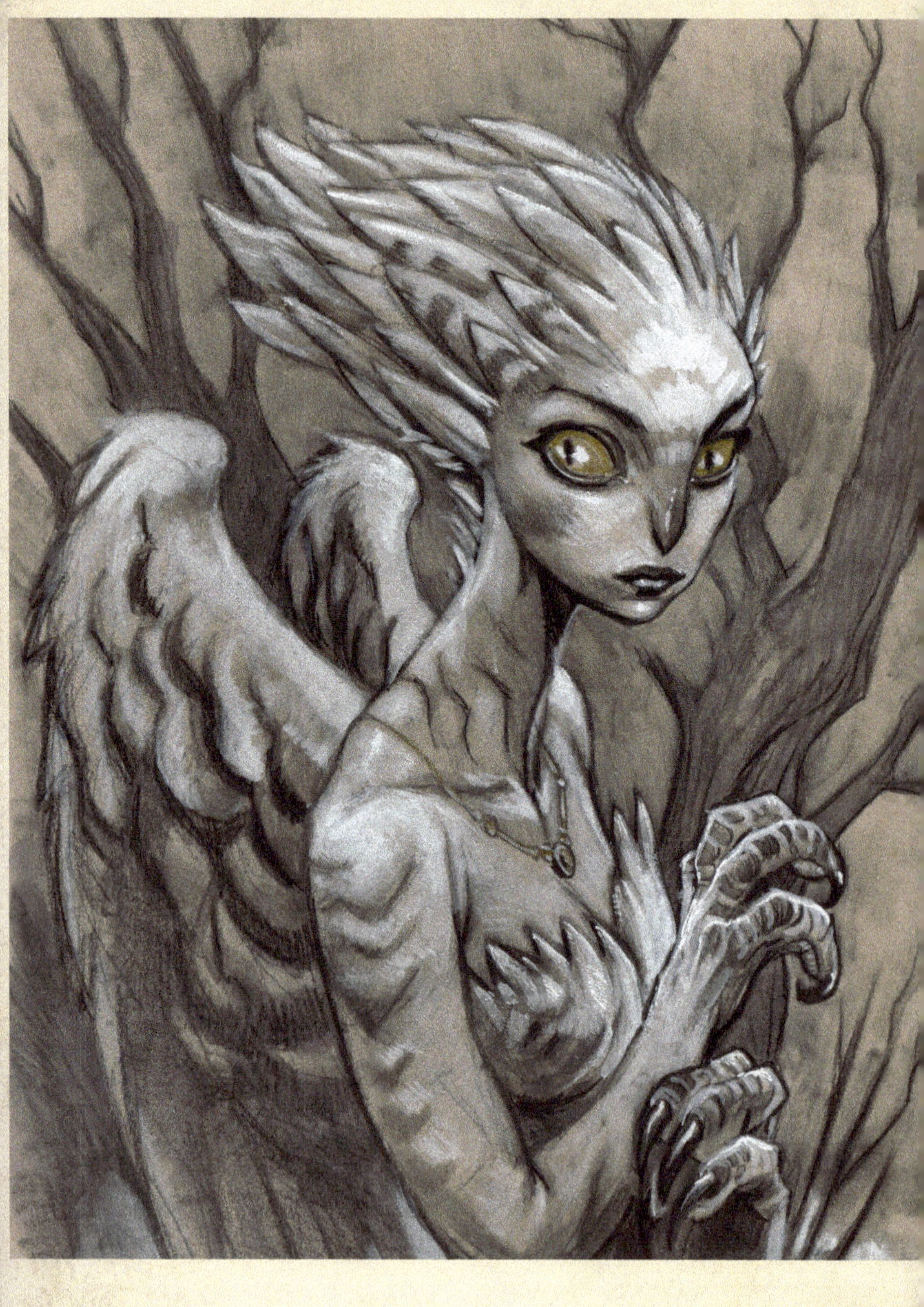

The Innocent

Deep in the Near forest woods surrounding Thornclaw Mansion, far into the edges of the sprawling estate, there lives a creature, both beautiful and fearsome. Sightings of her are so rare, that no one knows her habits or where she nests. Hearing her call in the night is considered a bad omen as the lives of those who have heard it often come to an untimely end.

Those that have survived an encounter with her say she is most likely as scared of you as you are of her, but watch out for the claws anyway.

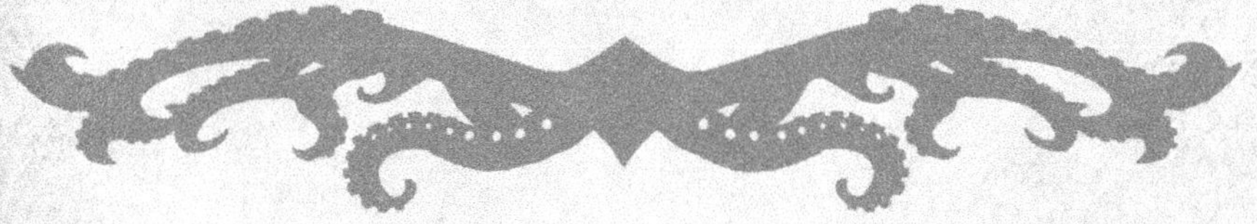

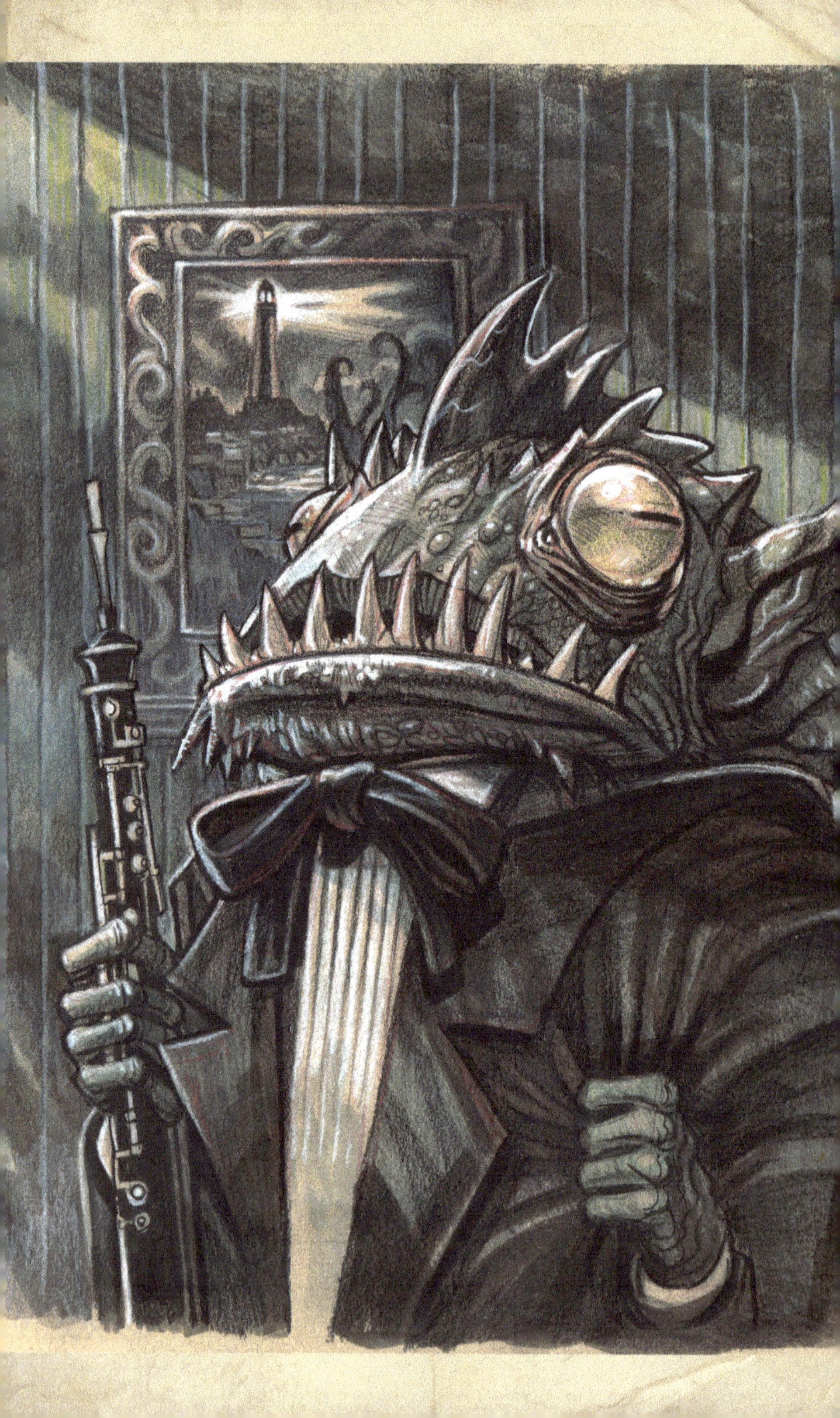

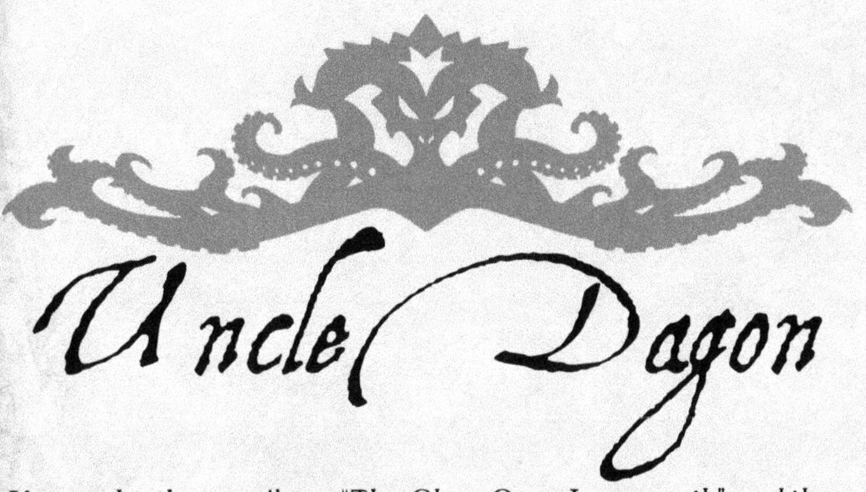

Uncle Dagon

Known by the monikers "The Oboe Over Innsmouth" and the " Sultan of Yog Sothoth," this otherworldly famous oboe player and jazz bandleader is in demand at all the clubs throughout the unknown dimensions beyond time and space. At the Playboy's request, he and his band are frequent players at the Antediluvian Club's unlighted chambers. His blasphemous music oft described as a "disconcerting and discordant cacophony," and "a muffled, maddening beating of vile drums and the thin monotonous whine of accursed flutes" is known for driving his audiences to the edge of madness.

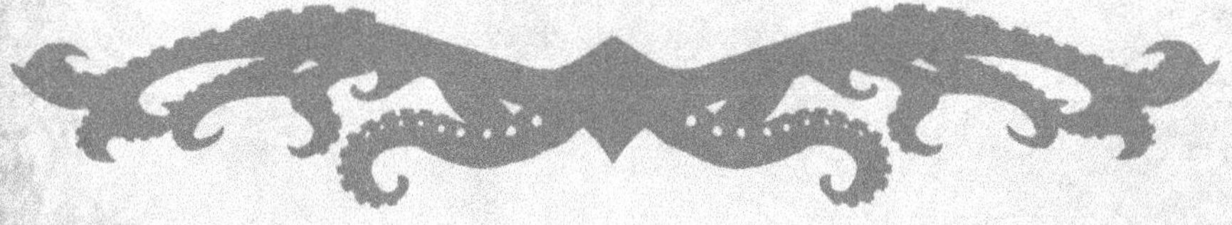

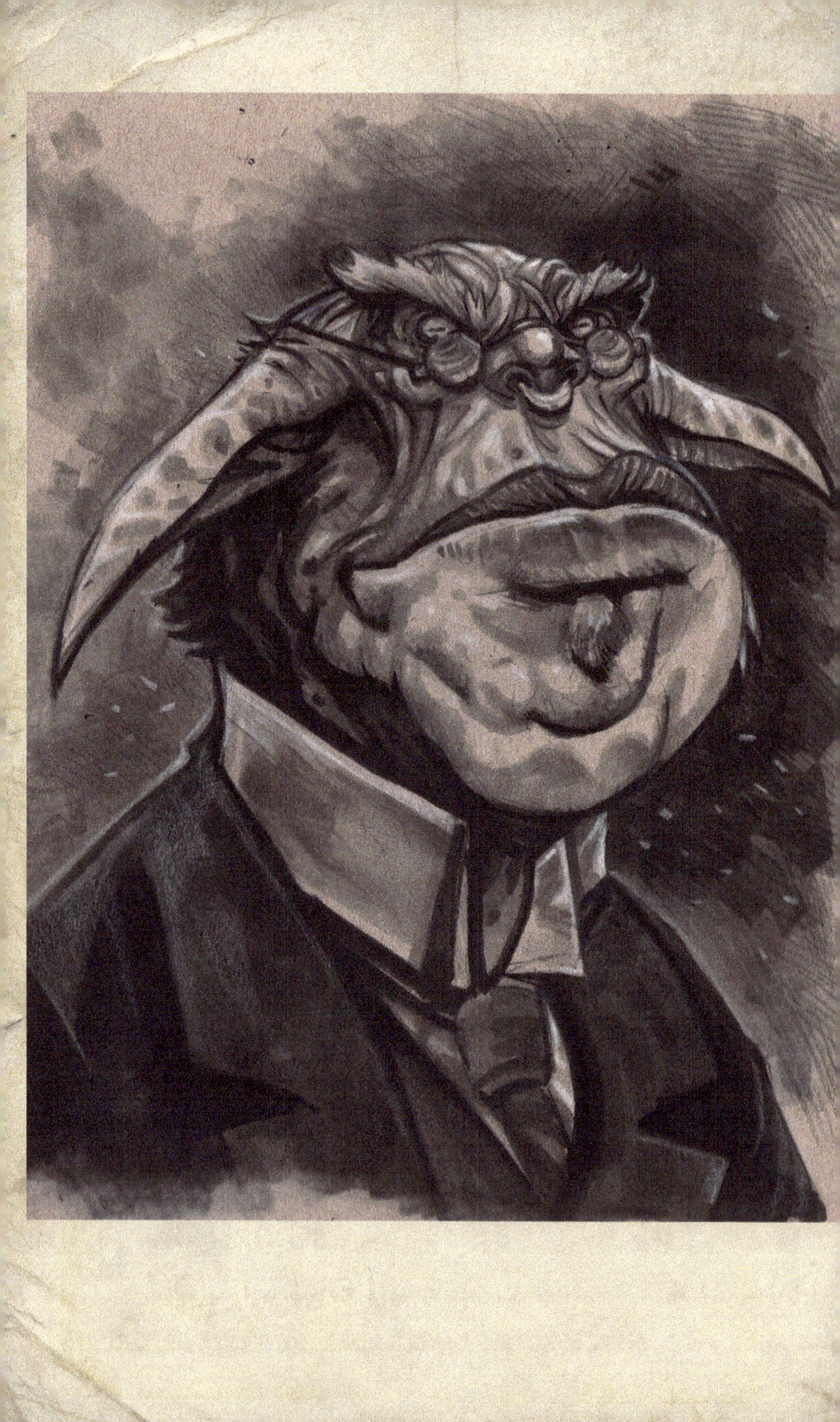

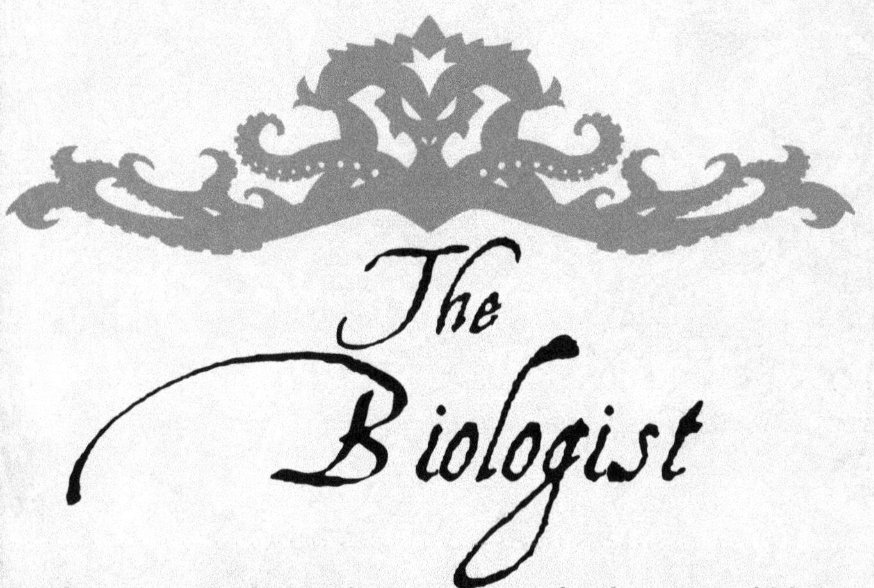

The Biologist

He has long sought out the answers to the diversity of life in the worlds of Thornclaw Manor. His research casts doubt on the Darwinian nature of life in the Multiverse. He has seen disturbing and obscene creatures develop through bizarre alterations in biology that defy logic or simple evolutionary process. He also casts doubt on the idea that there is any kind of "intelligent design." The maddeningly chaotic development of life suggests that if there was a "designer," he or she must be either out of their mind or an omnipotent yet blind idiot god.

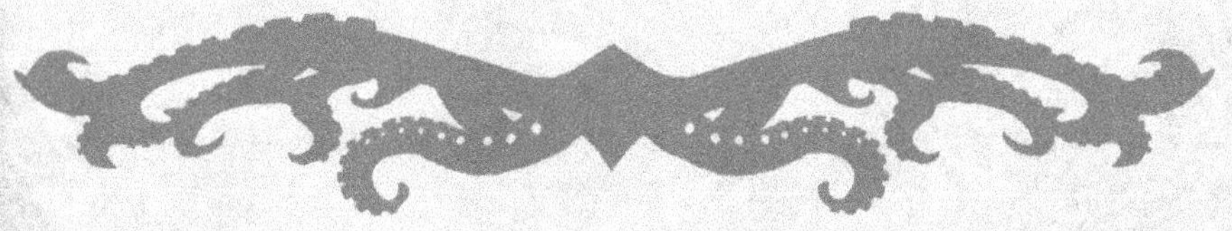

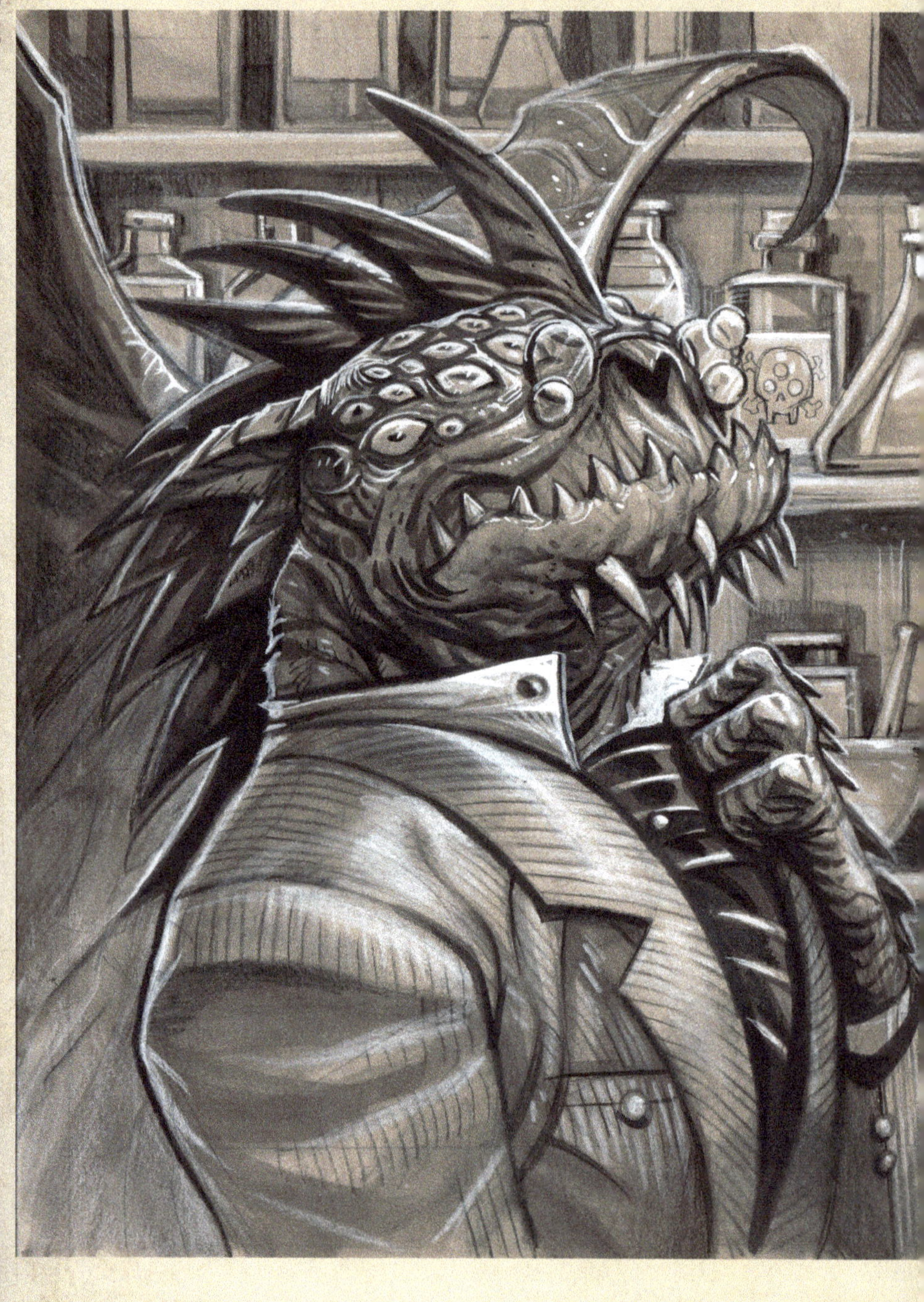

The Apothecary

He sits deep within his lab brewing up concoctions and technological innovations to serve the purposes of the Thornclaw family. His elixirs are known for many effects: inducing love, curing ills, inciting riots, and instilling madness. In his shoppe, surrounded by countless bottles of unsettling liquids and unnameable devices he toils long hours working to aid the Dowager in the lengthening of her already long life. The Apothecary is also known to keep strange company as he seeks ingredients from often unsavory beings from around the universe.

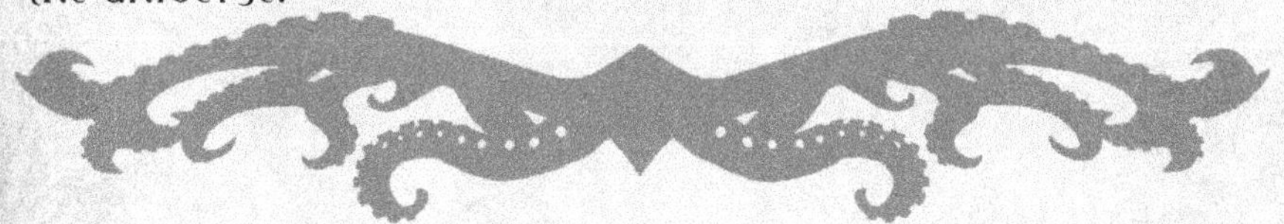

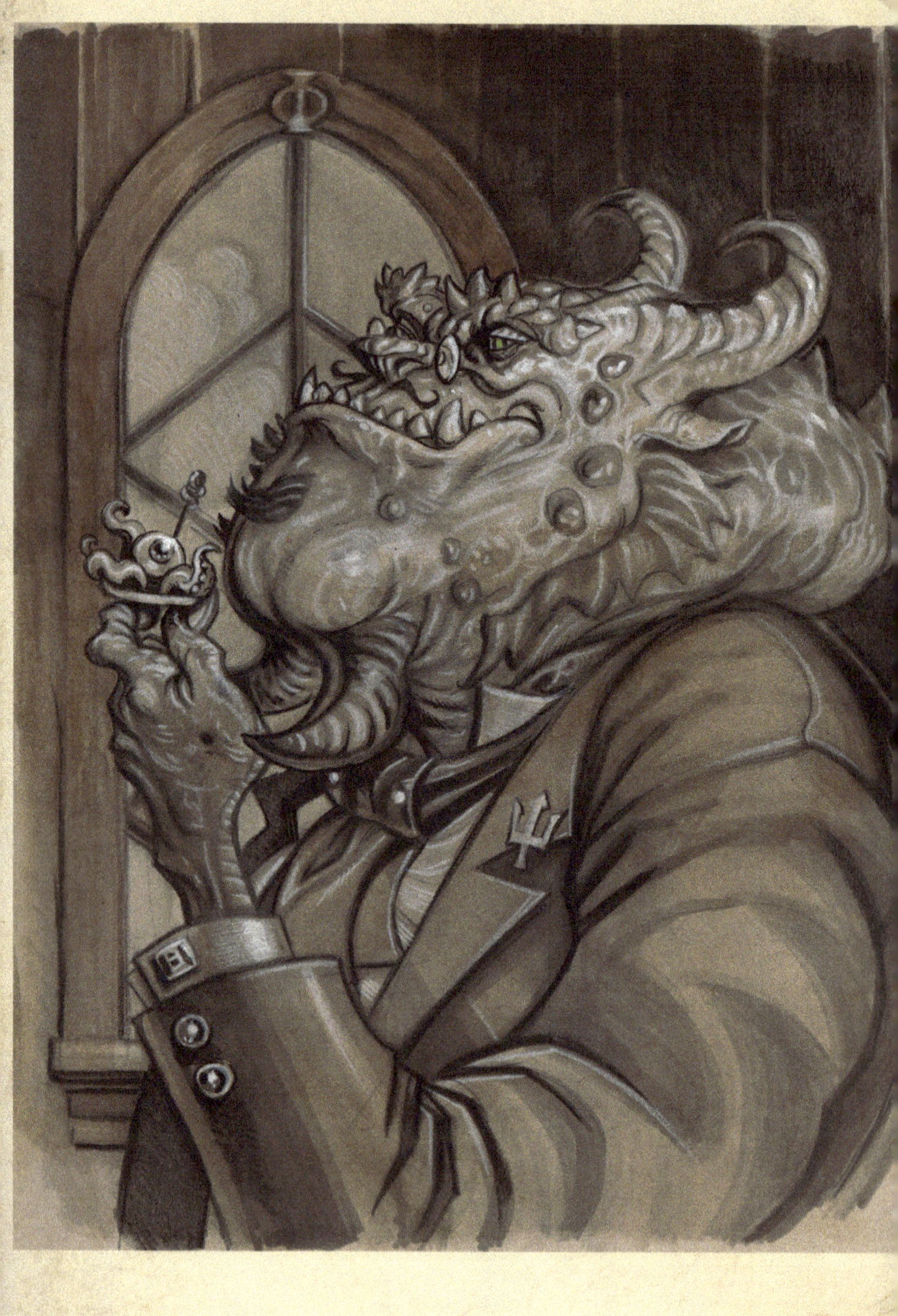

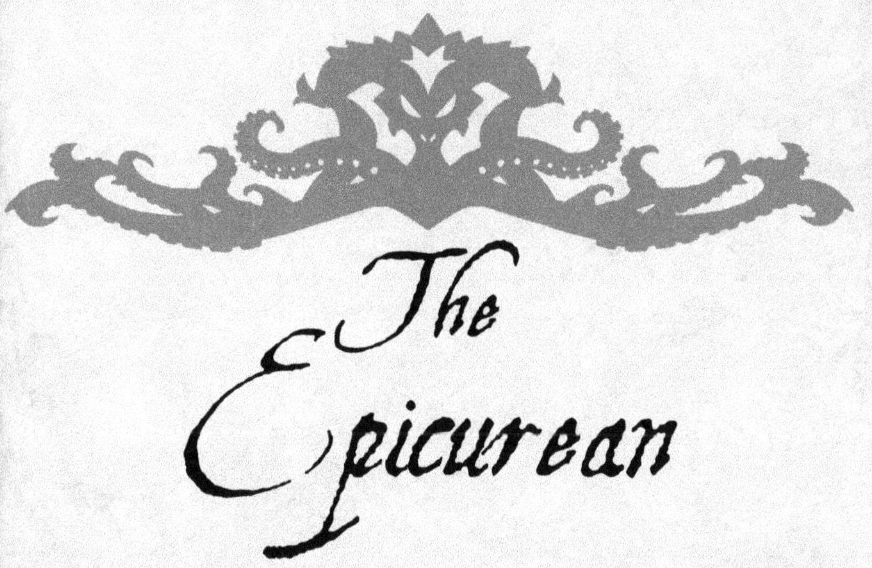

The Epicurean

A dionysian lover of obscure and disturbing delights, he will travel to the furthest lengths, with cost never a question, for new flavors and experiences to tantalize his multitudinous disquieting tastes. His restaurant reviews can make or break a world-class chef and his celebrity column in the paper can eviscerate even the most eminent of lives. Everyone who is anyone is always certain to make sure that when he invites them to dinner, they aren't on the menu.

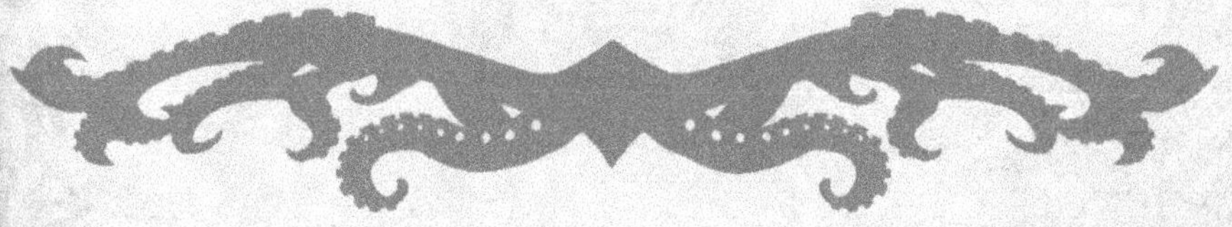

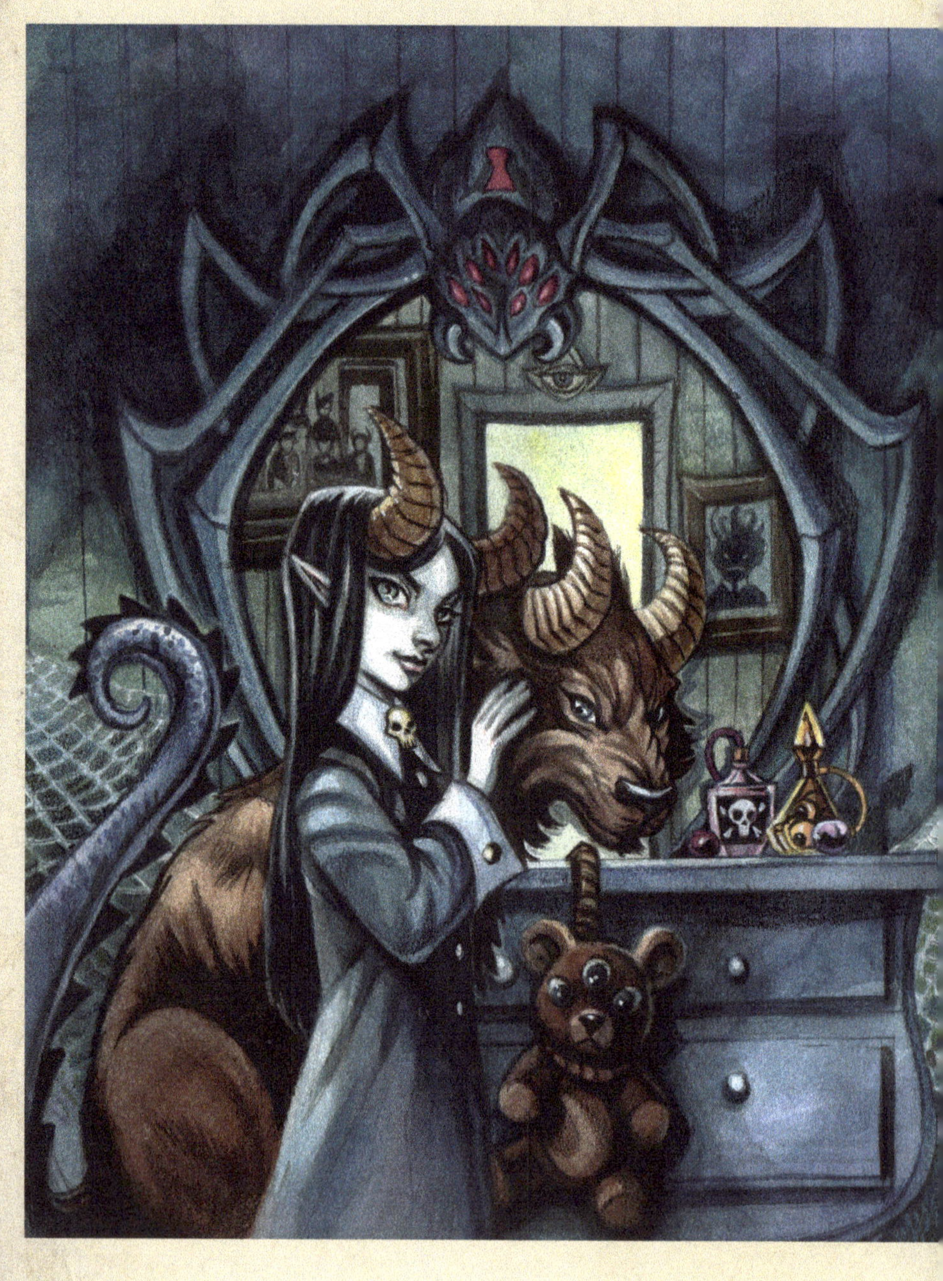

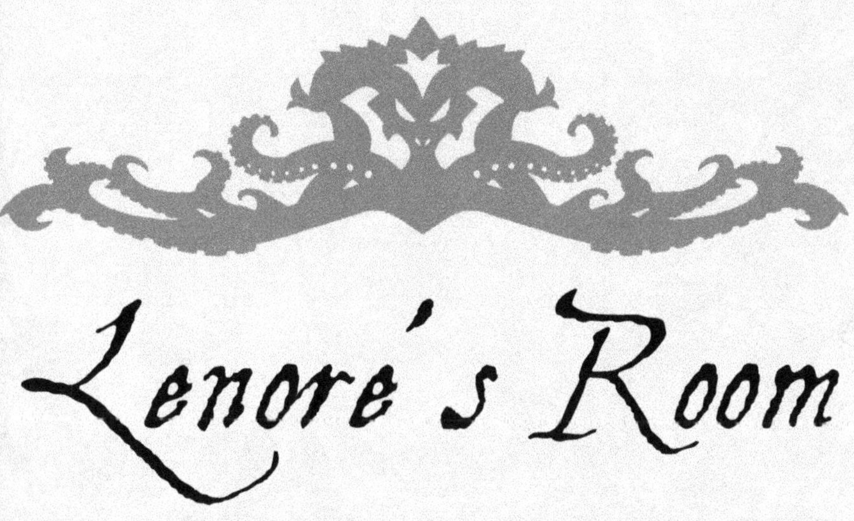

Lenore's Room

Somewhere in the old manor is Lenore's playroom, filled with toys and doom. Together with her pet direwolf, she plans traps and mischiefs for any unfortunate who might cross her path be they friend, foe or family. There are countless people who would love to get their hands on her, but they know that any harm that comes to Lenore would be returned tenfold by the Dowager who loves her little granddaughter Lenore like no other.

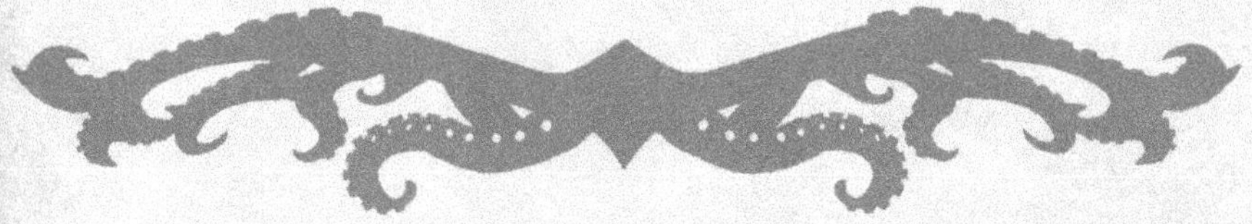

The Menagerie

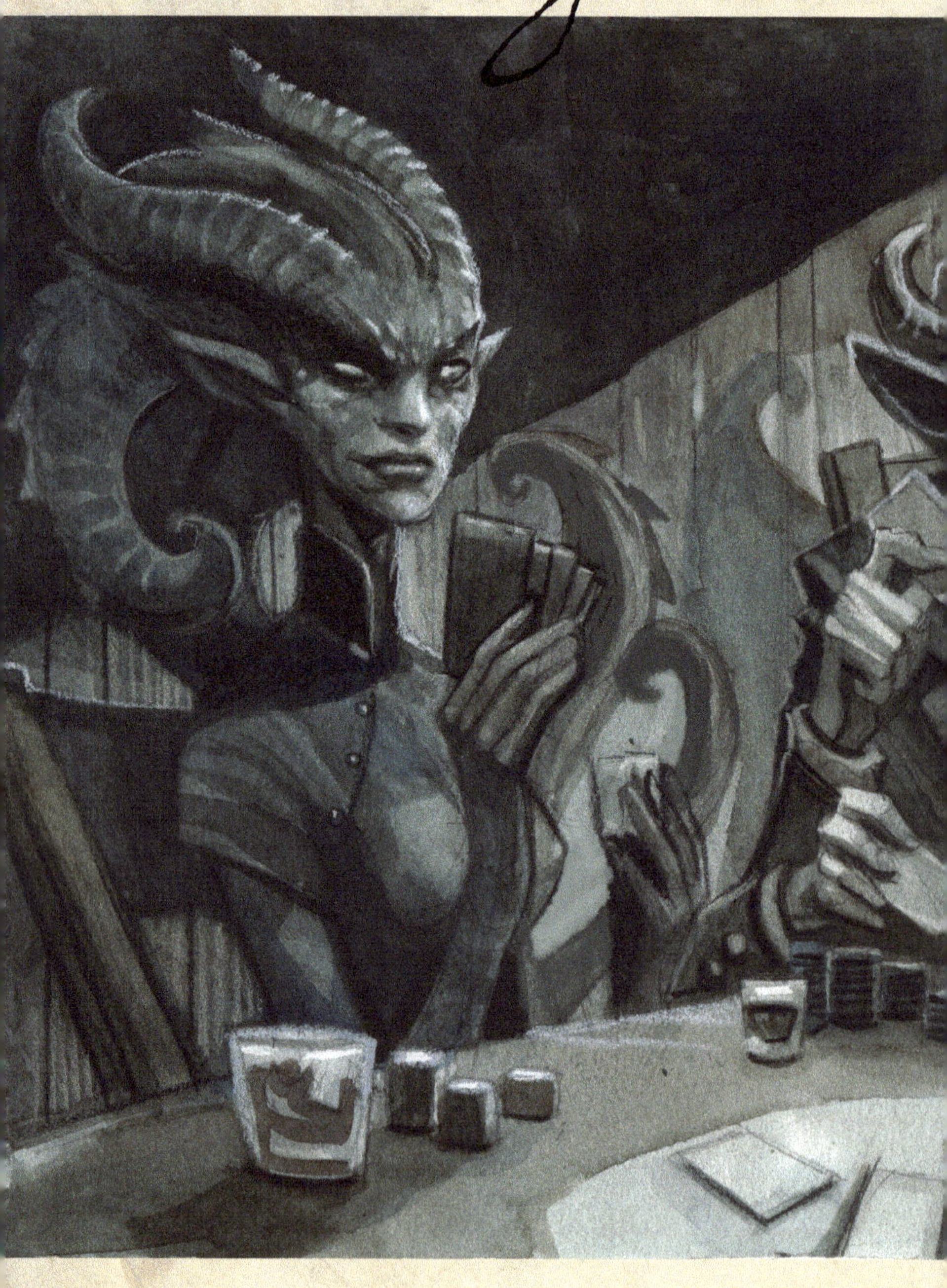

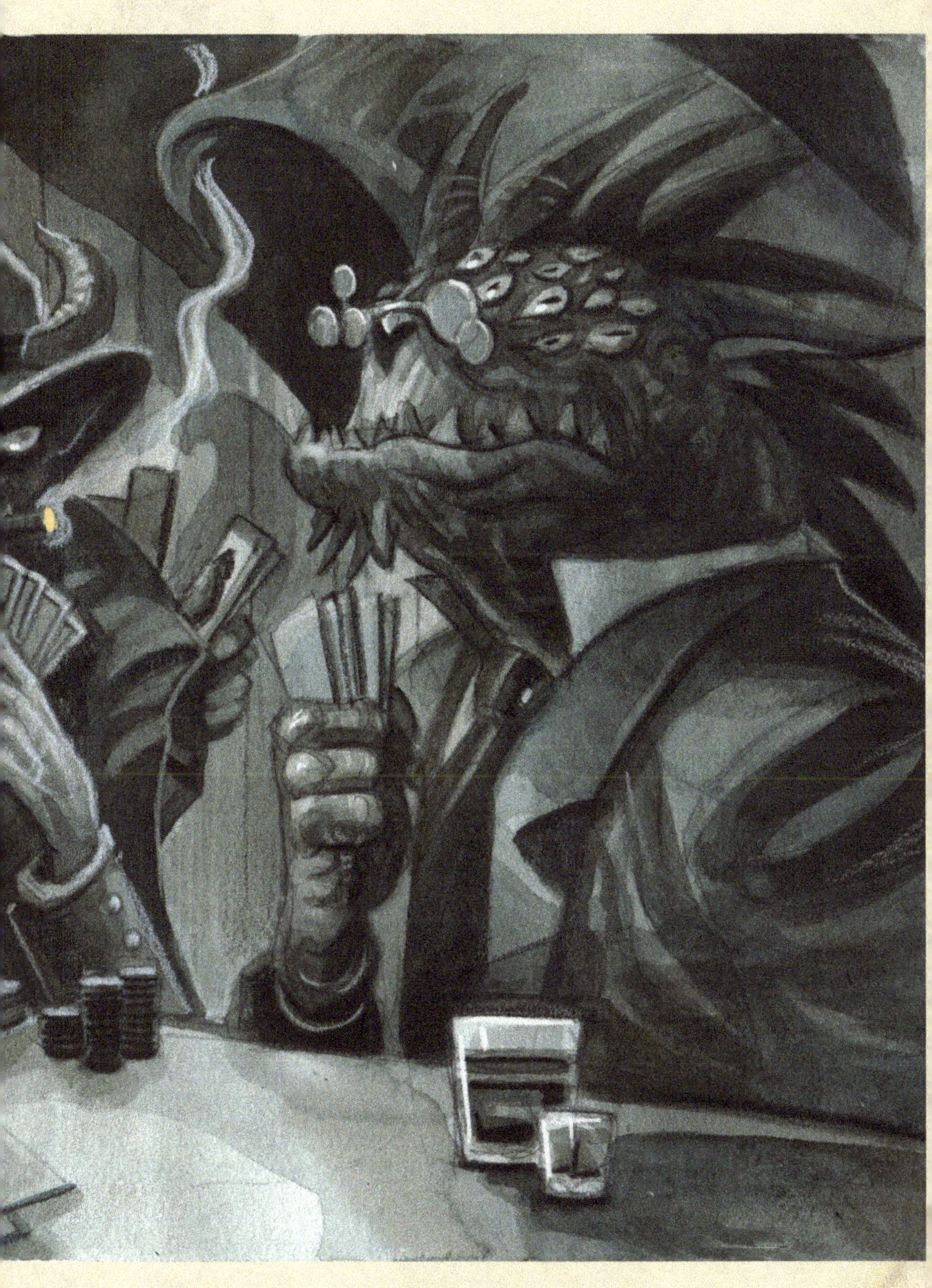

The Extended Family,
Sketches, and Concepts

The Tourist

She loves to visit the surface worlds for the beautiful flora and fauna that is so different from her underwater cities array of creatures. Her inability to breathe air also limits her ability to communicate so she tends to keep to herself.

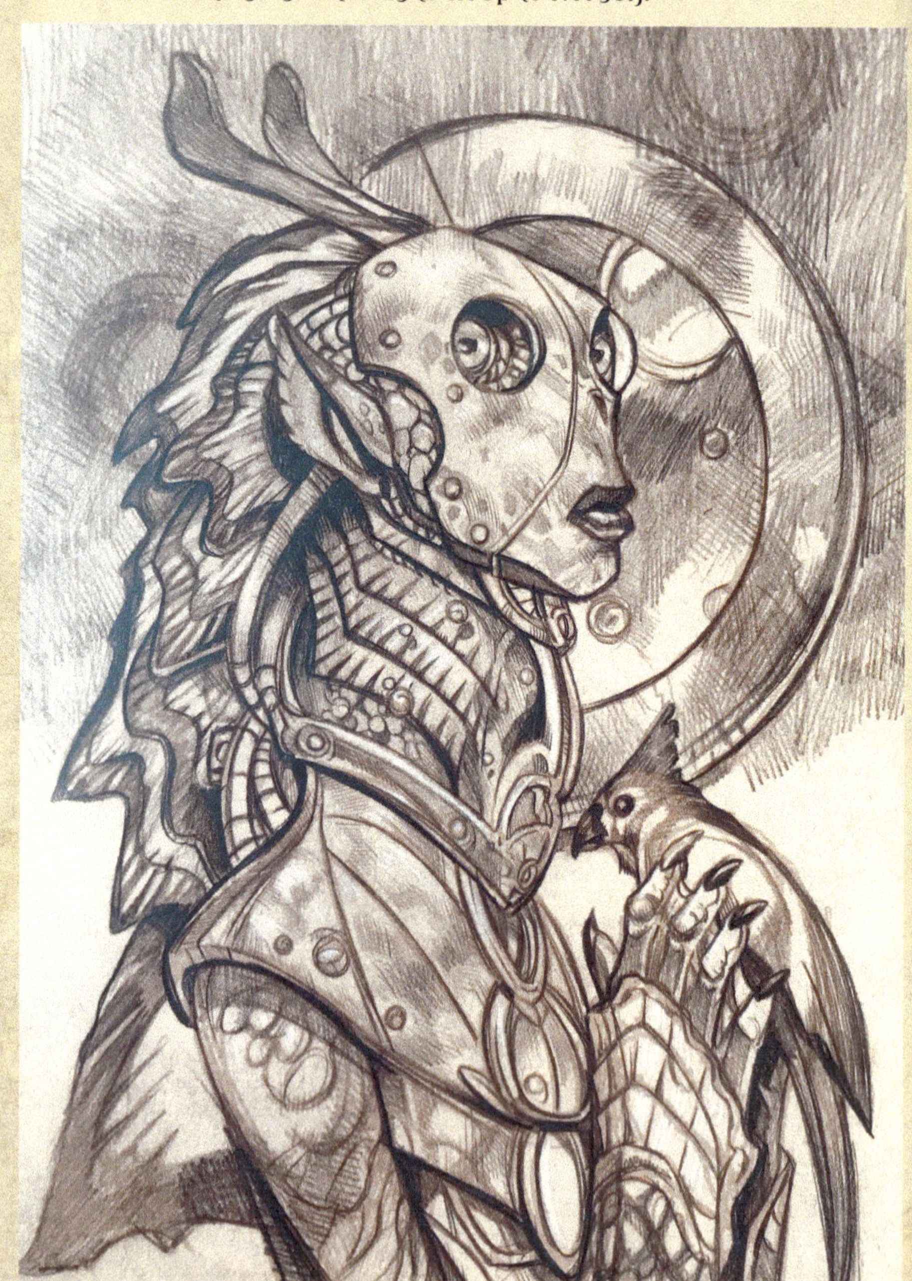

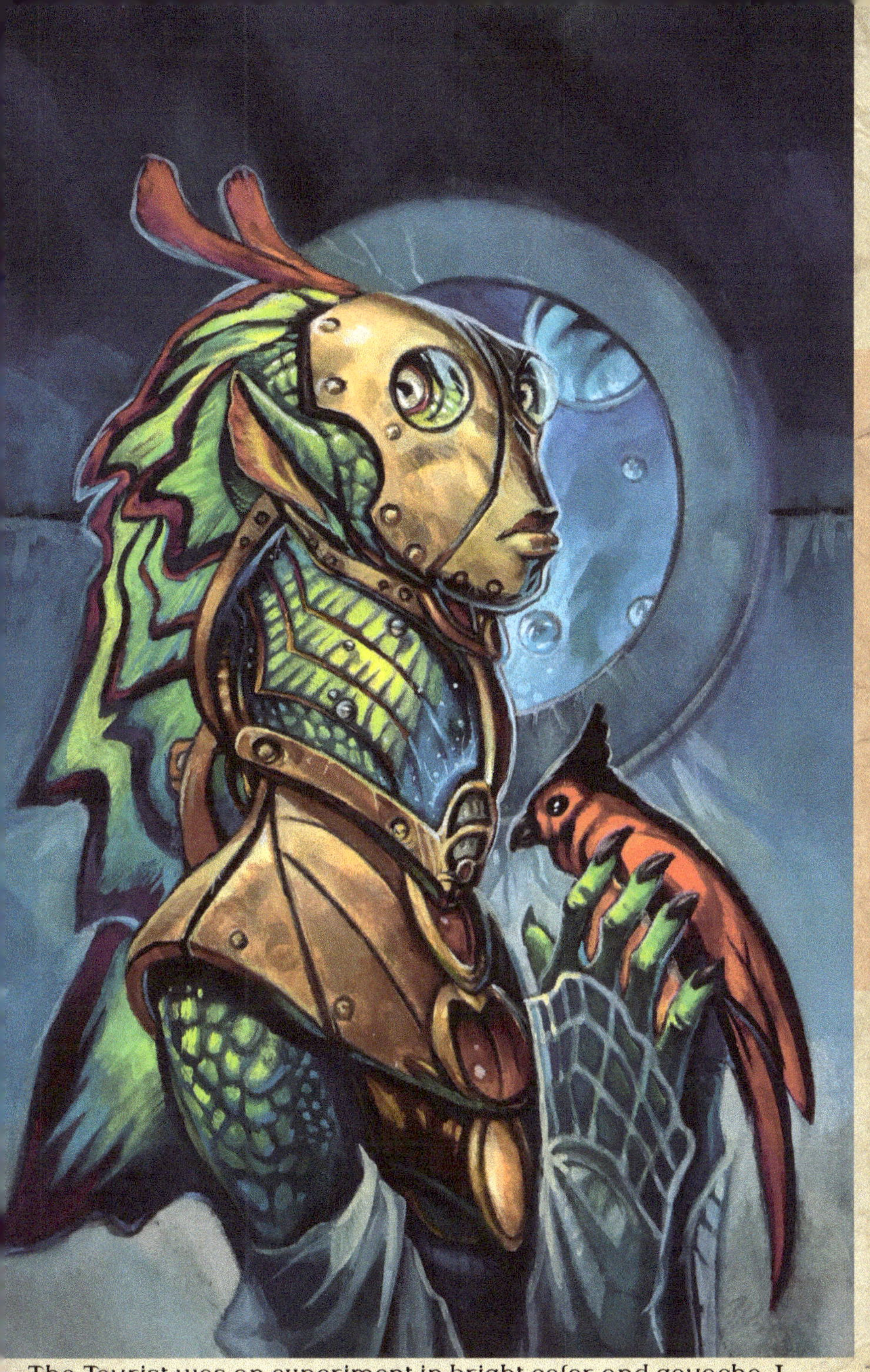

The Tourist was an experiment in bright color and gouache, I love the painting, but there was too much color for the Thorn-claws so I decided to just keep her to the side. There might be an opportunity to do more full-color versions of the Thorn-claws but I didn't think it would be good to change the color style so dramatically.

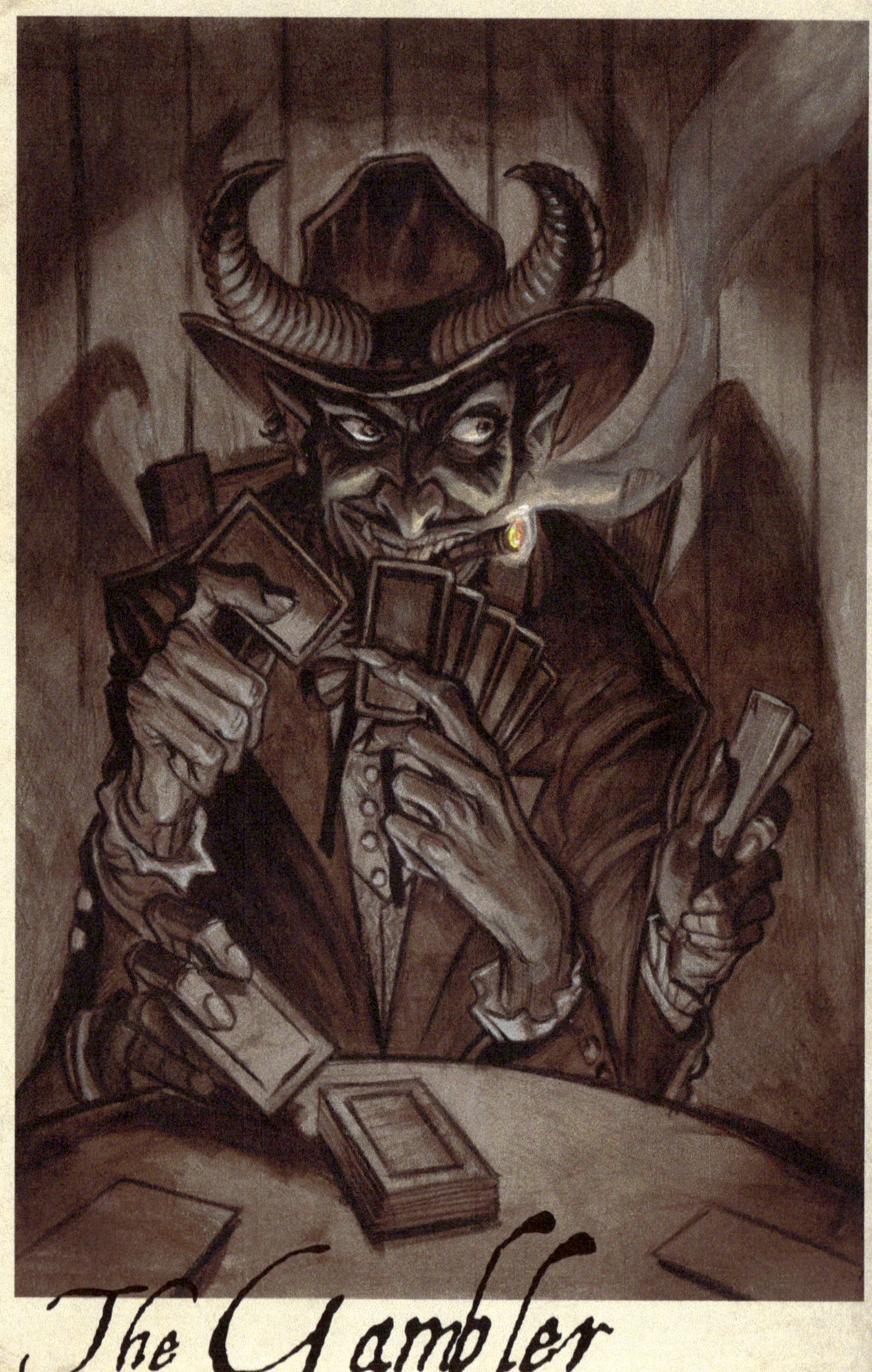

The Gambler

The Gambler is still part of the Thornclaw world, and he is a fun one, but I wanted to save him for a different set.

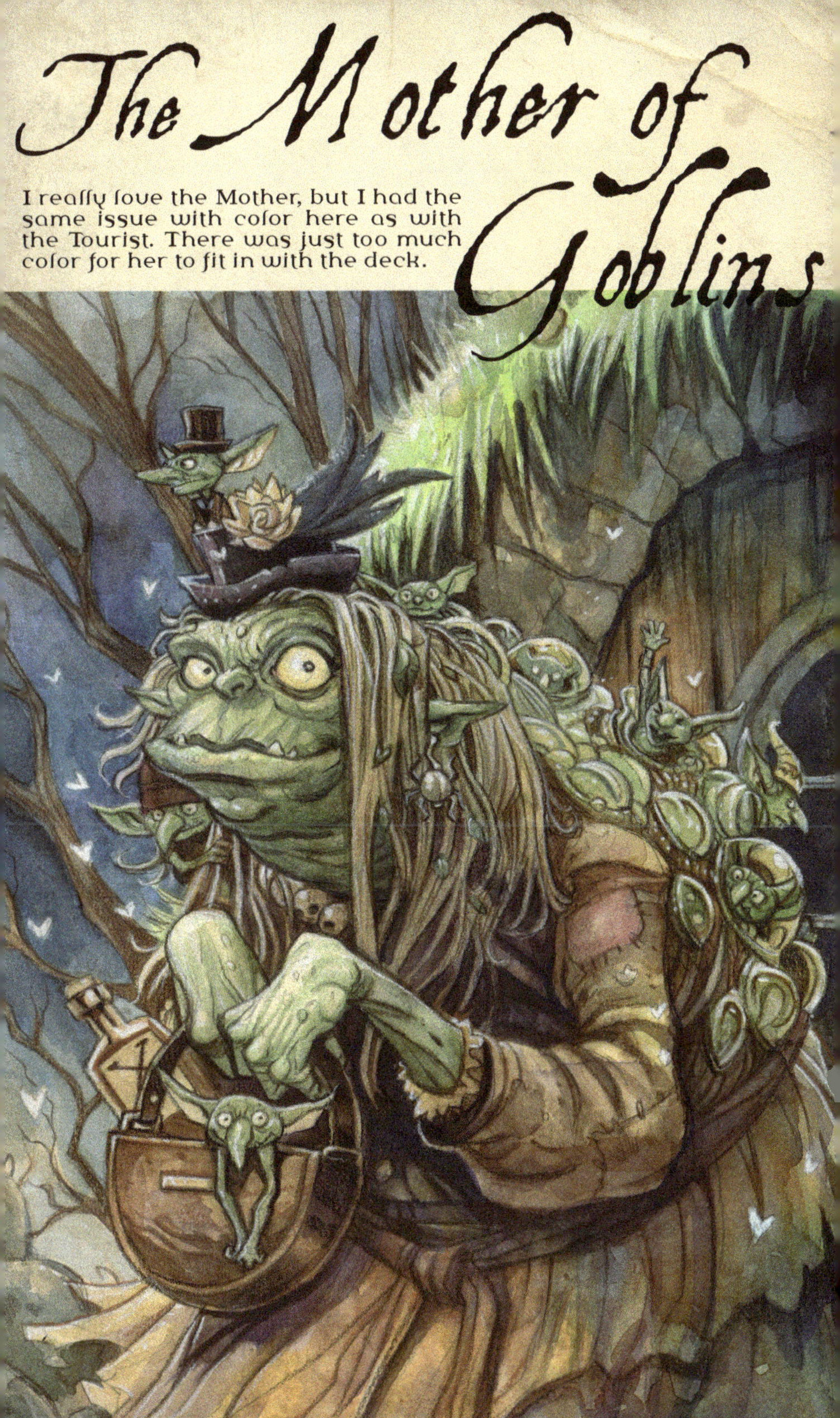

The Mother of

Goblins

I really love the Mother, but I had the same issue with color here as with the Tourist. There was just too much color for her to fit in with the deck.

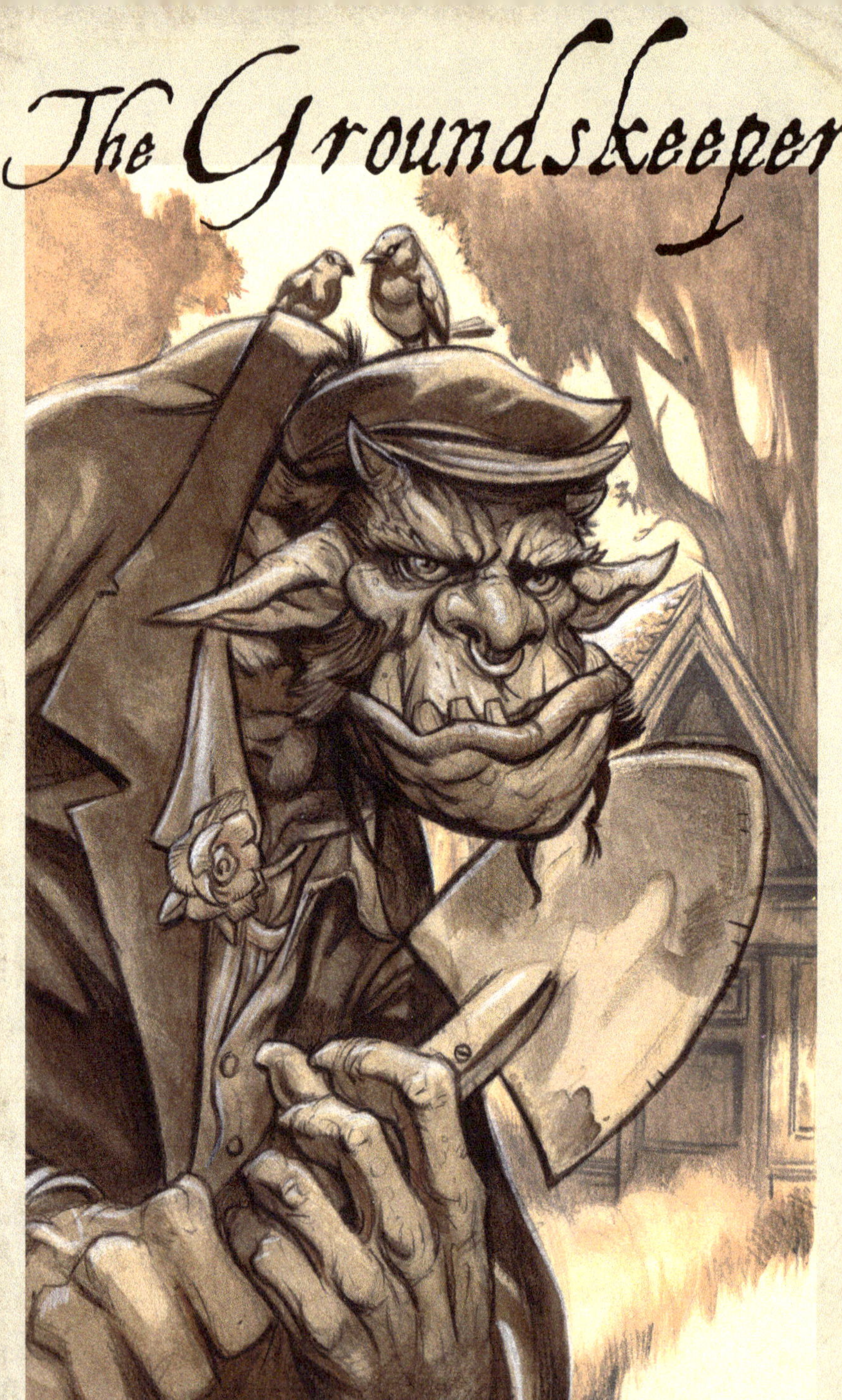

The Groundskeeper

The Groundskeeper and the Pirate Queen are two more family members who just didn't fit in the theme of the original decks. I imagine these characters live outside the social order in the Thornclaw Family, so they will wait for another Thornclaw project. The Pirate was executed with watercolor and the Groundskeeper, who is dangerously sweet, was done in acrylic.

The Pirate Queen

The Tree Nymph

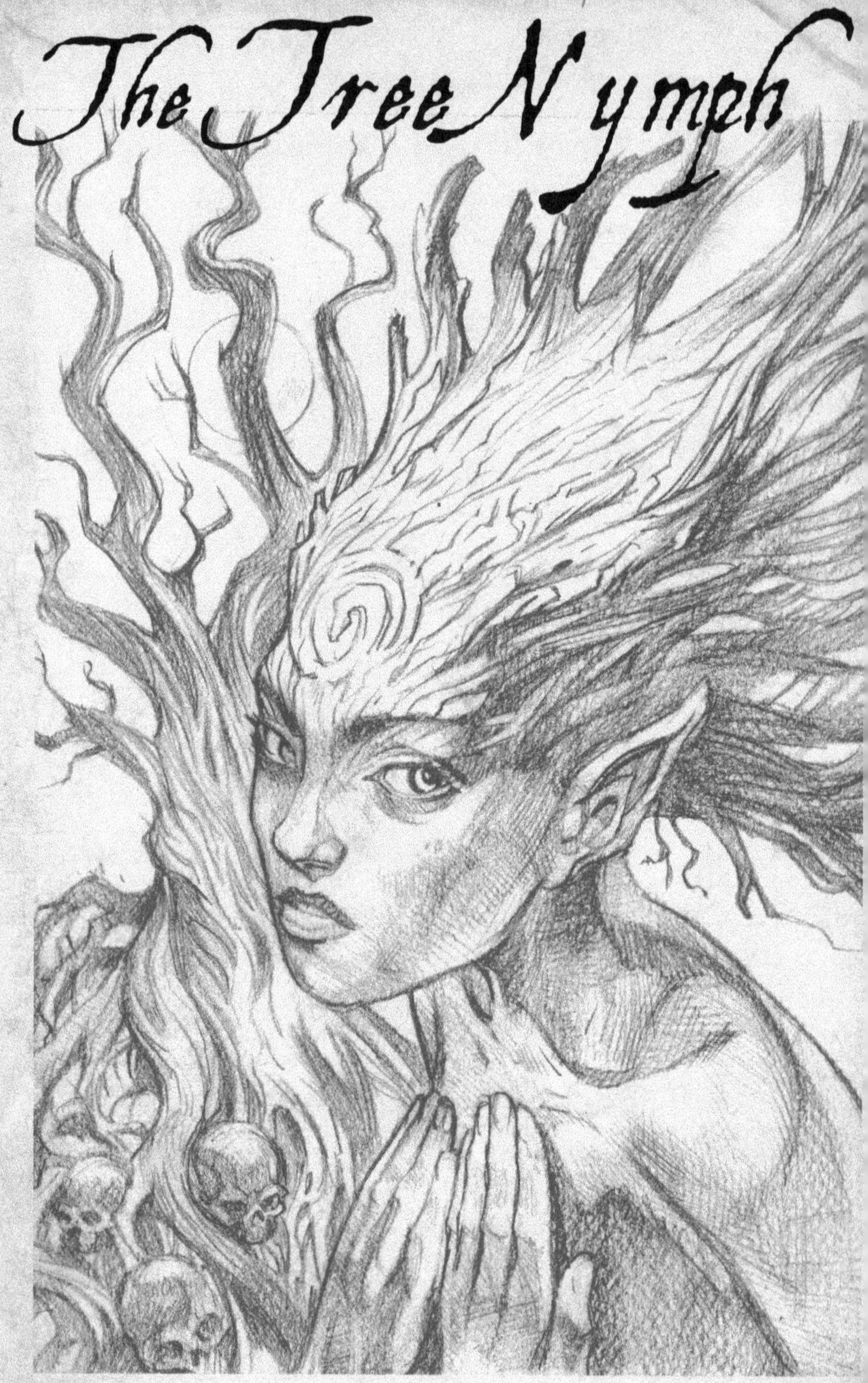

The Tree Nymph is an acrylic piece that I did as I was developing the first deck. She is very lovely, but because of the color issue, I left her out. I imagine she lives in the dark forest near the Innocent.

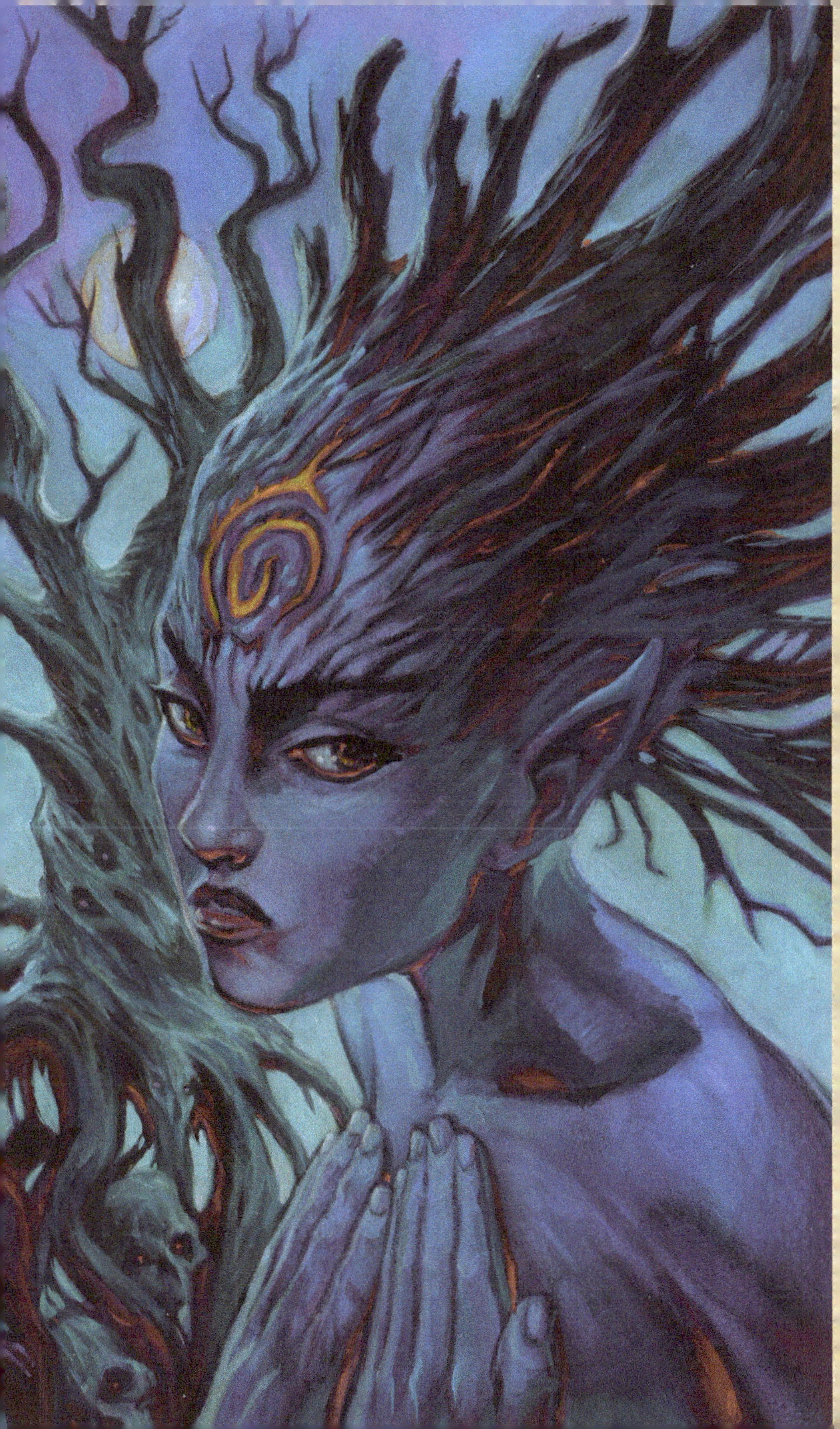

The Collector

The Collector is an early draft of the Lady Darque, a psychopomp who collects the souls of the dead. ultimately I wanted more personality in her so I did the current version but I still like this as an alternate portrait of the winged death.

The Deciever

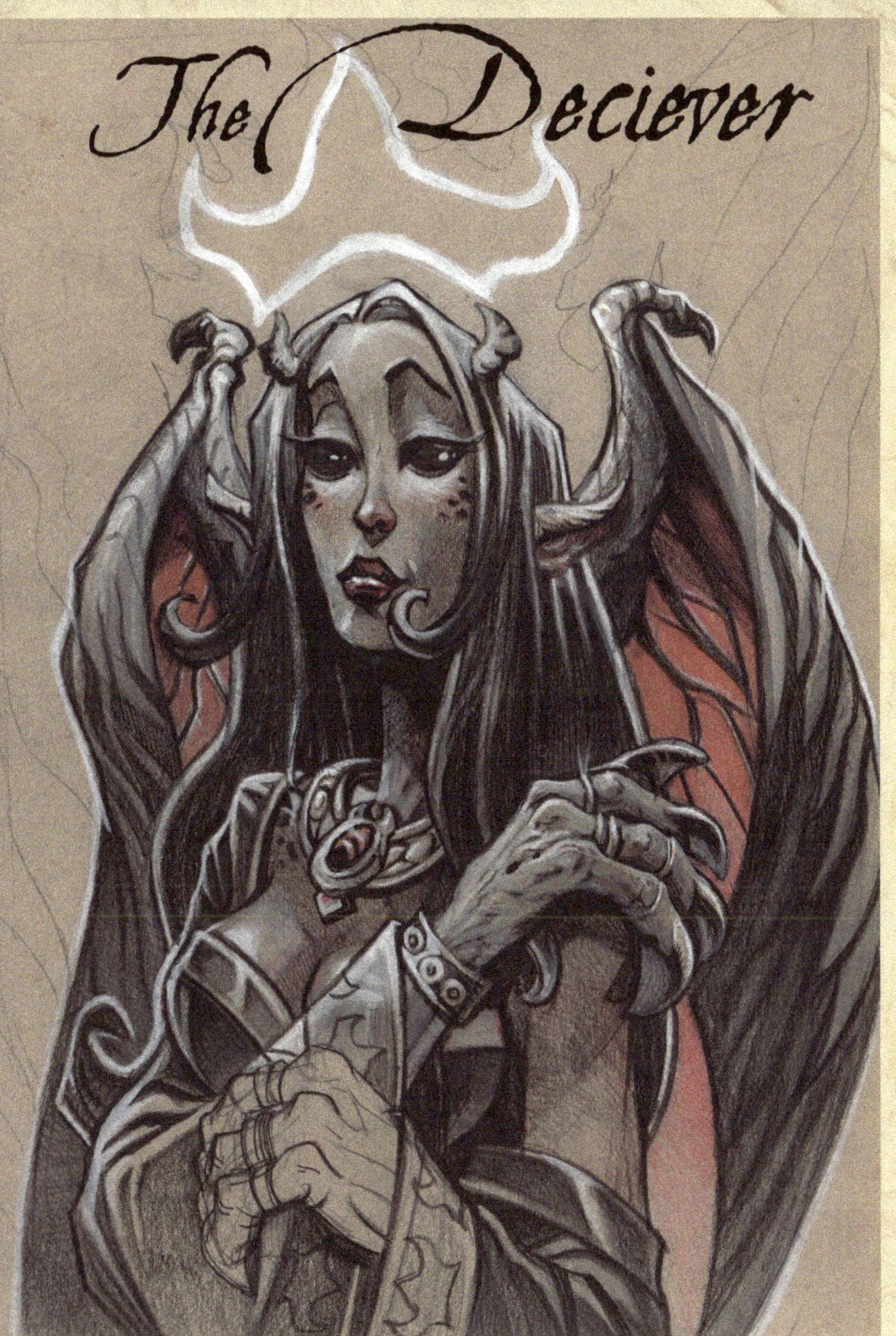

The Deciever is a concept I want to explore a little more. There is an entire part of the Thornclaw family that feeds on the distress and frustration that they can impose upon the humans they encounter. A nice drawing, but I felt that she was a little too showy to be part of the family and I want to take another stab at the idea.

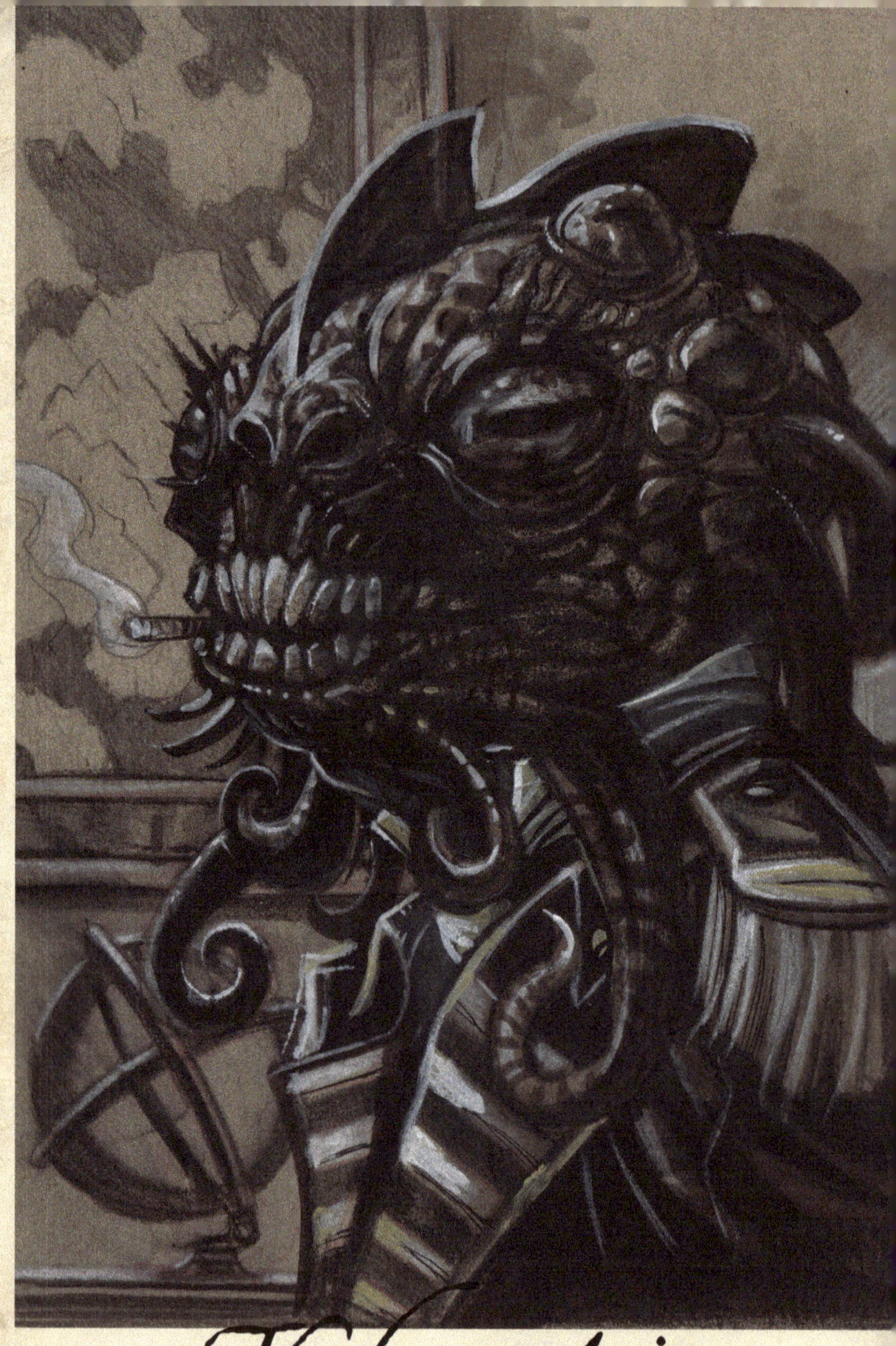

The Captain

The Captain was an early version of the Admiral, but I decided that I wanted the Admiral to be part of the cephaloid family of Thornclaws. The Admiral was inspired by an old British Admiral, the bushy mustaches becoming long tentacles.

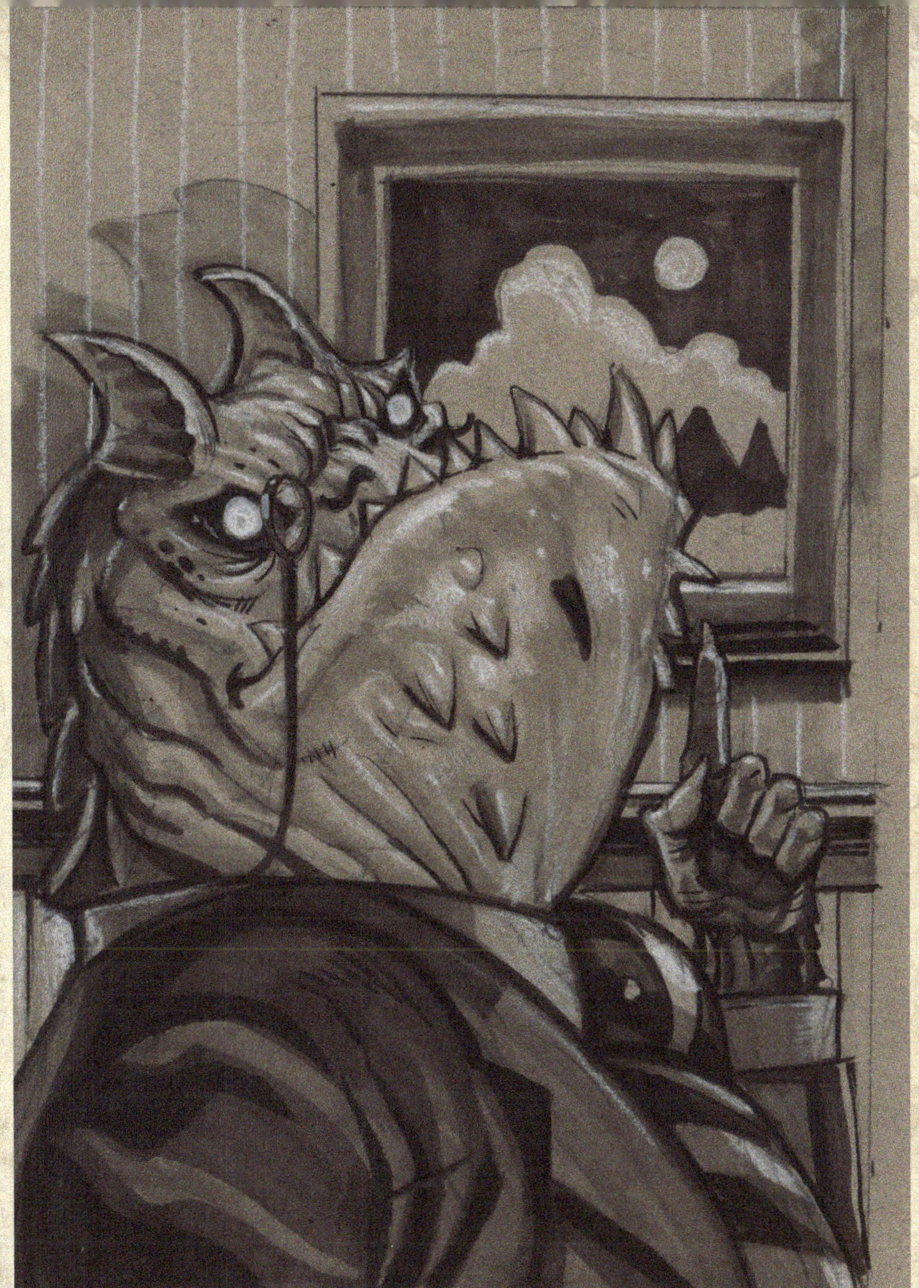

The Industrialist

This guy was a lot of fun to make but I want to create a more complex image for this guy. I imagine him pouring over his ticker tape machine hoping to find out whether his investments are up or down. He's a creative predecessor to the Gentleman and maybe a co-worker at the firm.

The Underworld

The Sneak is an example of life for the common creatures of the Thornclaw world. Surviving on scrounging and petty crime, the Sneak is a frequent associate of the Boss and some of the other underworld beings of Thornclaw. He's generally good at helping people find what they need, just don't get between him and his dinner.

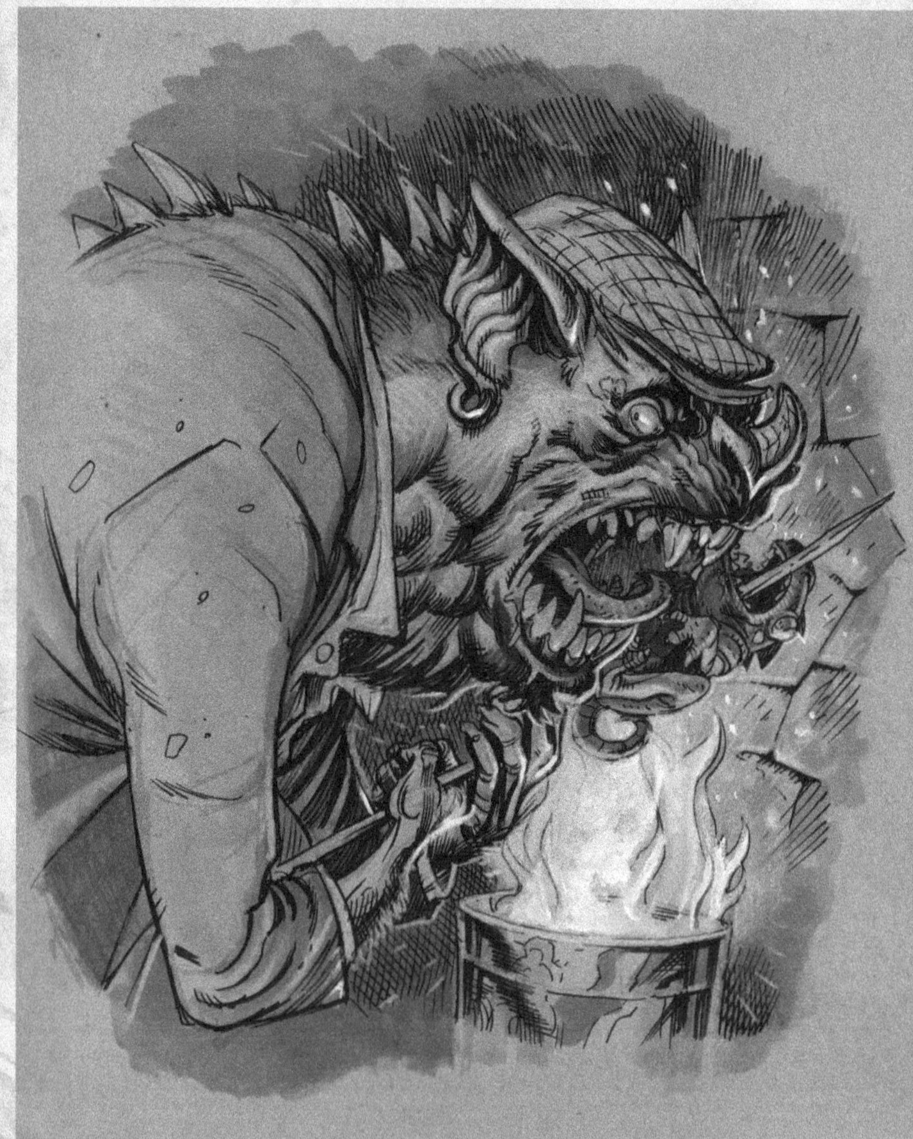

The streets of the small city near the manor are teeming with creatures from all over the known universe. They gather to be close to the center of power, to learn, to work, to trade, to make their weirdest dreams come true. For every wide-eyed traveler seeking their fortune, there are those who cling to the underbelly of society, who make their fortunes off of others' failure. These creatures of business probably work for the Boss or they won't live long.

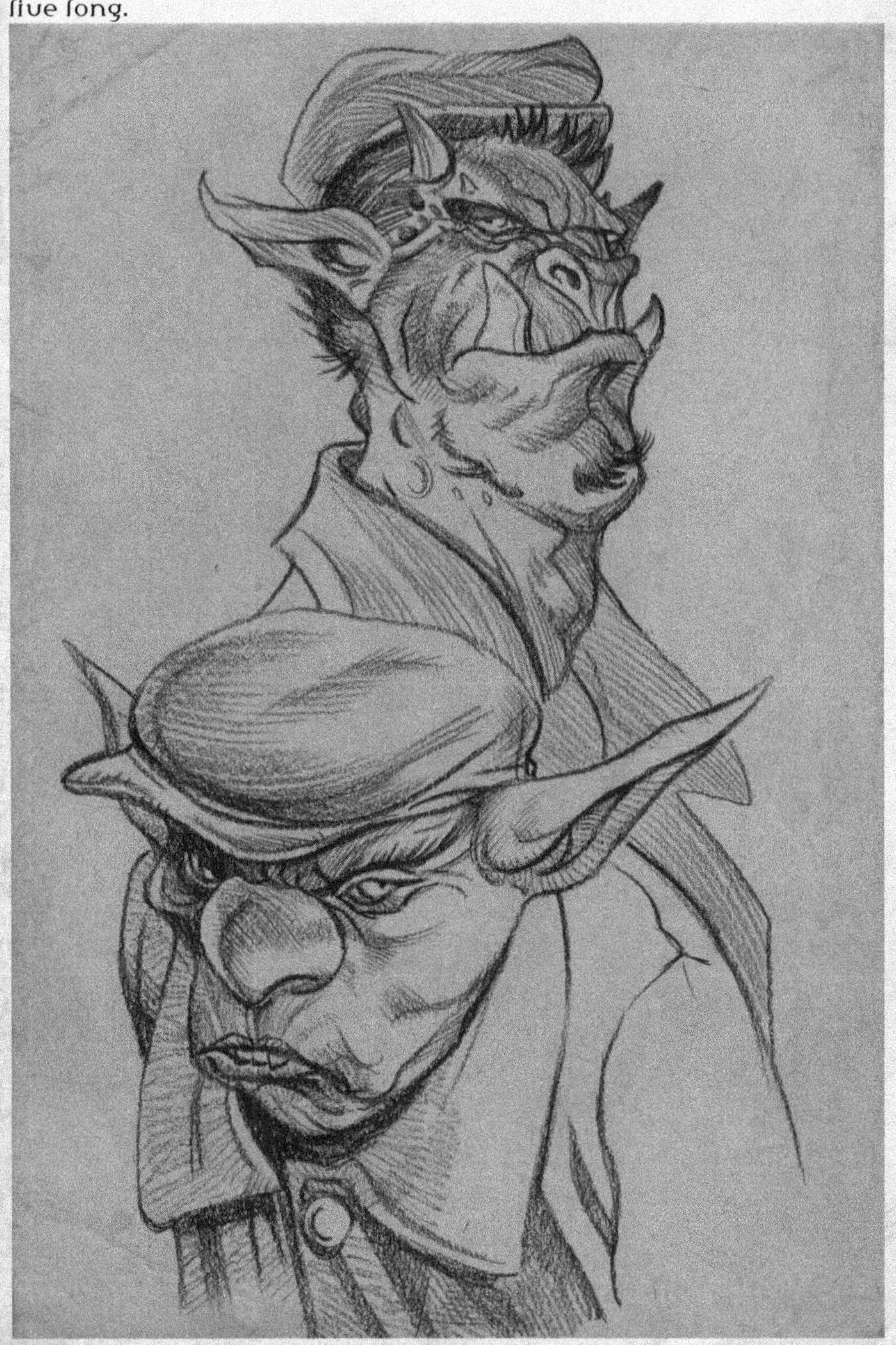

The Sketches

I love thinking about the Thornclaw world, and when I start imagining, I start sketching.

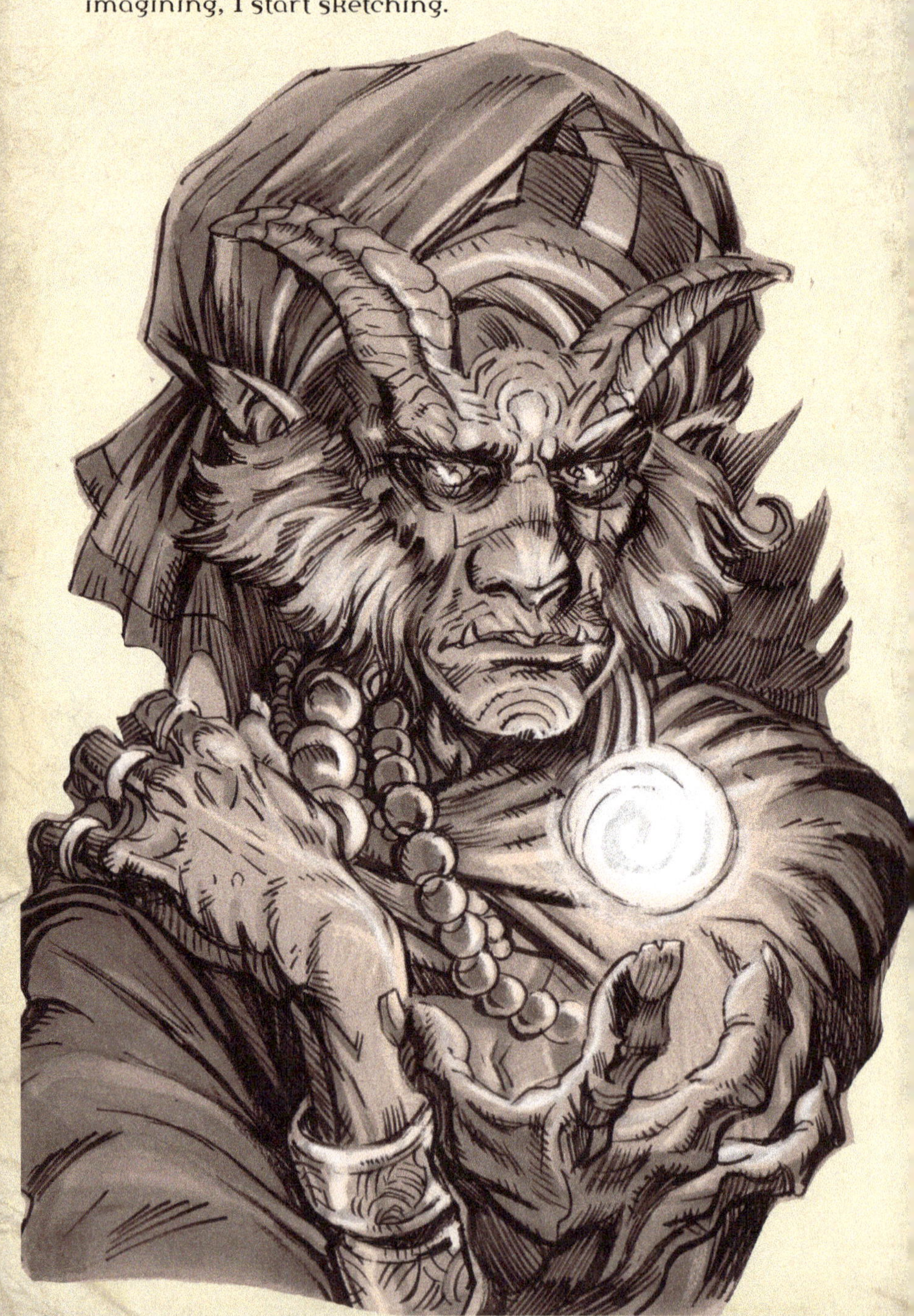

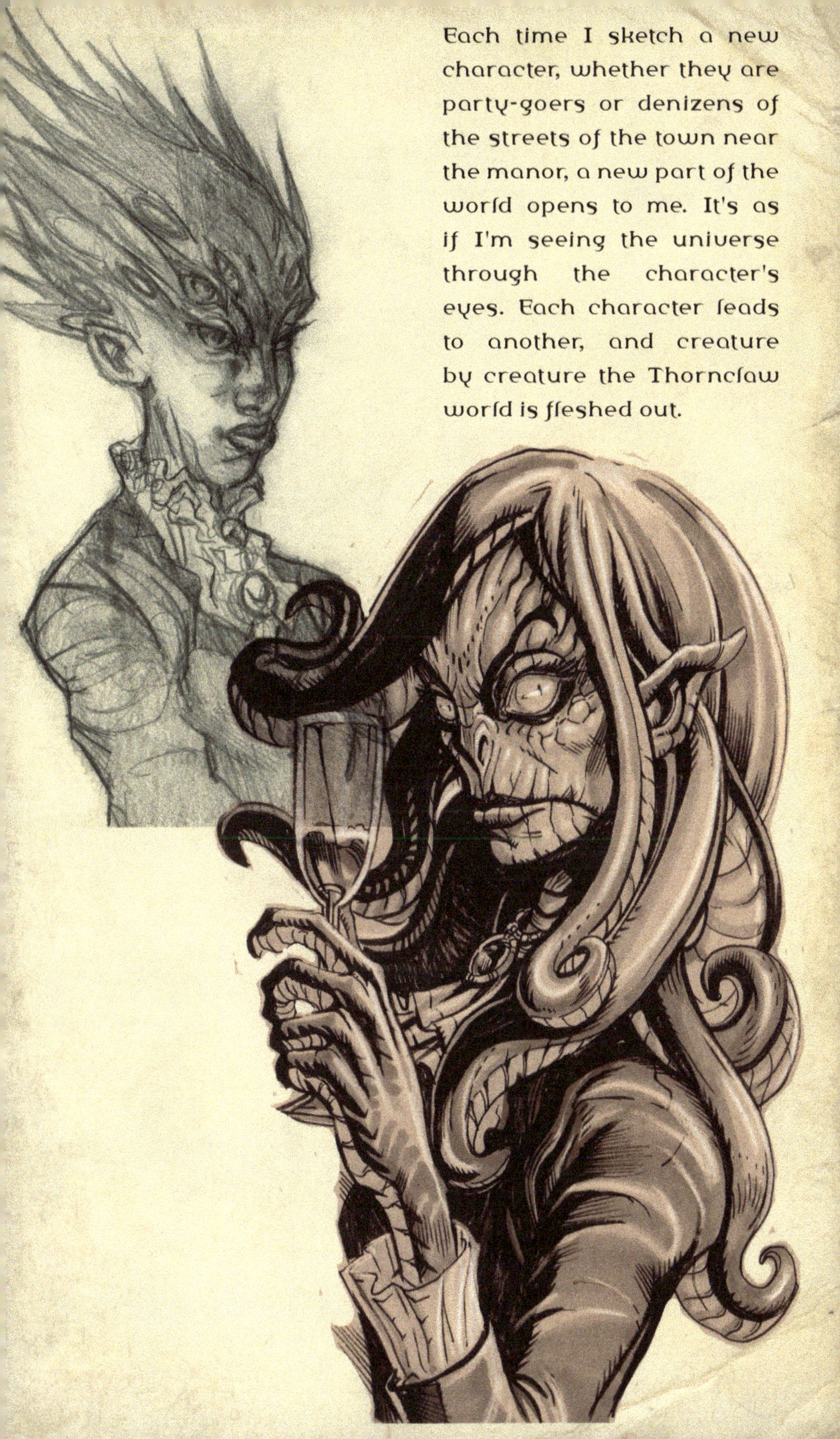

Each time I sketch a new character, whether they are party-goers or denizens of the streets of the town near the manor, a new part of the world opens to me. It's as if I'm seeing the universe through the character's eyes. Each character leads to another, and creature by creature the Thornclaw world is fleshed out.

Some of the Thornclaws are based on dark versions of fairytale creatures and others on interesting animals from nature. When i look around the world I am constantly hit with new inspiration, but the underlying basis of all of them is my attempt to create the personality of very human characters in monstrous creatures.

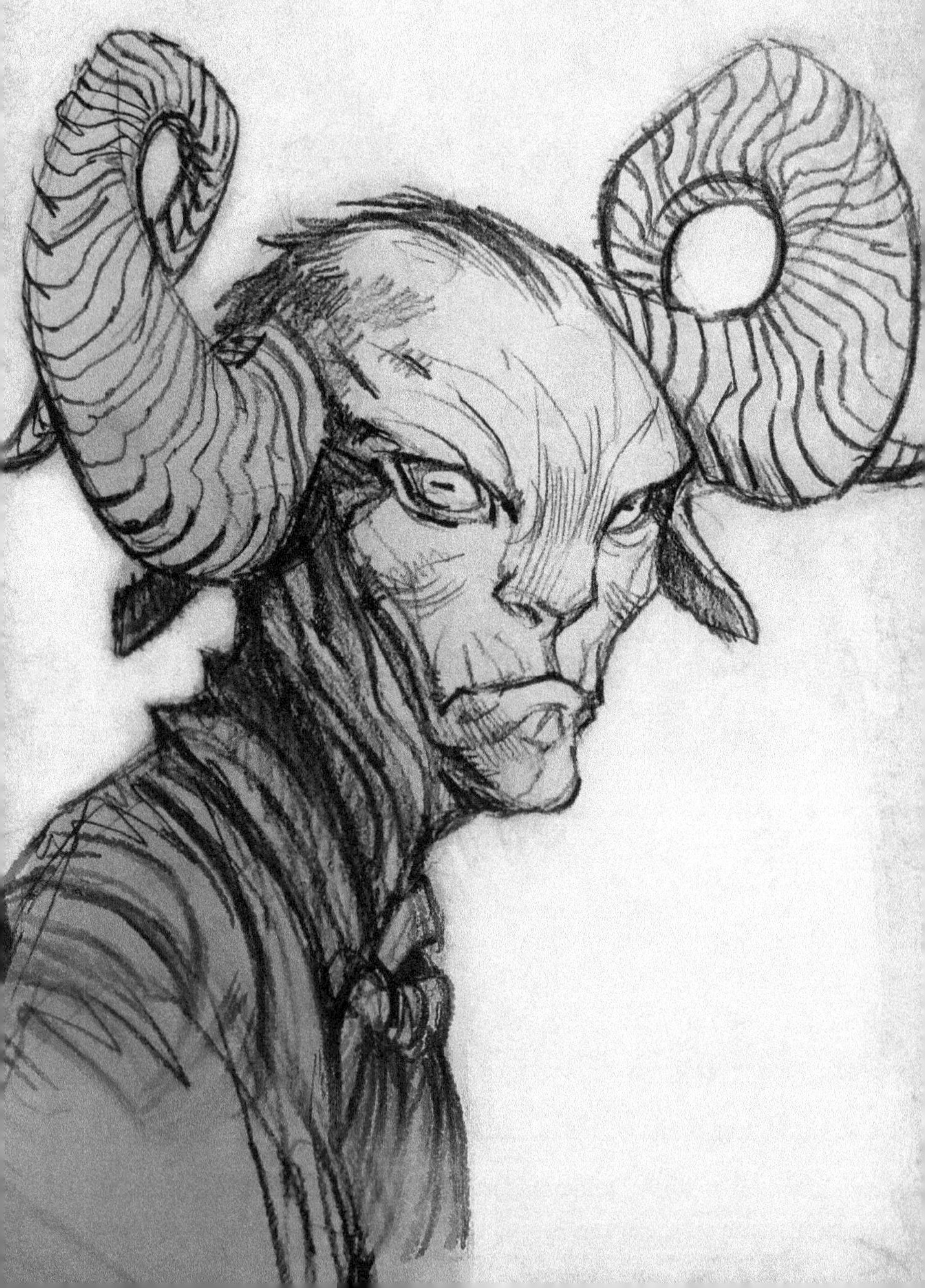

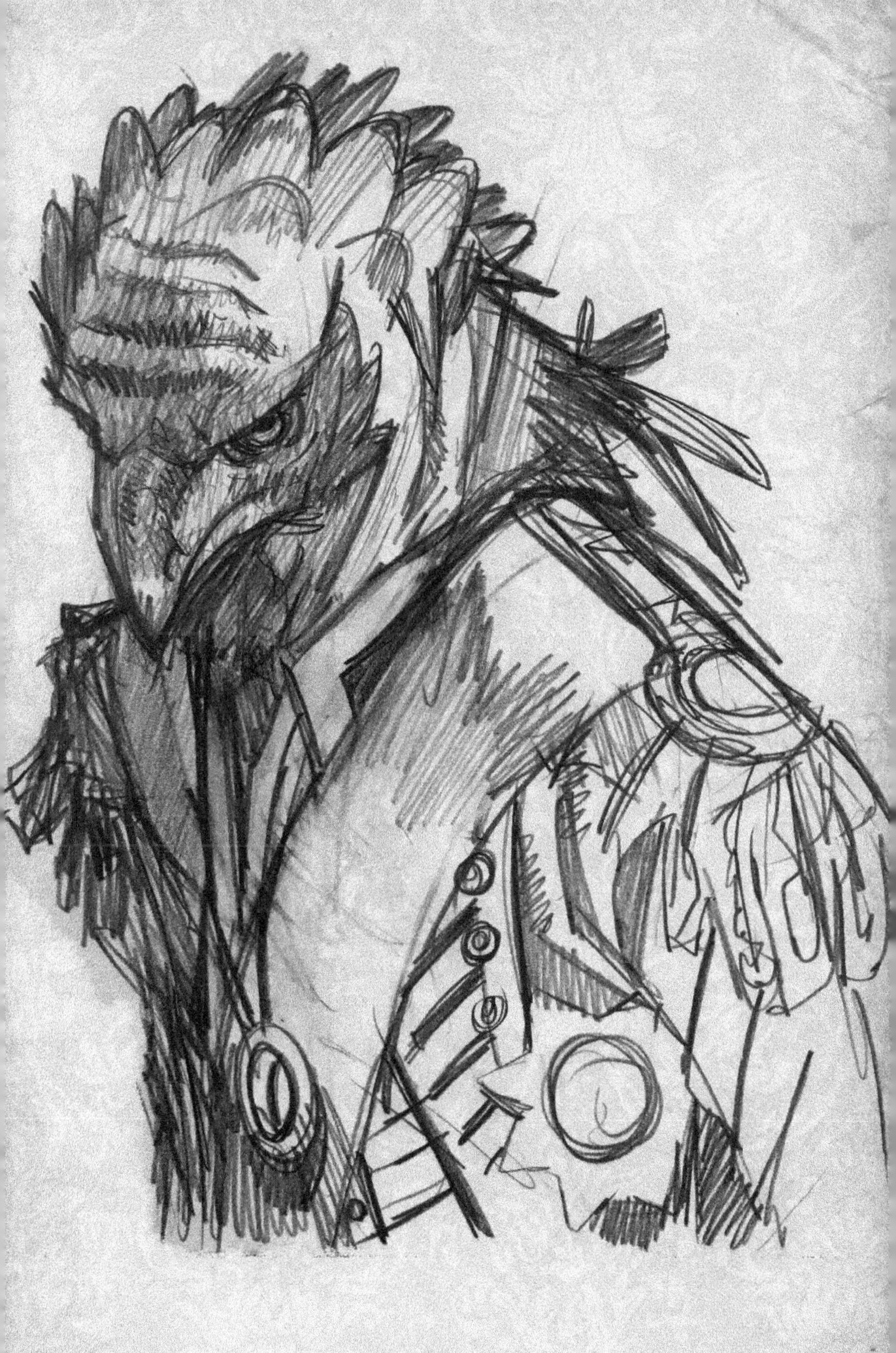

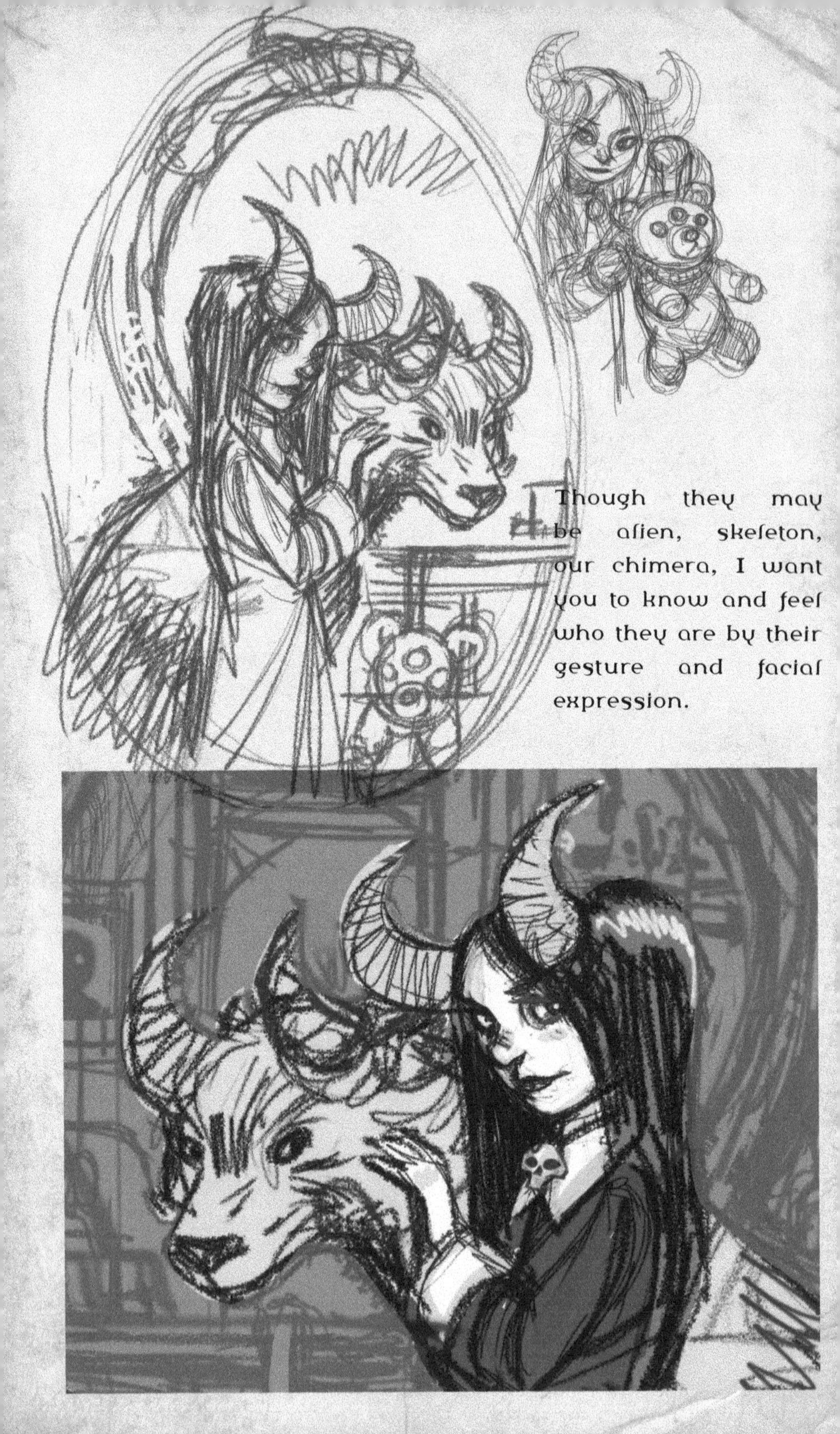

Though they may be alien, skeleton, our chimera, I want you to know and feel who they are by their gesture and facial expression.

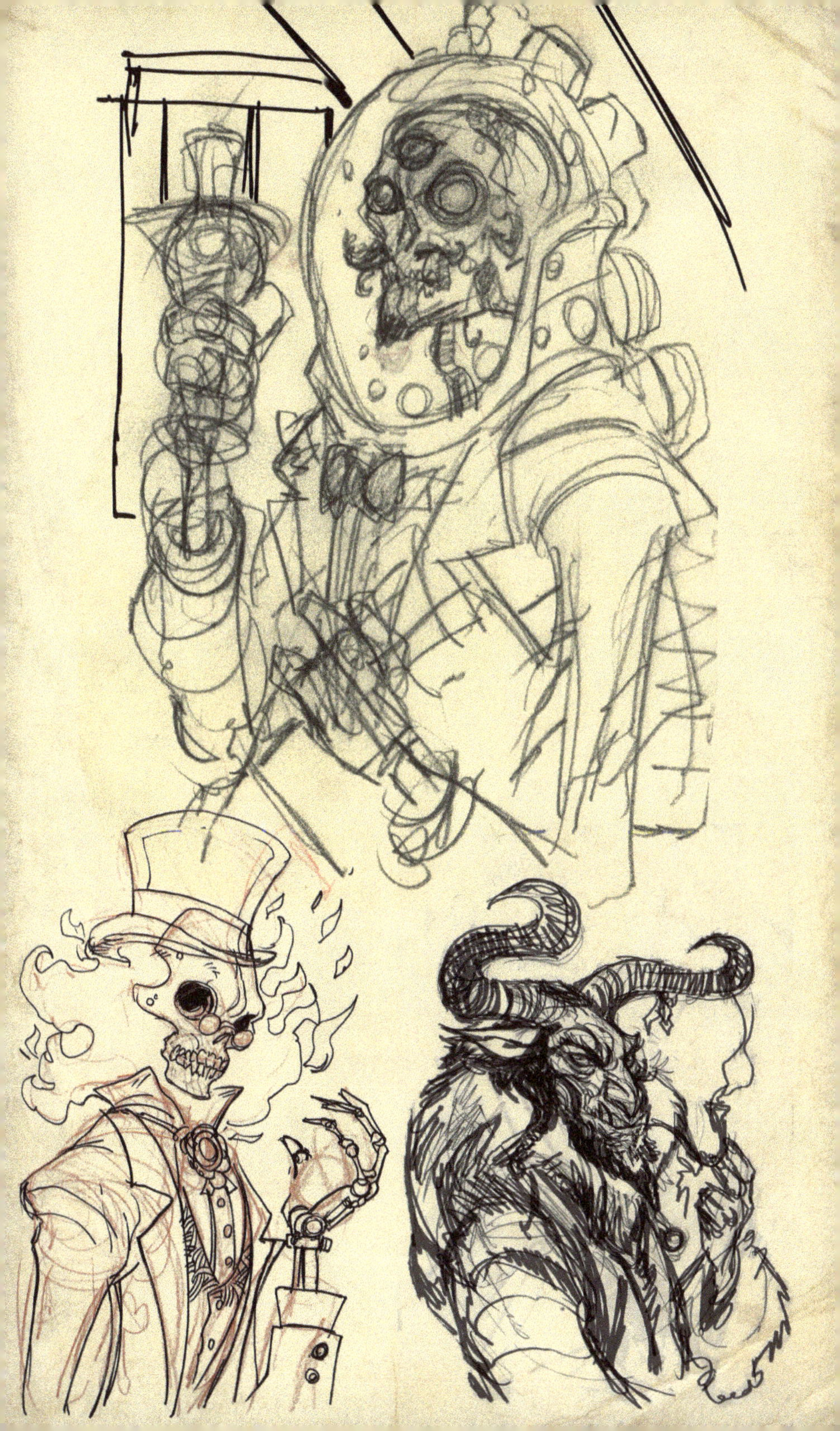

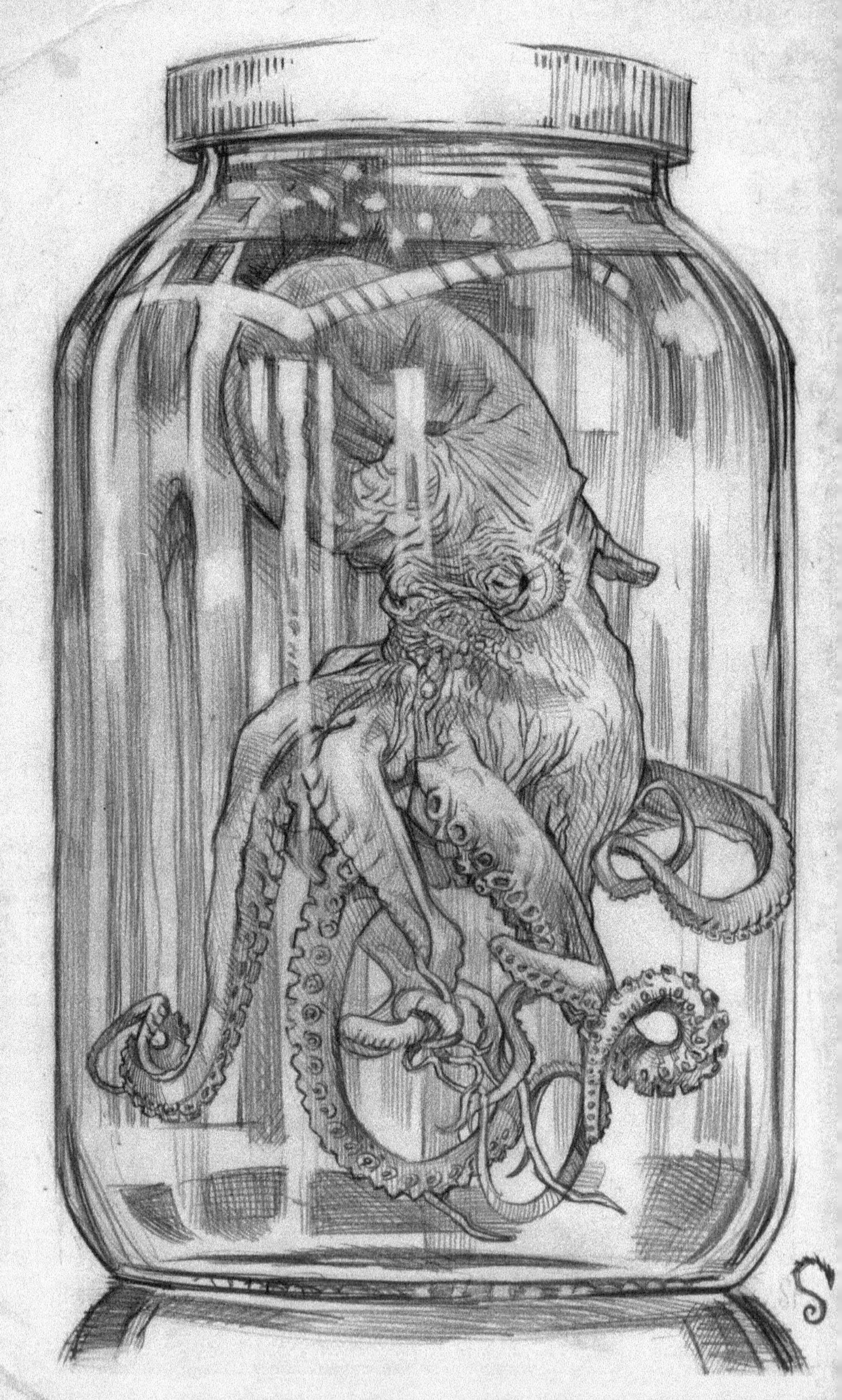

The Wanderer

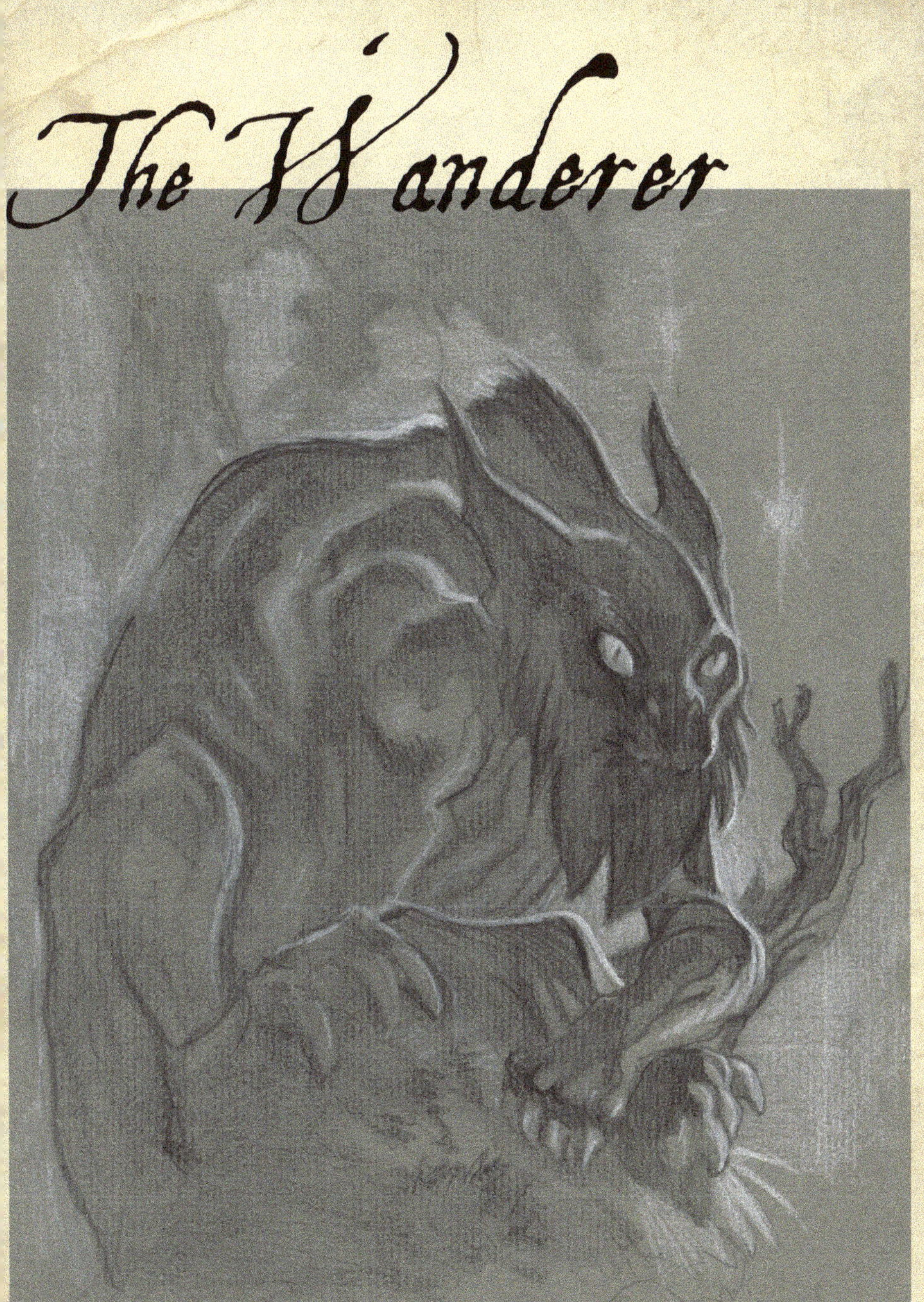

In the dark night the forests around Thornclaw Manor comes to life with all manner of wonderful beast. The Wanderer lurks among the bracnhes of the ancient trees and will follow it's prey. If you come upon him, he will ask you a question. If you answer correctly he will let you go, if you don't The Wanderer will eat well that night.

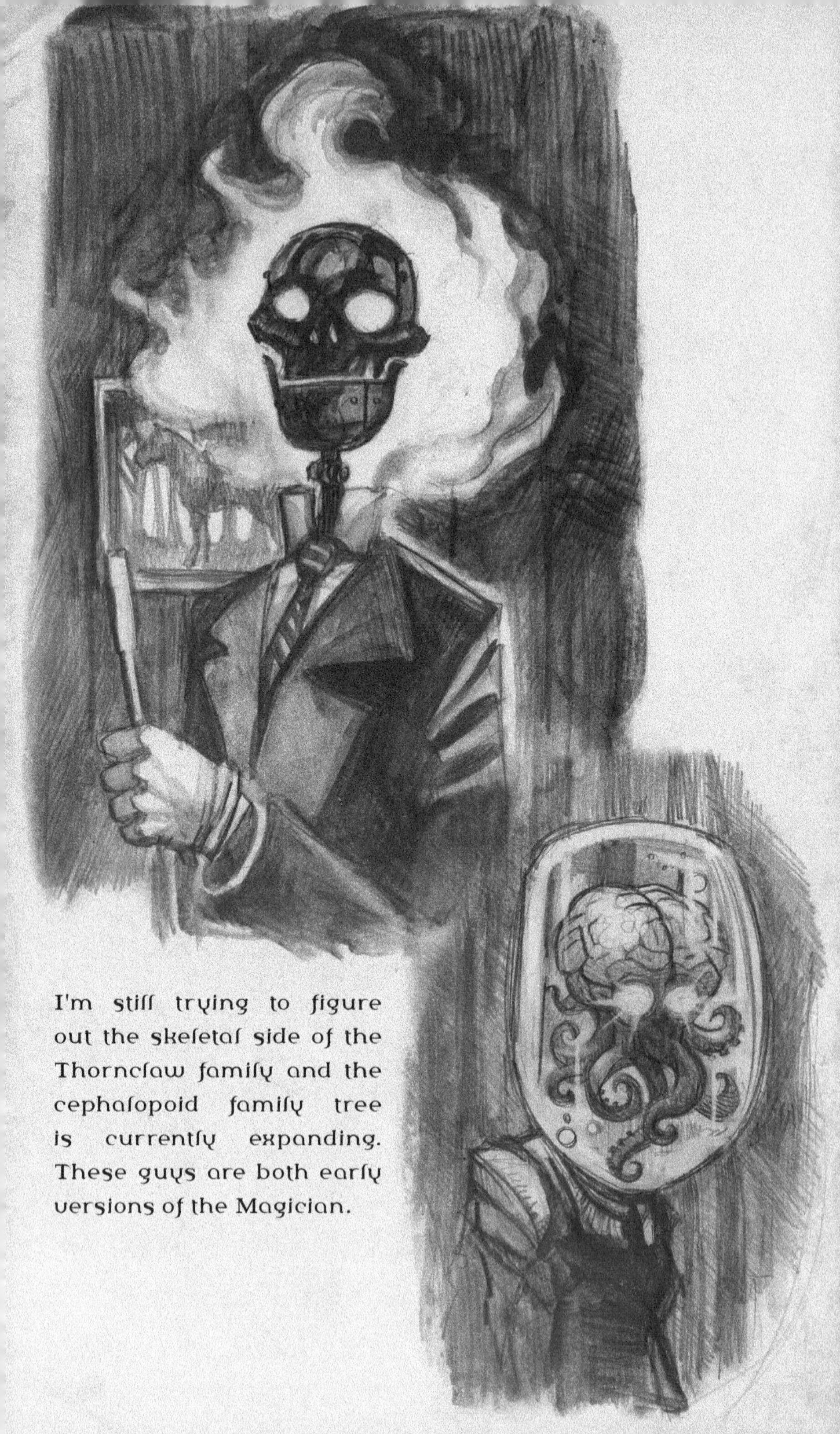

I'm still trying to figure out the skeletal side of the Thornclaw family and the cephalopoid family tree is currently expanding. These guys are both early versions of the Magician.

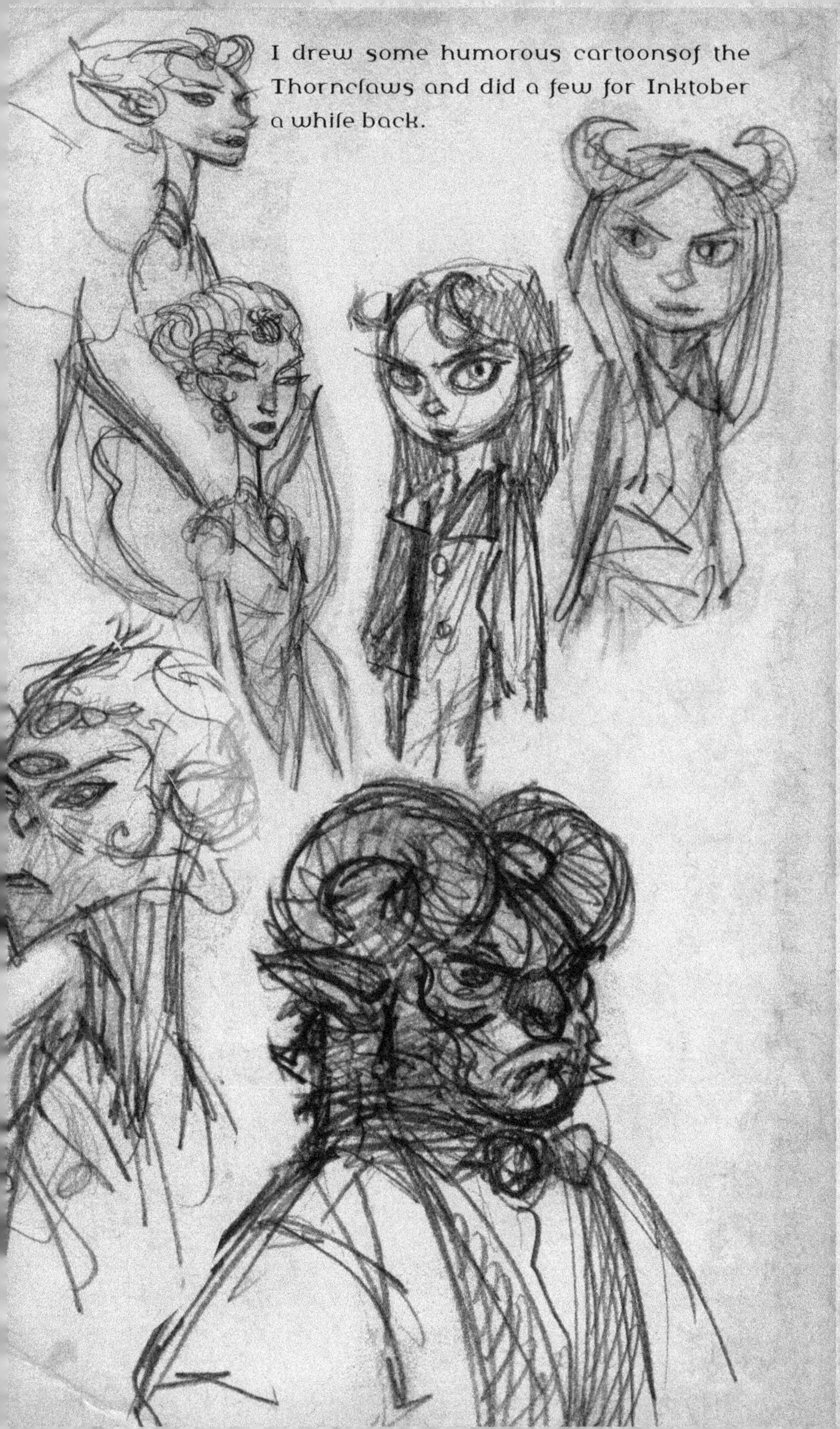
I drew some humorous cartoonsof the
Thornclaws and did a few for Inktober
a while back.

The Process

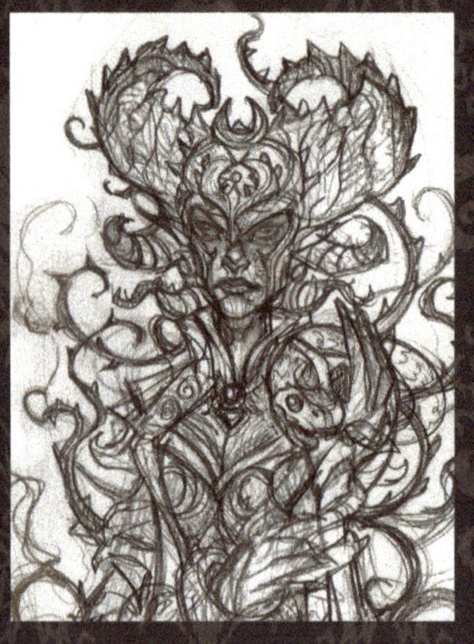

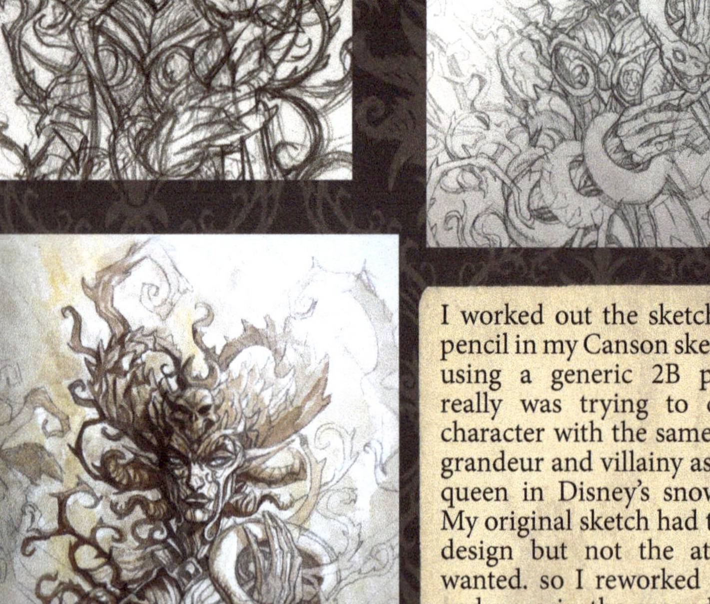

I worked out the sketches with pencil in my Canson sketchbook using a generic 2B pencil. I really was trying to create a character with the same kind of grandeur and villainy as the evil queen in Disney's snow white. My original sketch had the right design but not the attitude I wanted. so I reworked the face and pose in the second sketch. When I transferred the sketch to the new board, I used the principles of dynamic symmetry (kind of like the golden ratio) to design the piece against the outer edges of the paper.

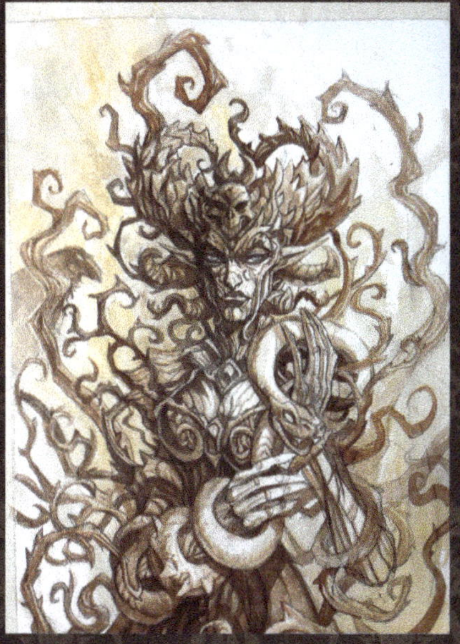

Once I've drawn down the pencil onto watercolor paper. The next step was to use burnt sienna watercolor in light washes to build up the values and tones.

The washes begin to build up and I start to add sepia ink for the darker areas and black in the darkest areas.

Once the underpainting is established, I can start layering in blues. Once one layer dries, I lay in water areas loosely with my brush and load my brush with pigment, I then allow the I've mixed the blue into the sepias to darken the color in the shadows.

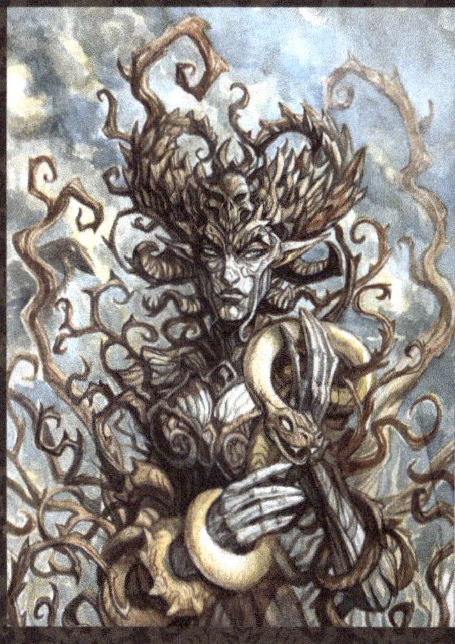

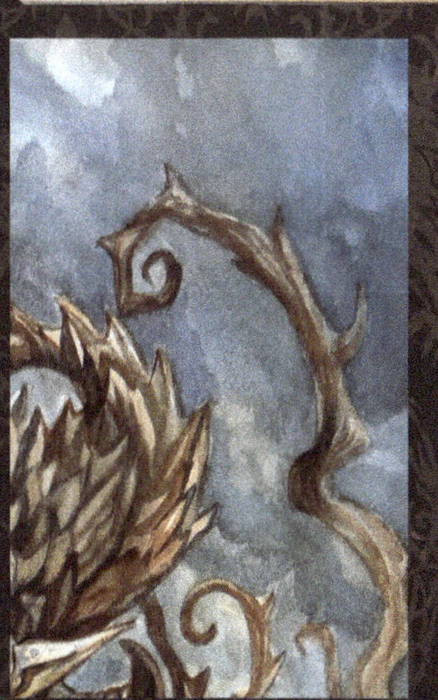

I use the blues in the sky to create an edge against the vines and the figure of the paper. Watercolor is all about controlling your edges.

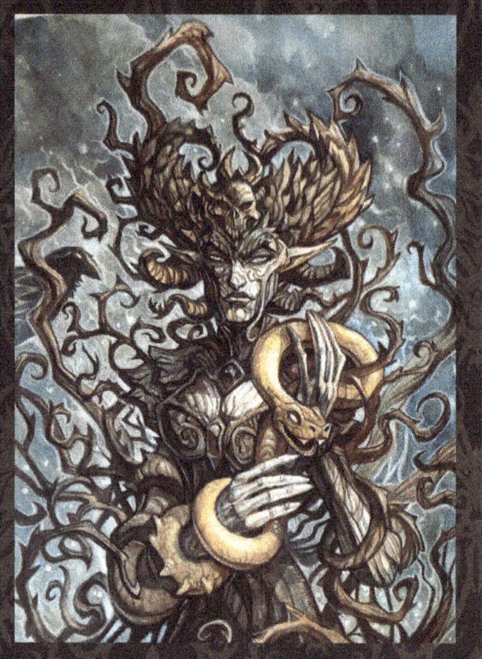

Once I've built up the watercolor and get the darks deepened, I use Prismacolor white and dark browns to sharpen edges. I'll also take white gouache (opaque watercolor) brush over the watercolor to create the will o' the wisps and lightning edges and other finishing touches. To get the darkest darks in, I use dark (Prussian) blue and black acrylic ink.

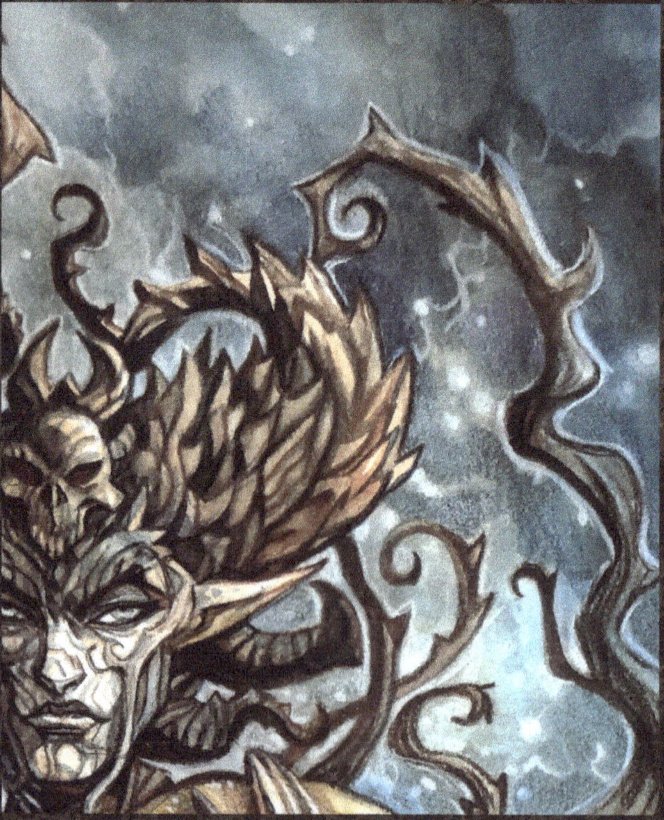

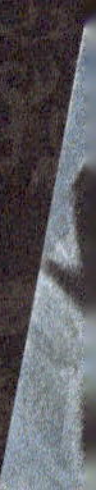

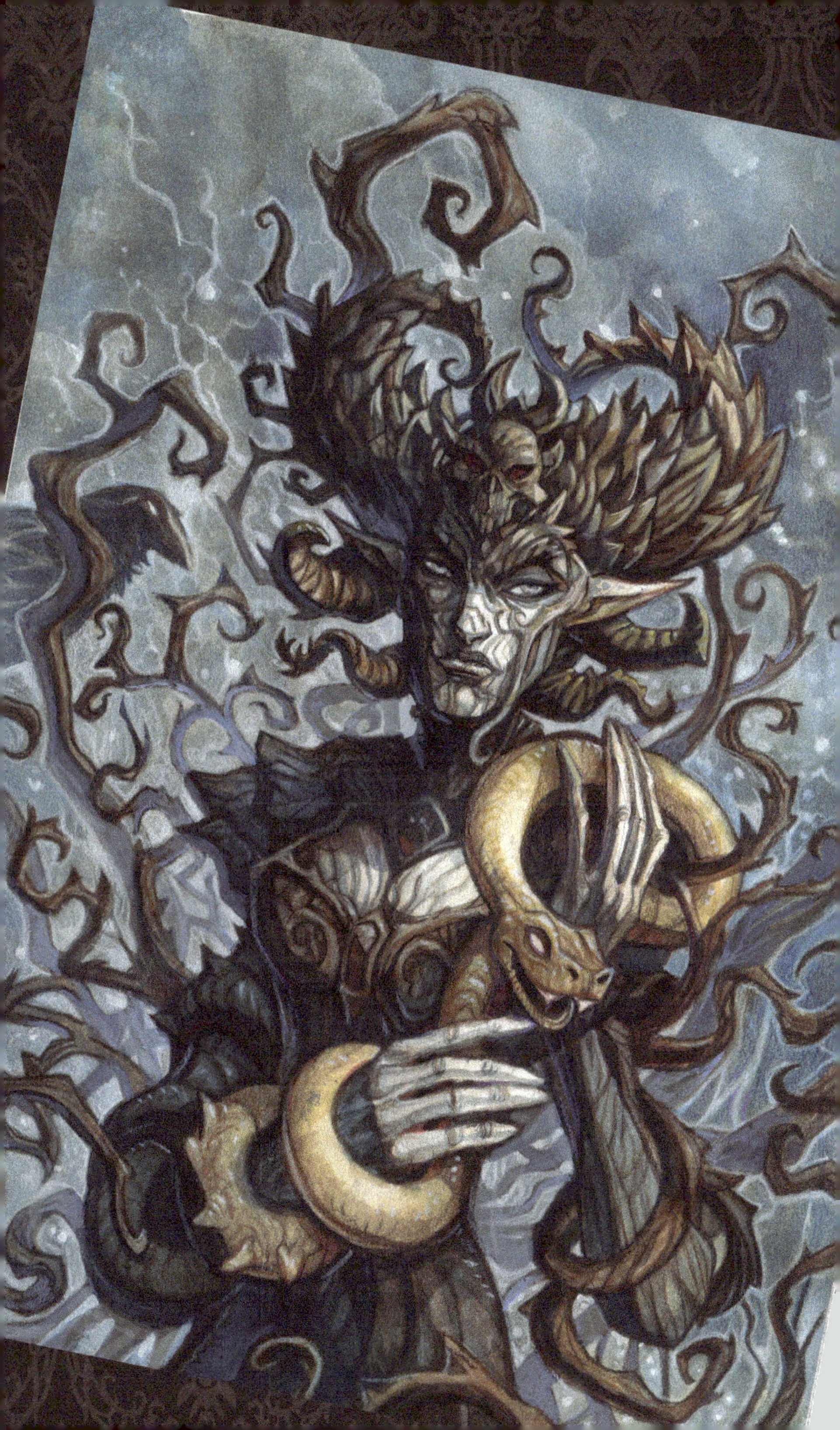

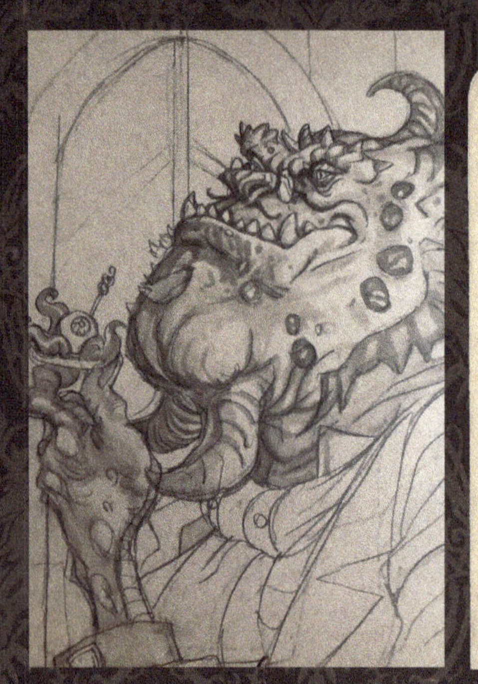

The Epicurean was done like many of the earlier Thornclaw family members; pencil, ink, colored pencil, ink wash and white goauche on toned paper. It's a simple process of building up from a loose pencil sketch with layers of tone and eventually white.

The Pirate is more of a traditional watercolor but still a bit of an experiment in media for me.

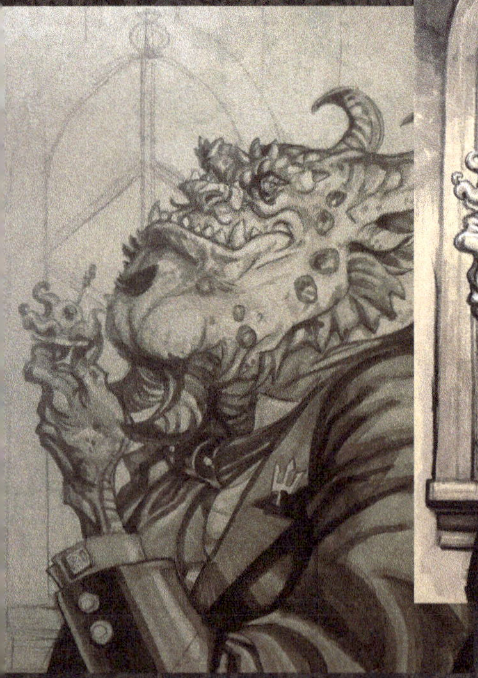

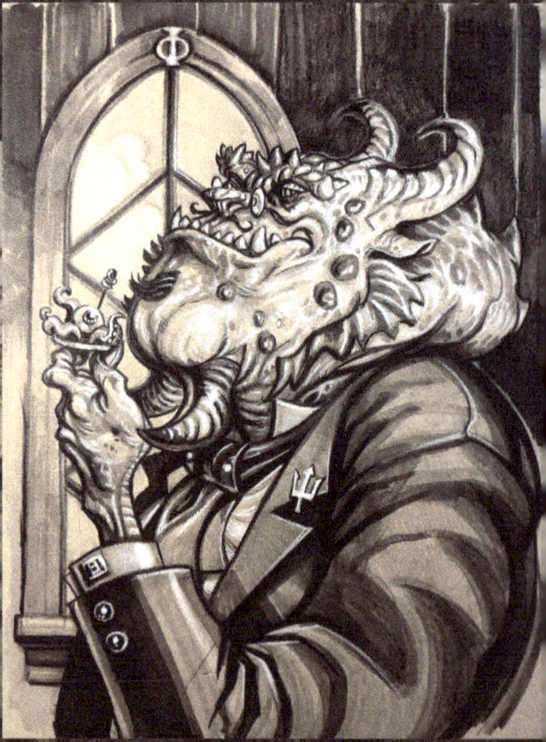

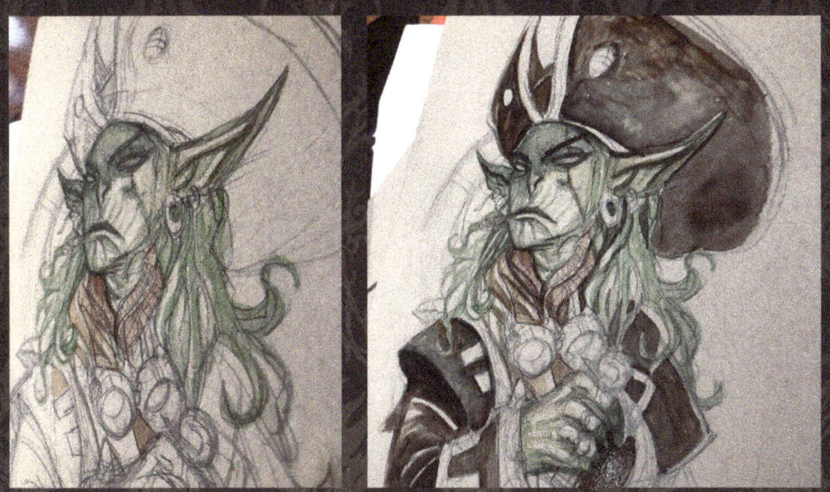

I used toned Strathmore paper as the ground and the watercolor worked beautifully. This was the first Thornclaw watercolor and it inspired many of the second deck characters to follow.

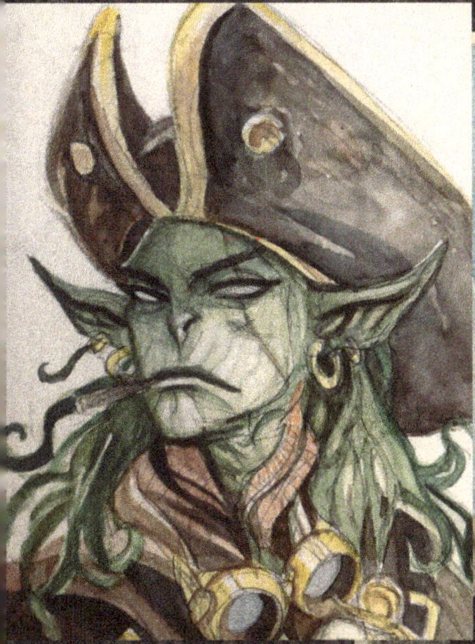

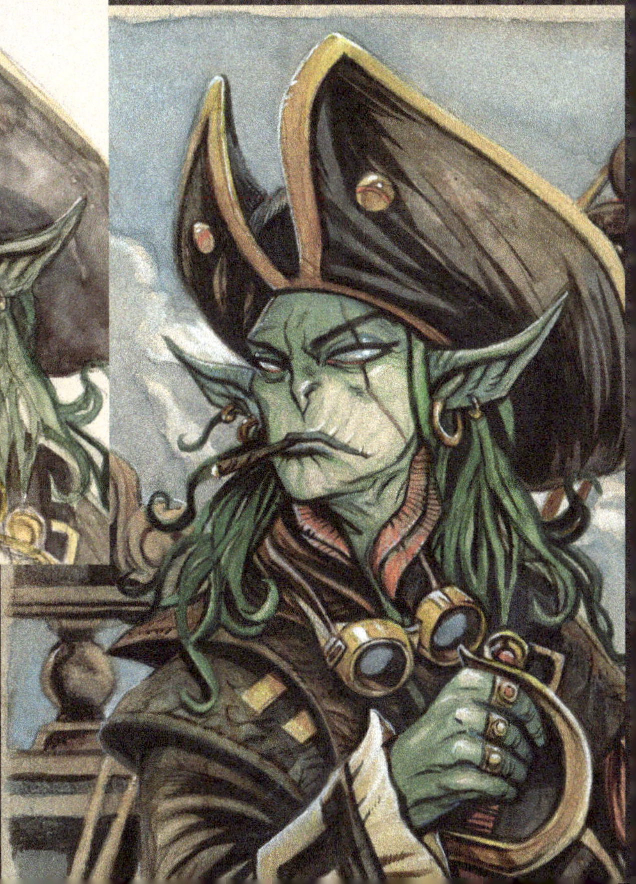

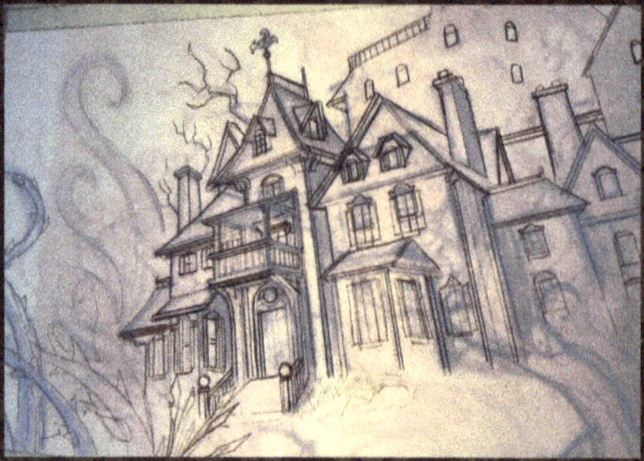

This first pic here is showing how I take a loose sketch and lightbox the drawing onto a thin sheet of Arches watercolor paper.

I develop the piece by adding colors into specific areas, making sure not to let the color bleed into areas of the art that need a different color treatment. I use brown as the darkening mix color for the blue which makes for a dark that isn't black, but has some energy to it.

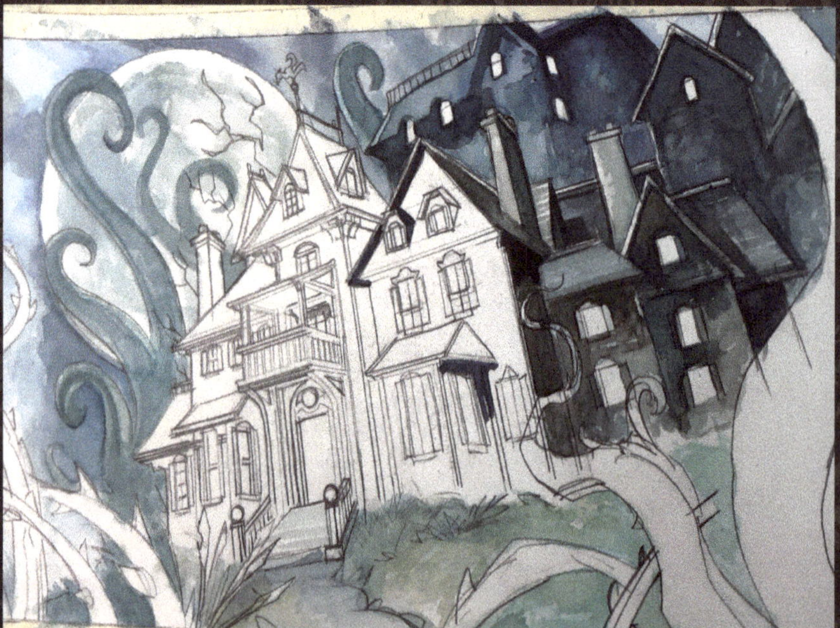

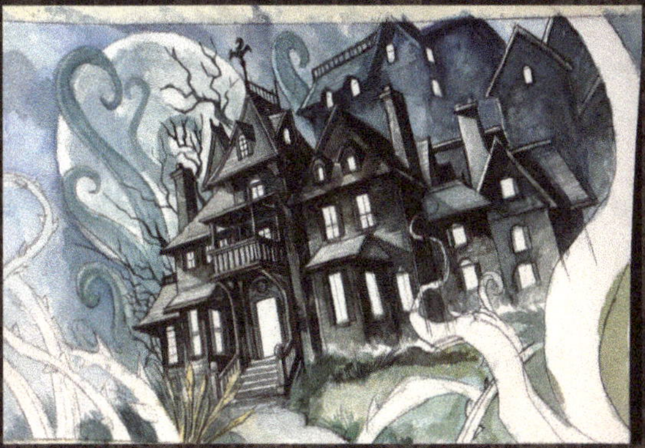

As you can see with the vines I wait to paint them in until I have all of the other areas colores and they've dried.

The final piece has a bit of softness to it but the edges between the different objects are clear and sharp.

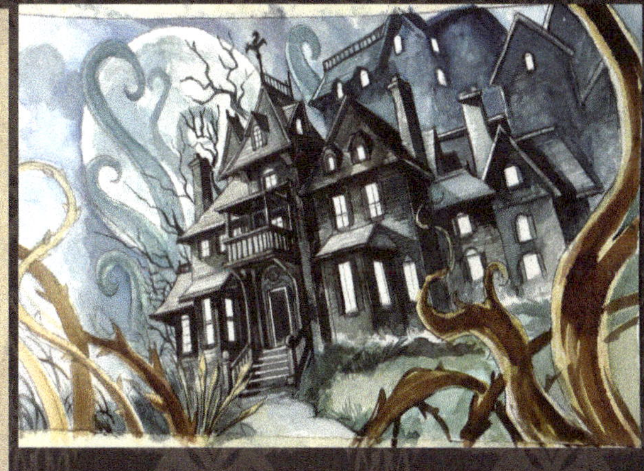

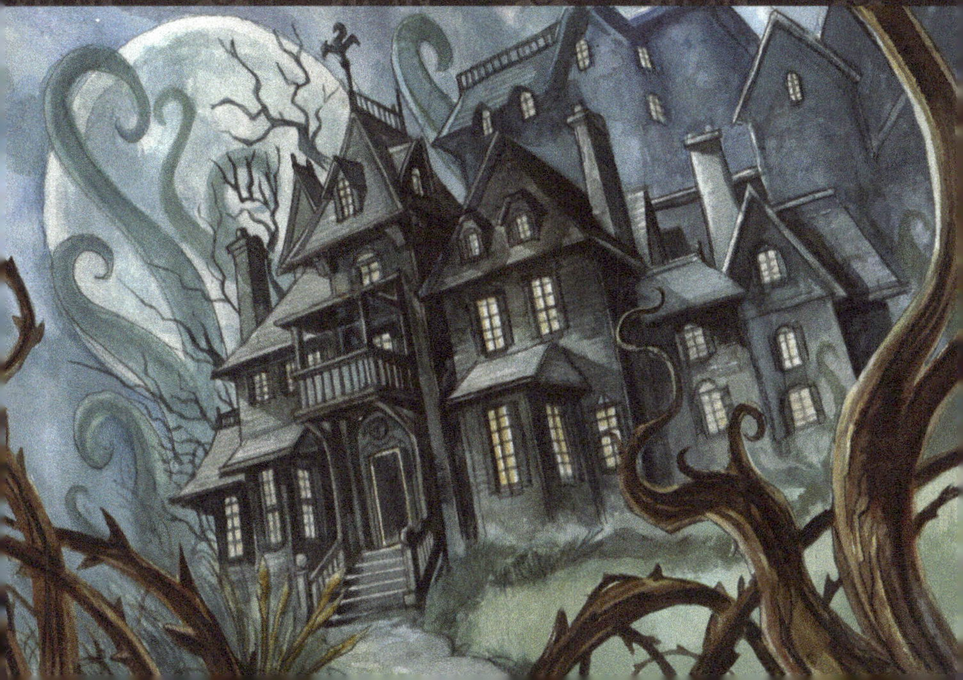

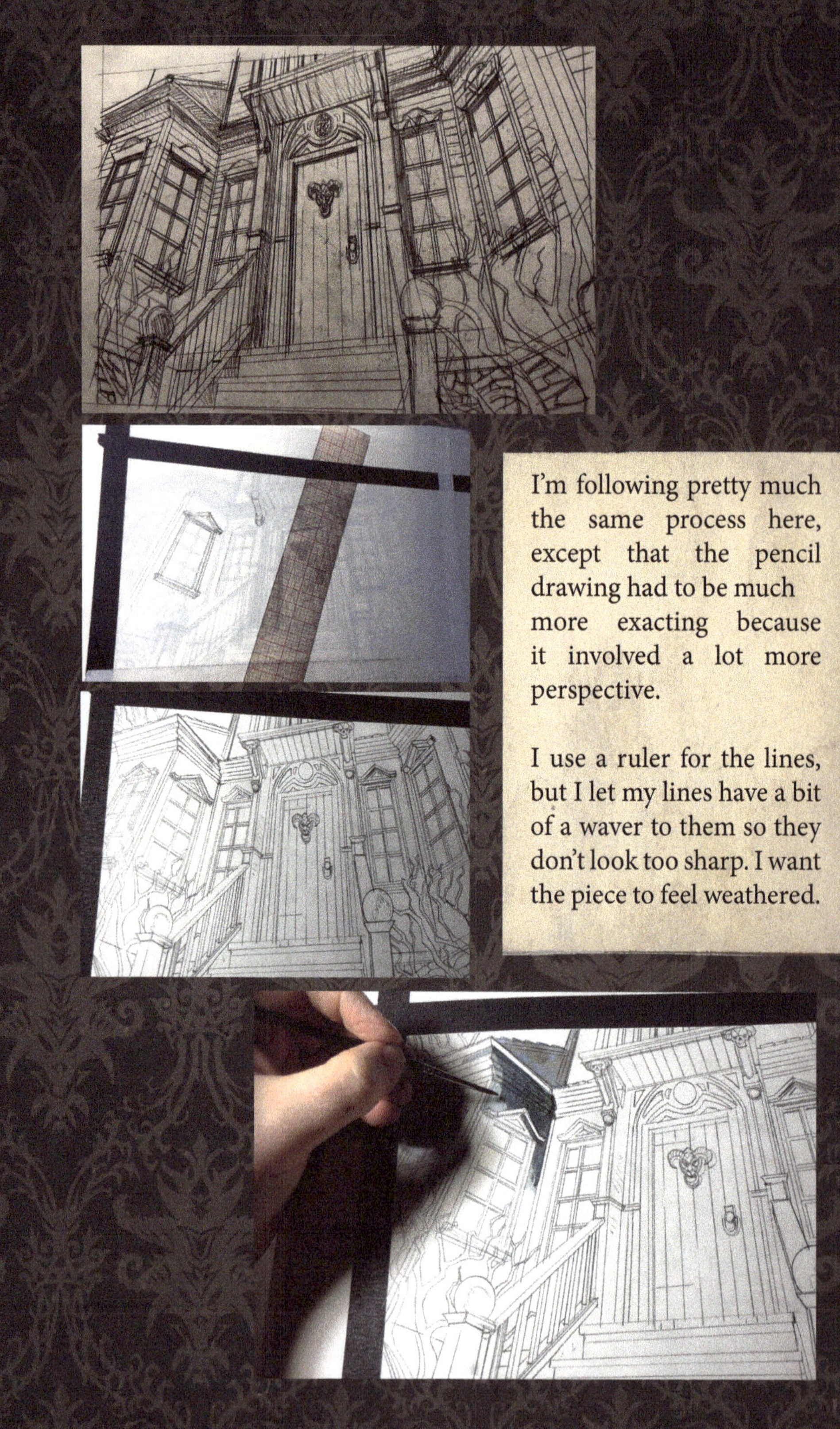

I'm following pretty much the same process here, except that the pencil drawing had to be much more exacting because it involved a lot more perspective.

I use a ruler for the lines, but I let my lines have a bit of a waver to them so they don't look too sharp. I want the piece to feel weathered.

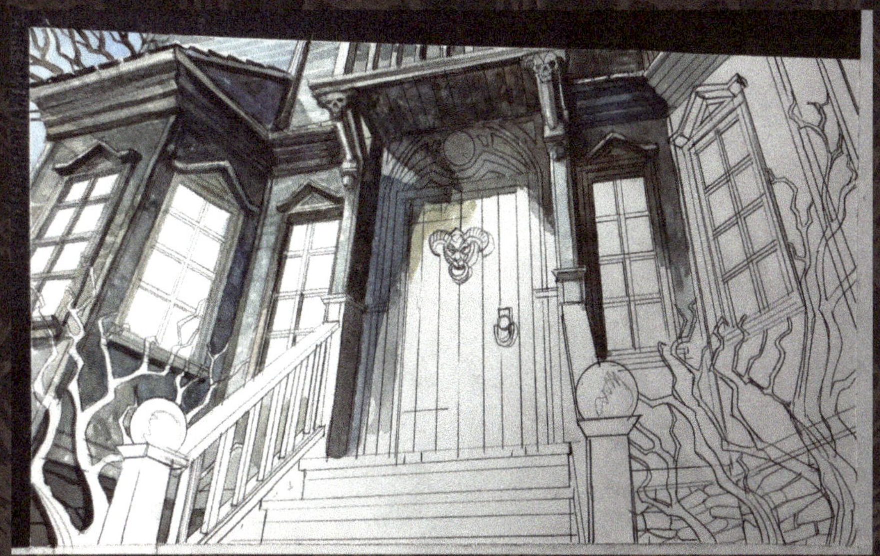

As I paint I go from section to section painting each area and moving on to the next rather than painting everything at once. I wait to do the windows last and paint them with only a little pigment so the white of the paper comes through. This gives me a glowing effect for the final image.

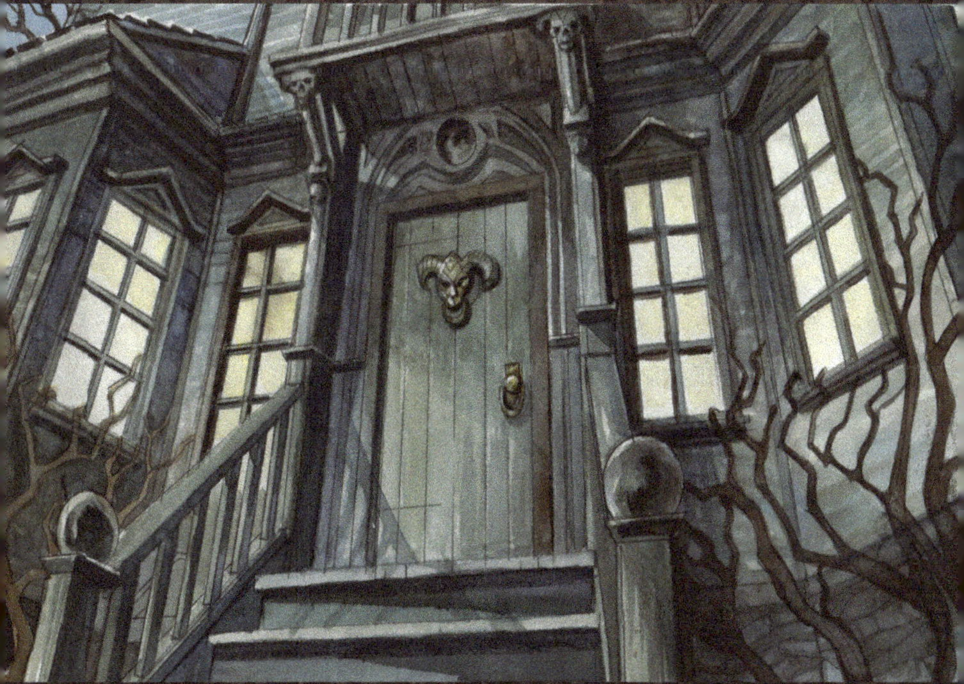

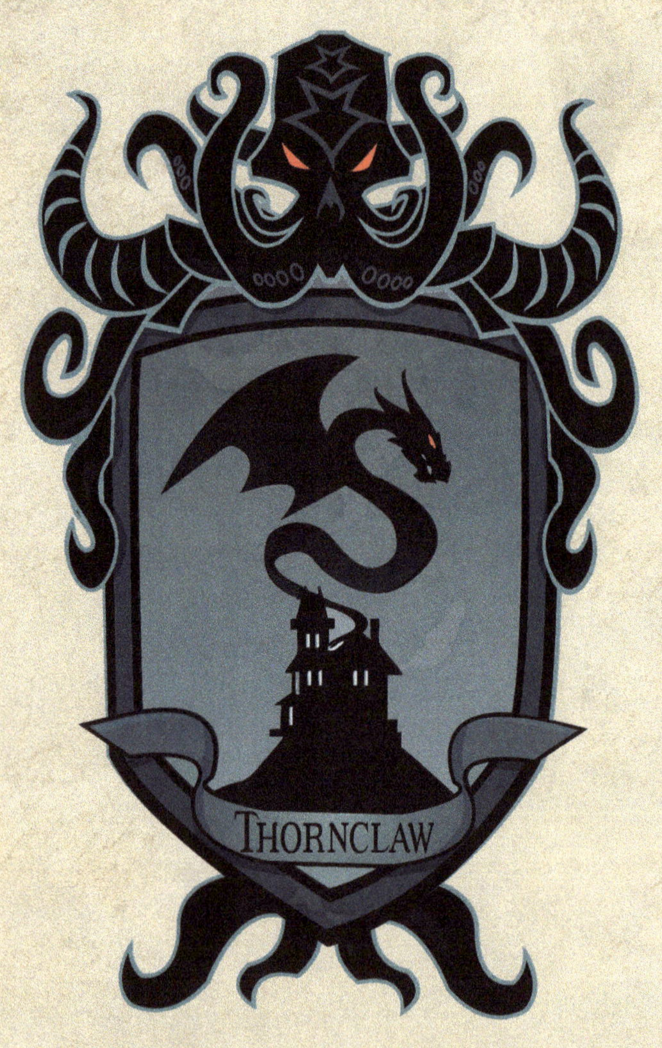
Thornclaw

Thornclaw Manor and it's monstrous family is a passion project that has been filling my sketchbook in between my comics and illustration work. It was born a few years ago while watching Downton Abbey with my wife, Mila. inspired by the world of Victorian and Edwardian British upper-class life, I sketched a period Cthulhu-like character - no reason, no client, just sketching. Then I made him a brother, and a mother, and then more and more family members....and the world of Thornclaw Manor was born.

Thornclaw Manor comes out of my love of myth, creepy fantasy, hours of my childhood sitting watching monster movies on Saturday afternoons, and the period of Spiritualism in the early 20th and late 19th centuries. In these pieces, you will see inspiration from the writings of H.P. Lovecraft, Poe, and Arthur Machen, Robert Bloch, Robert W. Chambers, real-life characters like Harry Houdini, The Fox sisters, my fascination with the occult, and the creepy dark woods of my upstate NY home.

The world is still growing and evolving in a non-Darwinian manner. The Family yearns to have novellas written about them as well as a game I've temporarily dubbed " The Soul Beneficiary." Please stay in touch with myself and the Family, as it grows there will be more art and more stories. Thank you for buying this book and making this world a possibility.

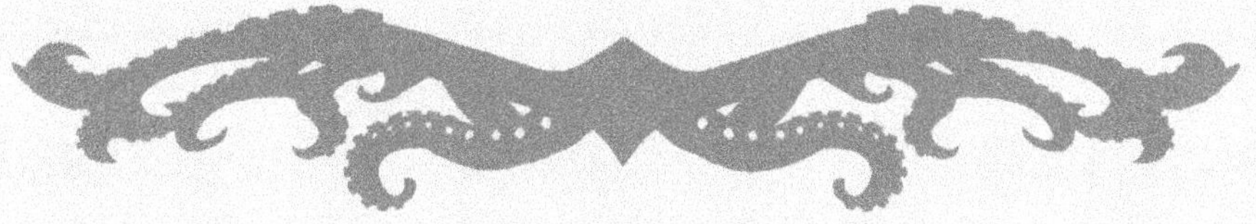

A preview from the upcoming Thornclaw Novel

Entering the Sorrows...

Up here Melody could see through the higher trunks of the trees, thinner than the lower parts, there was more space to see…nothing. It was dark everywhere. Brambles and vines with nasty looking thorns curled around the forest floor. In every direction she saw enormous trees, their trunks twisting up high in the air, their warped branches weaving in and out of each other, sparse leaves sprouting from the ends. The moonlight was barely breaking through the upper branches. Moonlight? Where had the day gone? It was morning when she left Thornclaw Manor. It was maybe late morning when that little monster Lenore ran away leaving her here in the Gloaming Forest to find he way to the Woodwitch's house alone. How could it possibly be night already?

As she pondered the mystery, she saw something glinting in the distance. Two things. Little glowing lights bobbing and weaving along the ground. Other lights joined them, all in pairs. Melody squinted at the lights as they got closer, bobbing and weaving, there were four, five no more pairs of the lights moving towards her. They reminded her of the alive-seeming lights the carriage driver was capturing in his lamp as they drove through the mists of the veil to enter the Dusklands adn the grounds of the Manor. There was something more ominous about these lights. As these lights got closer to her she could hear the rustling of the vines and the underbrush getting louder and louder.
As they got closer Melody could see, they were eyes! They were glowing eyes!

Creepy little things with glowing green eyes broke through the thickets near the base of the rock and began to climb the rock around her. Small four legged bodies rat-like, but larger than rats, hairier than rats with strange beady glowing eyes and nasty looking sharp teeth. Melody yelped and pulled herself close. But the things seemed to stop at her toes, circling around them and climbing over each other. They snarled and spat and drooled and hissed at her feet and she tried to curl her toes up farther than ever.

"Looks a little thin for eating, though, dontcha think?" As voice came from behind her.

"Er, I don't know," a second voice answered," Better let the boss decide. 'Sides, it's been a long while since we got any two-legged food."

Melody turned.

There, behind her at her head level, were two of the most peculiar beings she'd seen yet. One, dressed in an old victorian style suit complete with vest and pocketwatch hovered on gossamer insect wings.It's skin was pale, grey white and its large grin was in a protruding lower jaw with a set of sharp looking but snarled fangs. His eyes were…he had no eyes, or a nose, just his large mouth and pointed ears. Melody's skin crawled just looking at him.

His companion was toadlike, squat and bumpy-skinned with a wide ugly mouth that looked uncomfortable forming words. His teeth were yellow like someone who had drunk too much coffee. He was also wearing a dark baggy suit with a top hat and a red bowtie. His skin glistened in the moonlight as if he was covered in a thin layer of slime. He was riding a dog of sorts, a mangy dirty thing with big ears like a fox and a long snout. Mud and drool hung down from its mouth where its teeth were bared. Though the pair creeped her out, she thought she knew what they were…. Ganglees! The creepy evil fae that her father had told her those stories to warn her. He wanted to prepare her. He knew that someday she would be here. The thought warmed Melody and made her feel taken care of.

But at the moment, Melody had to deal with these things and she didn't enjoy the idea of being viewed as food.

"I'm not food! Melody responded angrily much to their surprise.

"It talks!" They squealed. The winged one almost fell from the air.

" I'm a "she" not an "it" Melody explained, "I'm a person."

"A person, out here?" Oh nonono! There are no "persons" in the The Sorrows! There is only monsters like us Ganglees and our prey." The winged one said, and the other shook it's head in affirmation.

"And you look like a plump good dinner," it admitted, a long sinewy tongue reached out between its lips like a dog licking its chops.

" I would appreciate it if you would stop calling me dinner."

"I would appreciate it if you would stop talking, I don't much enjoy talking to my dinn…er….meal?

"Now come along!" The little flying creature reach out to grab her arm with its cold clammy pale hand. She swatted it away.

"I'm not a meal either!"

"Then what are you? You are here, surrounded by the kings troops, in our forest. If you arn't prey, then what are you?"

"I'm Melody, Melody Hawthorne."

"Well, Melody Melody Hawthorne, you are now dinner."

"Grab her!"

The creatures on the rock began to climb onto Melody's exposed ankles and onto her jeans legs. She was glad she'd changed out of the dress she had been wearing at the the manor this morning. She could just imagine how awful it would be to have these things crawling into her dress and up her legs.

She shrieked as their little sharp claws snagged her skin and they bared their little dirty fangs.

A branch hung down from a nearby tree just within Melody's reach. She grabbed it, it was just old and rotten enough to snap off in her hand and she turned it on the rat beasts climbing up her legs swatting them with the stick. They fell into the mud at the base of the rock squealing , wrestled around a bit to run themselves over,and immediately begin climbing back up.

She kept swatting them until they were off her and she had made a perimeter around herself at the top of the rock, still surrounded, but holding them at bay with her stick.

"Ooh it's a fighter!" grinned the one with no face rubbing its hands. The King will be pleased!"

Melody growled at the no- face creature.

"We'll bring you back to the King and he can decide how to handle you."

"Maybe he'll throw her into the pits! We'll see how she fares before we cook her!" The toad-like one blurted.

"That would be good fun indeed." the no- face Ganglee replied as his little clawed hands grabbed at Melody's arm.
The toad creature's mount rushed at her with a speed that surprised Melody for all it's awkwardness of movement. They were trying to push her off the rock.

"C'mon, lets go, food, maybe the king will give you a chance to fight for your life. Then you can join the feast rather than be the feast! Heh heh!"

Melody struggled as the creatures grabbed and pushed at her. Individually they would be too small to bother her, but between the two larger ones and the rat-things, Melody slipped off the rock and into the mud below, landing atop a few squealing rat things as she fell. Melody grimaced at the sound and feel of the rat things anbd had to contain a squeal of her own. Luckily, her falling surprised the Ganglees and gave her a chance to gather herself and run.

She stood up and just took off. Well, she tried to take off. The mud around her feet again pulled at her making her every effort to run difficult at best. She slogged away from the creature, but it was dark and full of vines and sticks and rocks. Running wasn't an option, so she slogged as best she could.

The Ganglees recovered quickly. She swung her stick at the things on her legs, but the flying one grabbed at her hair and head. When she switched to flailing at the flying one, the creatures on her legs would push and scratch at her to make her move as the dog-thing nipped at her legs under the command of frog boy.

"That's right That's right! Let's go!" The flying one who seemed to be the leader cajoled her as the toad-guy together with the rat-things pushed at her legs.

She didn't feel so much like she was running away as she was being herded.

She was being harried so much she couldn't tell where she was going or what direction.

She screamed, " Help anyone! Anyone out there?"

"Be quiet Missy!" the eyeless fae advised, " No need to wake up the whole forest. You are our find. Don't want to get others involved. Just be a good girl and do as we say."

Good girl. Melody had heard that before…too many times. It meant shut up and stay in your place, you don't have any say here, sit on the chair in the corner and we'll decide where you live and who you live with, where you go to school, who your friends are.
We'll decide who you get to be.

"Enough!" Melody dropped her stick and quickly grabbed at the flying Ganglee. He was surprised and didn't expect it, so she was able to snatch him out of the sky. She pulled him in close to her chest, the other ganglees grabbing and scratching at her legs, but she held him firm. He began to scrape at her with his sharp fingernails and his mouth opened as if to bite at her neck. She stumbled backward. She'd been in fights before. At her old school, there were a few scuffles, it was the reason she had ended up at the Clarks. She didn't like to fight, she didn't want to fight, but sometimes the other girls were vicious especially to anyone the least bit different. Usually, it was just a little pushing and shoving in the play-ground after school when the older kids were waiting for their parents to pick them up.

This was serious, this was her life on the line and she wasn't going to win this fight.

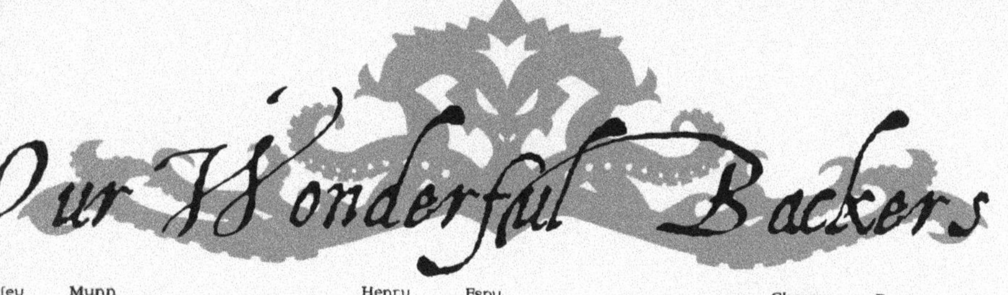

...ley	Munn	Henry	Espy	Cheree	Bonner
...n	Enström	Adam	Skava	Fred	Hooper
...ert	Andrew Smith	Kimberly	Fritzler	Kent	Hall
...el	Rotman	steve	Seeper	Shane	Davis
...aniel	Peterson	Chris	Slota	Ash	Glue
...n	Wilson	Laura	Norman	Eric	Zdilla
...es	Kleefeld	Jessica	Marie Boehman	Manuel	Deutsch
...sey	Aleksandrovich Ivanov	Stephanie	Paustian	Gareth	Edwards
	Page	Matt	M McElroy	Ray	Lago
...ua	Leake	Harry	Bauer	Steven	Walker
	Lovett	Ruben	Almaraz	Tracy	Fretwell
...el	Govar	Hannah	Shayler	Steven	Tottenhoff
	Balfour and family	Gianluca	Rota	Matti	Viren
...n	Rosen	Marek	Benes	Matt	Black
...k	J Bush	Julie	Carpenter	William	F Coconato
...stopher	Burdett	Elianne	Brazeau	Dr.	Gregory Ellis
	Klemer	Manuel	Fraunholz	Nir	Laor
...ny	Mohler	Olegs	Vasiljevs	Ryan	Smith
...en	Miles	Stephen	Erin Dinehart	Adam	Tran
...e	Struharik	Caroline	Dickman	Kevin	Ruppel
...n	Fernandez	Ben	Palumbo	Tony	Tran
...f	Pattie	Johnny	sesma jr.	Matthew	Wang
...d	Mattson	Chris	Kawagiwa	Robert and Margaret Reed	
...an	Ho	Clare	Armstrong	Sebastian	Suarez
	Neat	Sean	Bowers	Mariah	Mariah
...y-Melissa	Wilzewski	Aaron	Alexovich	Kazuhiko	Nakahara
	Lau	Navin	Monteiro	Claire	Rosser
...than	Akeley	* ung.m888@gmail.com		Keri	Reininger
...na	Kaye	Rhiannon	R-S	Alexandra	Long
...asz	Kandybowicz	Elisia	Tichy	Walker	Hecht
...es	Williams	Rick	Argiro	Yves	Diggelmann
	Choi	Mark	Beard	Jamie	Stewart
...s	Gabalins	Samuel	Swanson	Rob	bennett
...ony	Sabino	Christopher	Fedelia	Hokan	Holmquist
...n	Griggs	LK	The Teardrop Shop	Ryan	Young
...ette	Rivera-Watts	MARTON	BATORY	Jeremy	Lenski
...stopher	Gunning	Greg	S Mueller	Kyle	D Paradis
...rew	Sanford	Adam	Vermillion	Eric	Adamson
...ID	SISSON	Elton	Lau	Dubrouskii	Egor Igorevich
...r	Iliaha	Ronald	F Schauer, Jr.	Mitchell	Hall
...ny	Kieft	Ron	Eklund	Tri	M Vu
...and Anisyah	KLock	Joseph	Montague	Michael	McDonald
...nna	Pajtash	Raymond	Sneddon	Sylvester	Stroud
	B Thomas	Andreas	Baur	Sarah	Longshore
...a	Z Hyde	Jeffrey	Daniels	Rand	Witz
...y	Berkowitz	Javier	Quintero	Shawn	L Brown
...and Melba	Piedrahita	Sebastian	Babinski	Brian	Rice
...worm1965		Agustin	Silvera	Alessio	Bergamini
	Kruse	Beth	Ferrara	Matt	Ryan
...ley	Blodgett	C	D Entwisle	Heather	Farrington
...ene	L Cryer	Michael	Makarius	Damien	Larminé
...ert	Landtman	Matthew	Anderson	Mark	Westbrook
	Harkin	Tim	Thompson	Nicole	Black
...lyn	Haase	Duane	Perkins	Colton	kitt
...an	Wilson	Bobby	Corbitt	Shaun	Brooke
...ef	Marler	Matt	Savage	Matt	McCart
...n	Douwes	Jayson	Santiago	Matthew	Z Bastrukonis
...d	W Clark	Joseph	Pirrone	Monster	Fight Club
...h	Erfurth	Nicholas	Scholtz	Jesse	rosenberger
...mLucio96@yahoo.com		Adam	Blanks	Lisa	Kluempke
...stopher	Allen Goetting	Christian	Centurion	René	Messema
	Odebralski	Joey	Schichtel	Beth	Agostino
...ward	Seffner	Roy	Burke	Debra	Mauzy-Melitz
	MacLeod	Ian	Williams	Laurie	B Ellis
...s	Edwin Stevens	Timothy	Weber	Alessa	M. Abruzzo
	Carlson	Cordell	Dickson	Mike	Gaisbauer
...ssa	Feinman	* Rhel@pacbell.net			

These fantastic people helped make this book and the Thornclaw decks possible!!!

www.ingramcontent.com/pod-product-compliance
Lightning Source LLC
Chambersburg PA
CBHW052352030726
47602CB00002B/20